The Flowers of Evil

volume 4

Shuzo Oshimi

Les fleurs du mal

VERTICAL.

Contents

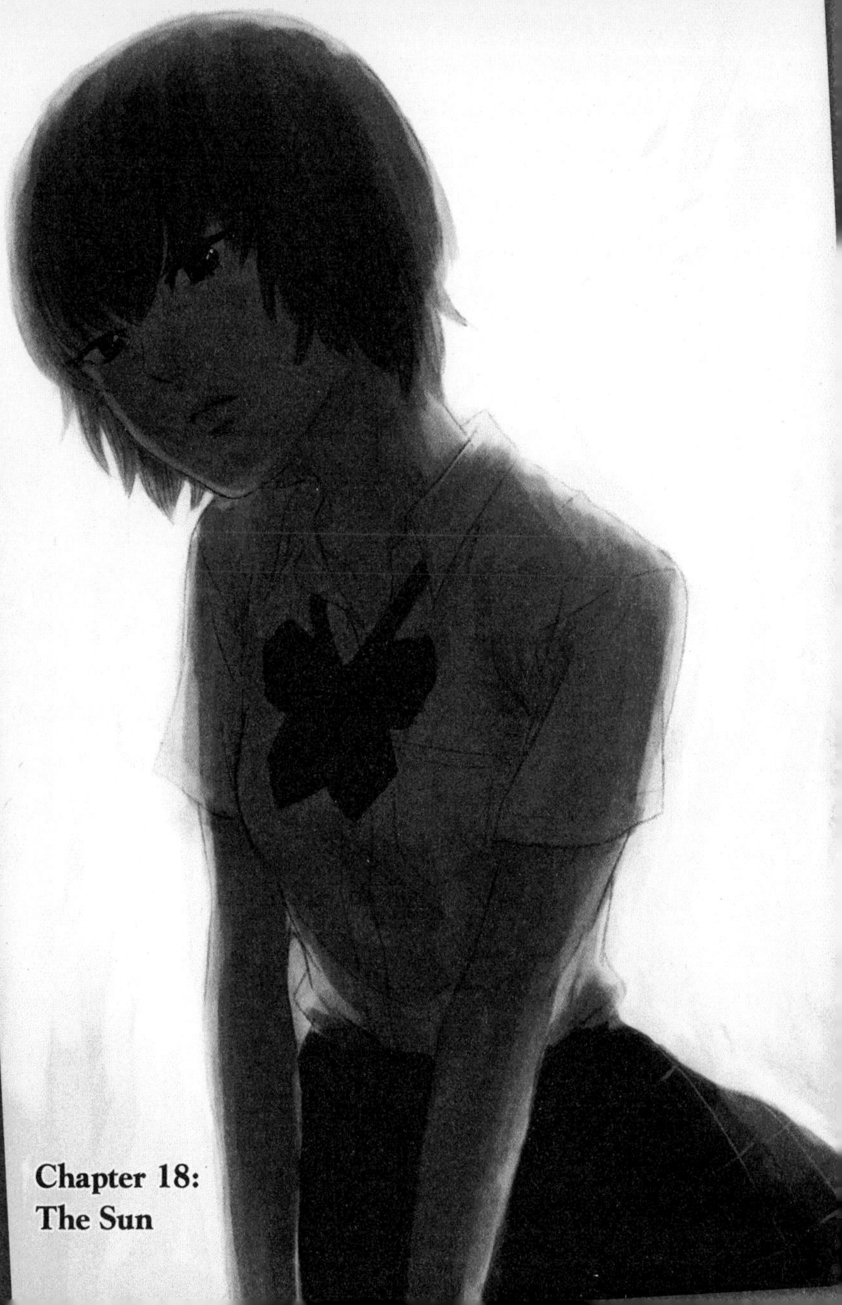

Chapter 18: The Sun

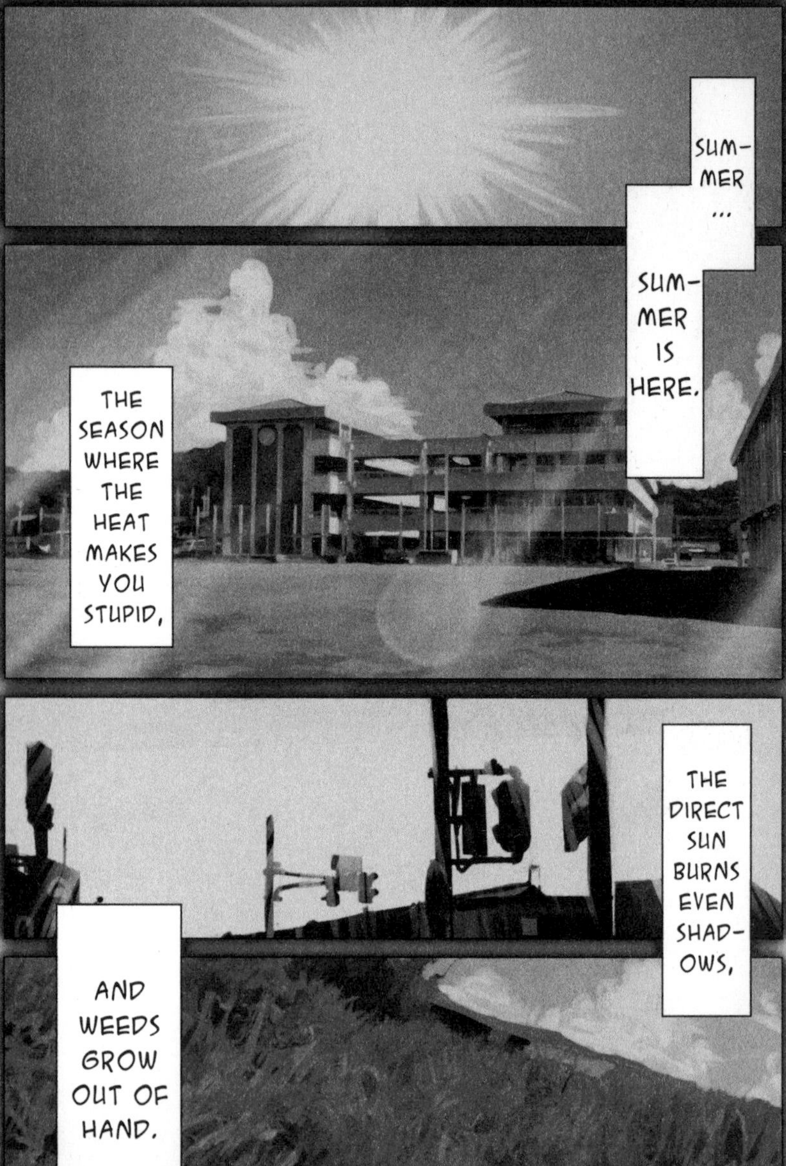
SUMMER...
SUMMER IS HERE.
THE SEASON WHERE THE HEAT MAKES YOU STUPID,
THE DIRECT SUN BURNS EVEN SHADOWS,
AND WEEDS GROW OUT OF HAND.

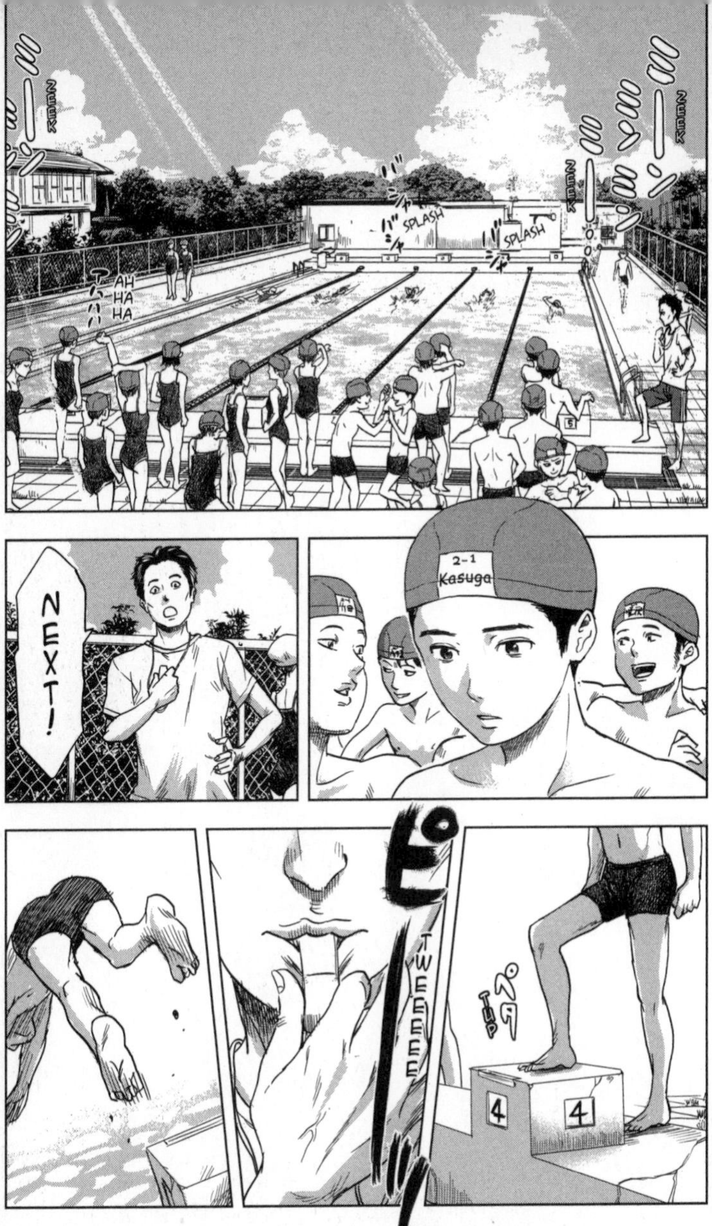
KEEEN
KEEEN
SPLASH
SPLASH
AH HA HA
KEEEN
2-1 Kasuga
NEXT!
TAP
TWEEEEE

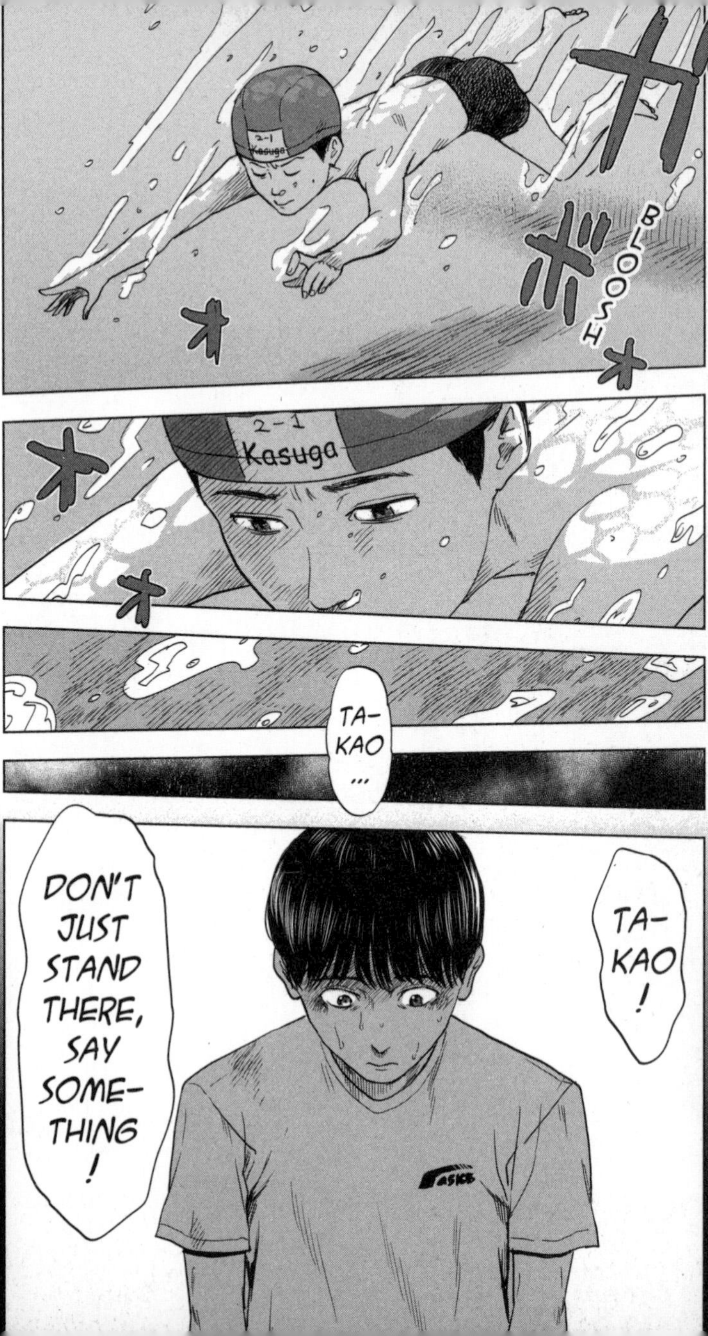
ガ
ボ
BLOOSH
オ
オ
2-1
Kasuga
2-1
Kasuga
オ
オ
TA-KAO ...
TA-KAO!
DON'T JUST STAND THERE, SAY SOMETHING!

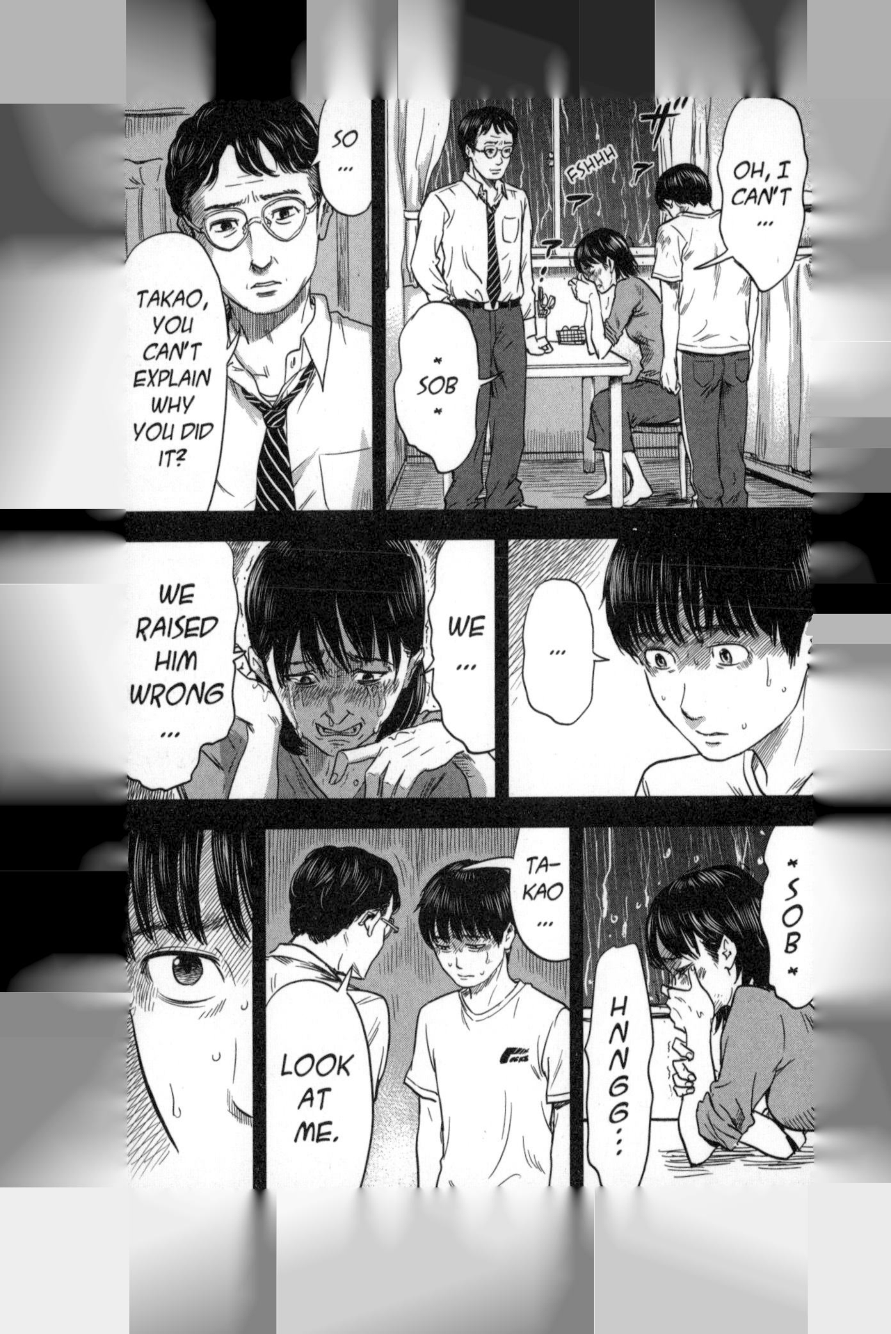
OH, I CAN'T ...
FSHHH
SOB
SO ...
TAKAO, YOU CAN'T EXPLAIN WHY YOU DID IT?
...
WE ...
WE RAISED HIM WRONG ...
SOB
HNNGG...
TA-KAO ...
LOOK AT ME.

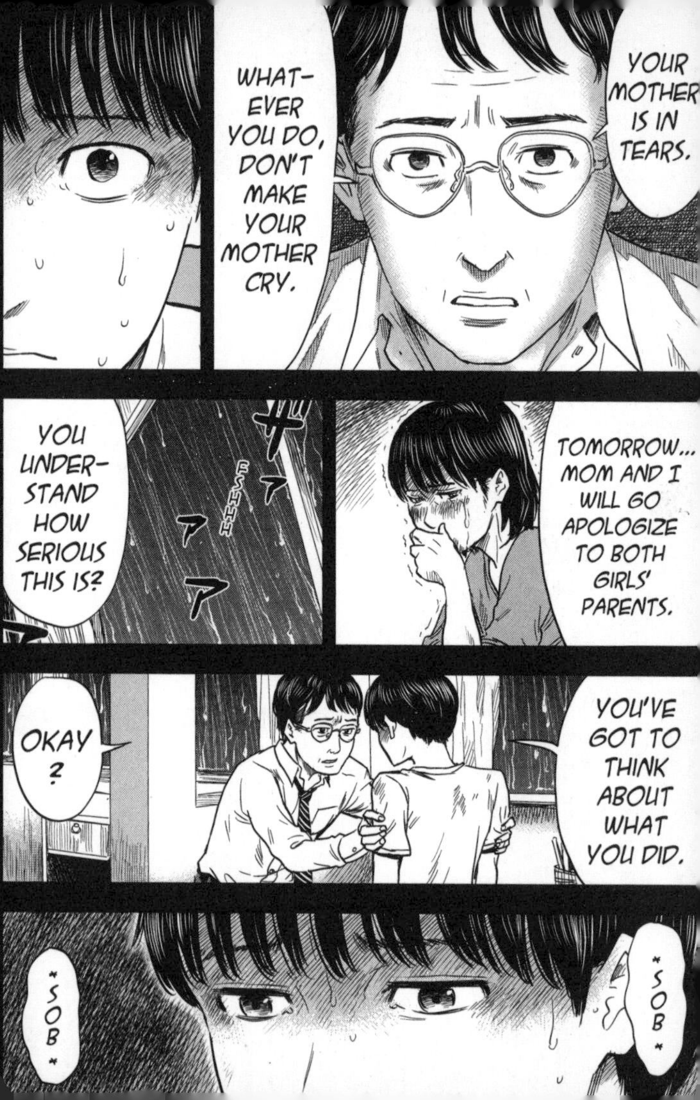
YOUR MOTHER IS IN TEARS.
WHAT-EVER YOU DO, DON'T MAKE YOUR MOTHER CRY.
TOMORROW... MOM AND I WILL GO APOLOGIZE TO BOTH GIRLS' PARENTS.
FSHHHH
YOU UNDER-STAND HOW SERIOUS THIS IS?
YOU'VE GOT TO THINK ABOUT WHAT YOU DID.
OKAY?
SOB
SOB

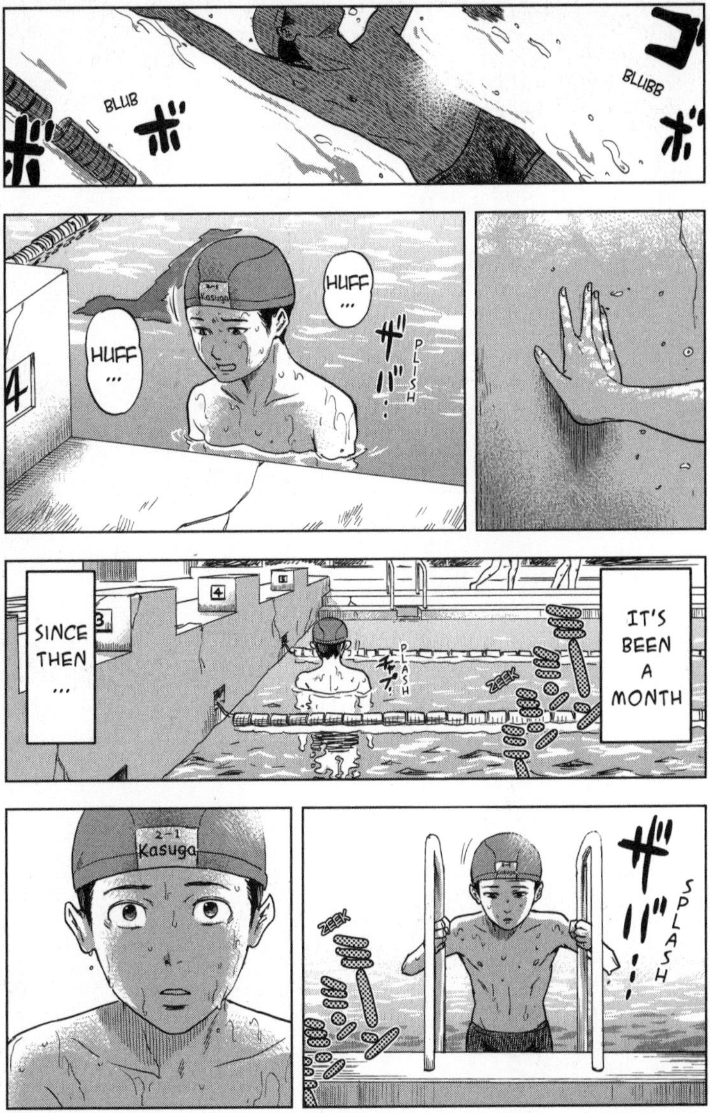
BLUBB
BLUB
PLISH
HUFF…
HUFF…
2-1 Kasuga
IT'S BEEN A MONTH
ZEEK
PLASH
SINCE THEN…
SPLASH
ZEEK
2-1 Kasuga

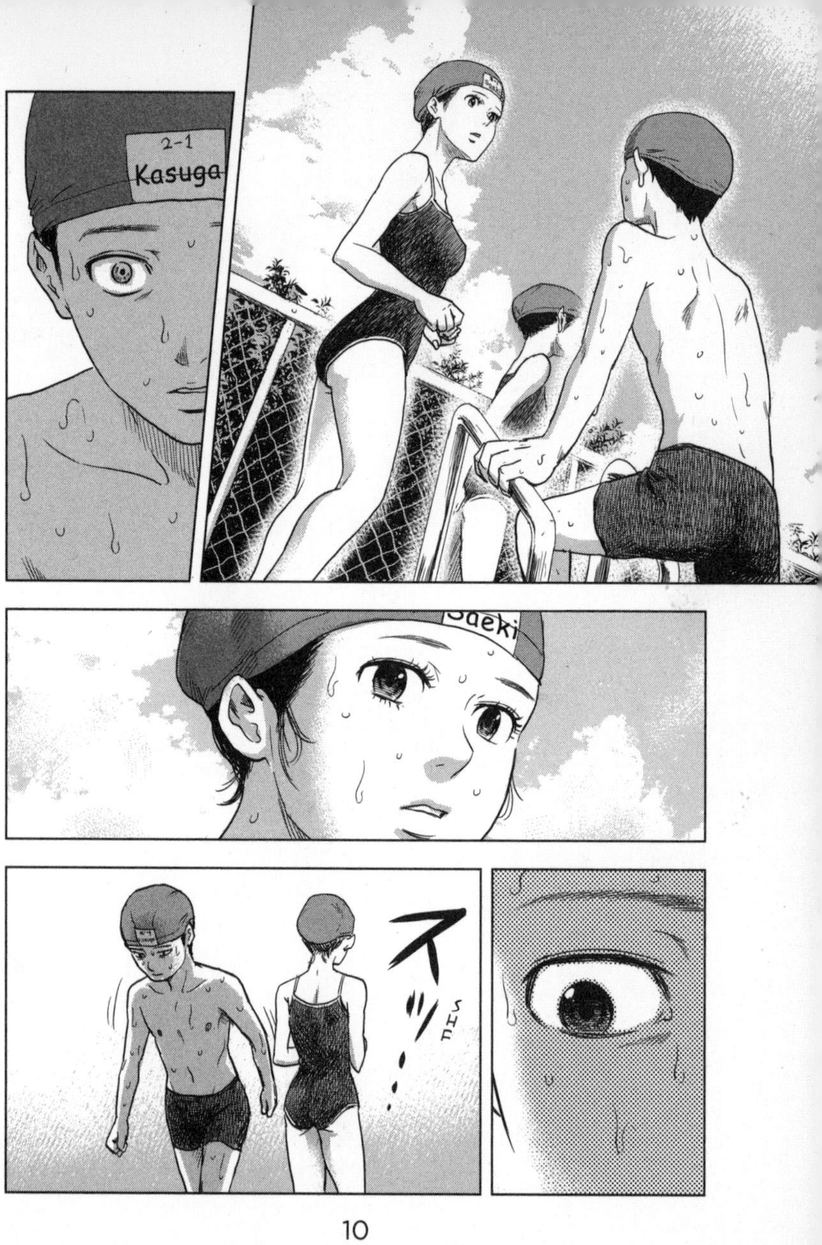
2-1
Kasuga
Saeki
スッ…
SHF

DANG...
SAEKI'S BOOBS ARE KINDA BIG.
CRAP, DUDE, KA-SUGA'S RIGHT THERE!
WHY, 'CAUSE HE'S HER BOY-FRIEND?
NO... I HEARD THEY BROKE UP.
THEY DID?!
HE'S BEEN SUPER GLOOMY LATELY, RIGHT?
YEAH... HIS EYES LOOK WAY DEAD.
WE OUGHT NOT TO MESS WITH HIM.
TW-TW-EE-EET!
HEY, YOU!

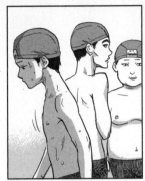

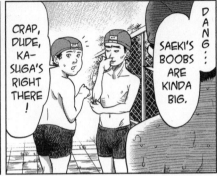

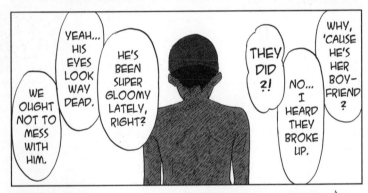

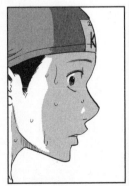

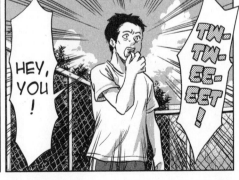

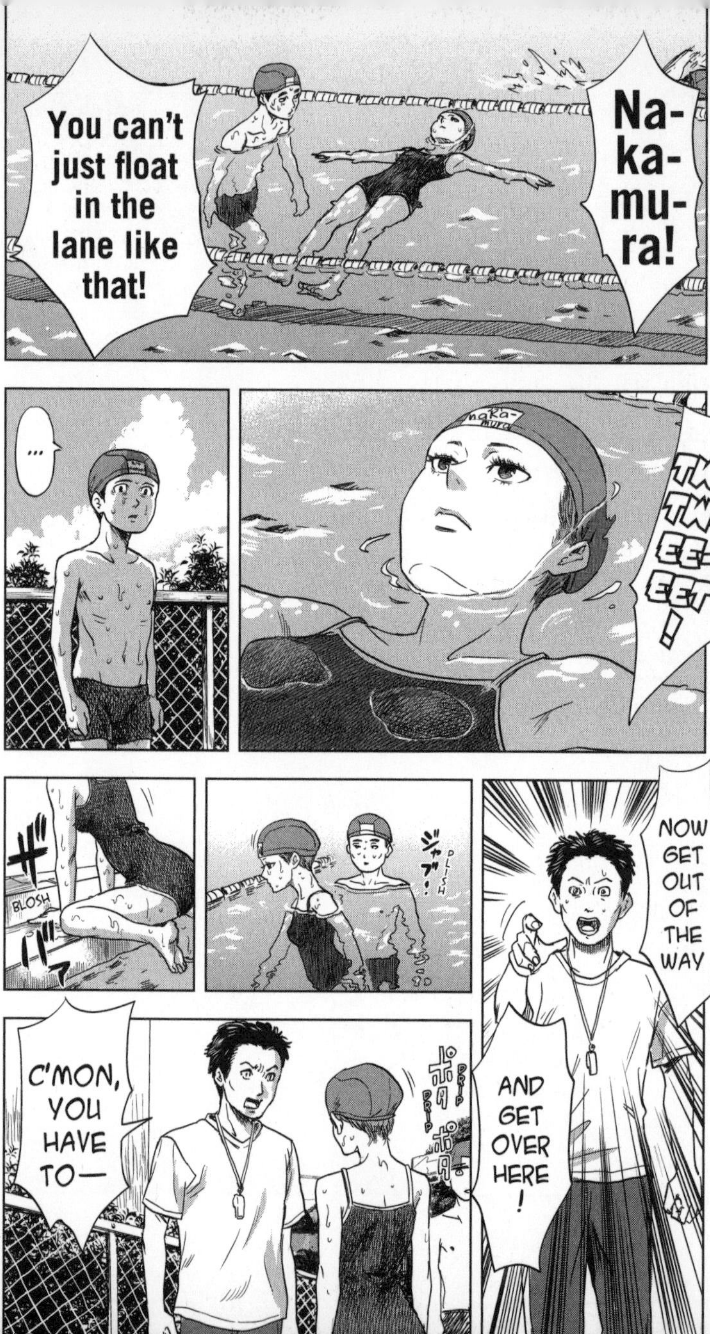
Na-ka-mu-ra!
You can't just float in the lane like that!
TW-TW-EE-EET!
naKa-mura
...
NOW GET OUT OF THE WAY
AND GET OVER HERE!
ジャブ!
DLISH
BLOSH
ポタポタ
DRIP DRIP
C'MON, YOU HAVE TO—

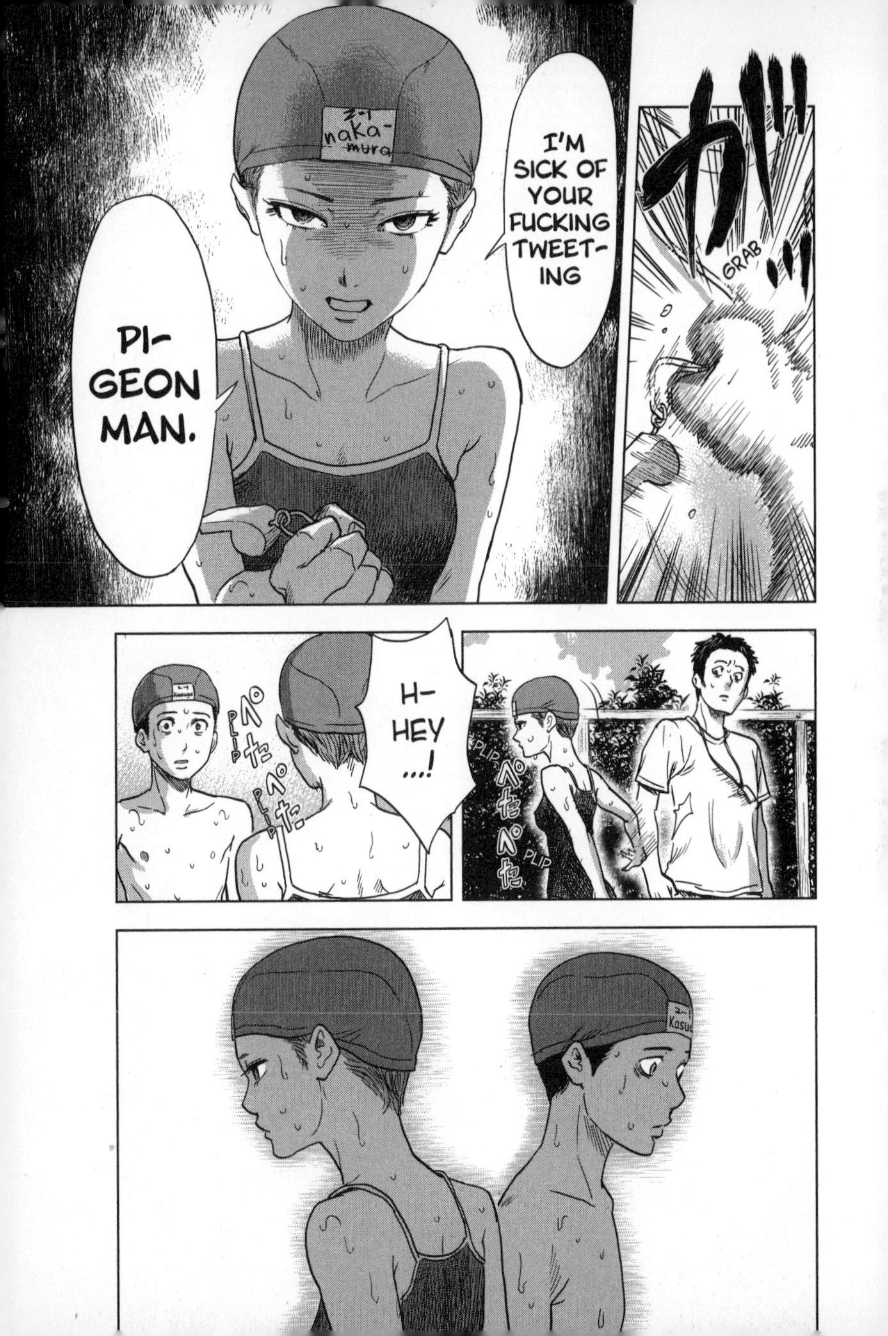

GRAB
nakamura
I'M SICK OF YOUR FUCKING TWEET-ING
PI-GEON MAN.
PLIP
PLIP
H-HEY ...!
PLIP
PLIP

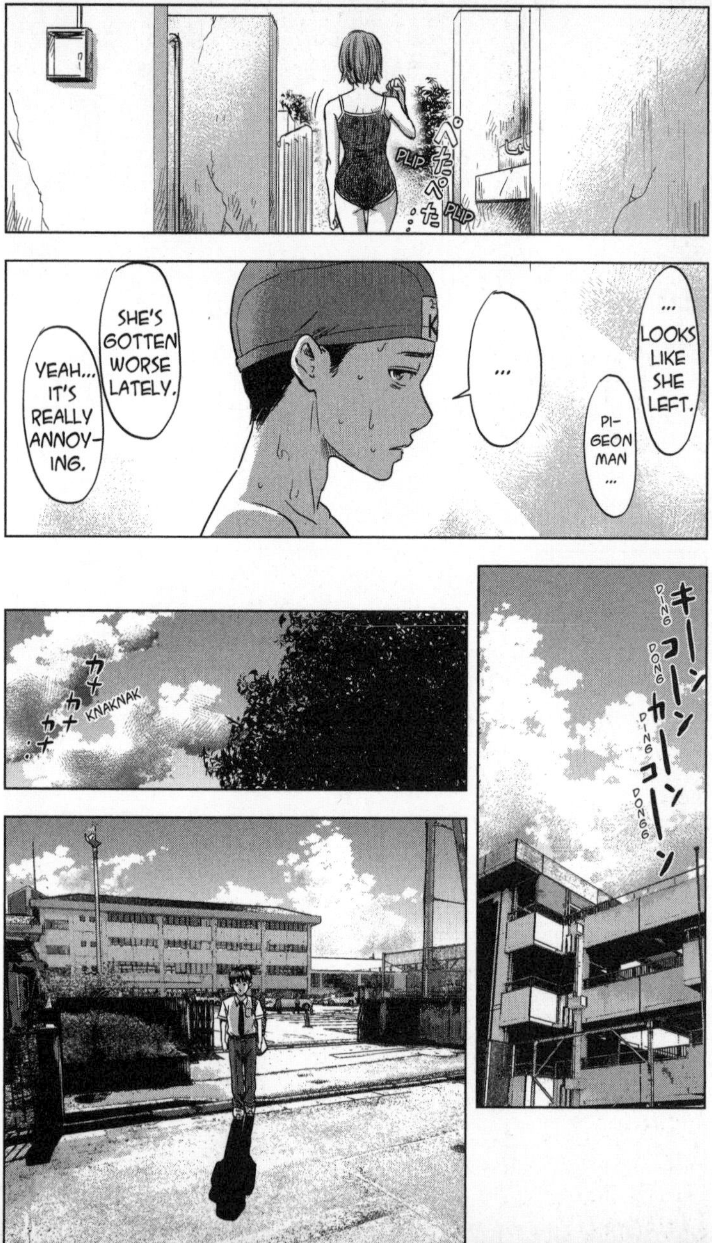
ぺたぺた
PLIP PLIP
... LOOKS LIKE SHE LEFT.
PI-GEON MAN ...
...
SHE'S GOTTEN WORSE LATELY.
YEAH... IT'S REALLY ANNOY-ING.
キーンコーンカーンコーン
DING DONG DING DONG
カナカナカナ
KNAKNAK

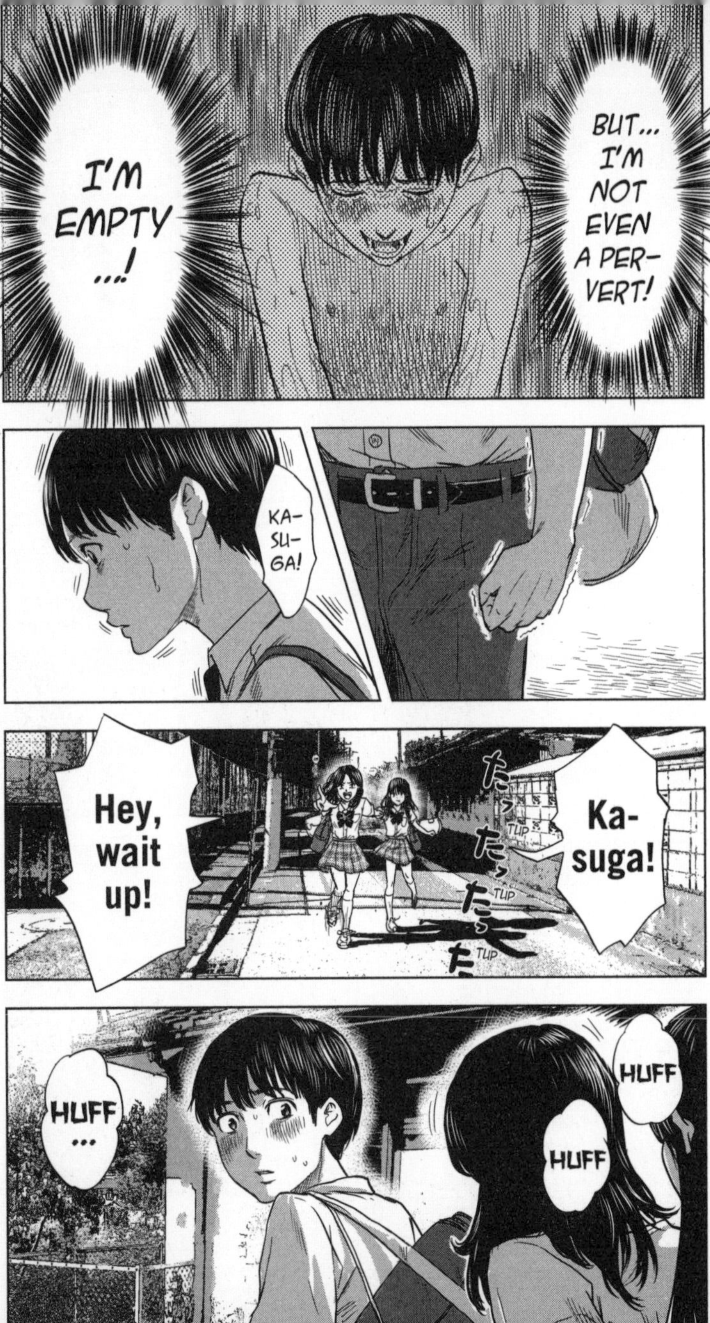
BUT... I'M NOT EVEN A PERVERT!
I'M EMPTY ...!
KA-SU-GA!
Ka-suga!
たっ
TUP
たっ
TUP
たっ
TUP
た
Hey, wait up!
HUFF
HUFF
HUFF ...

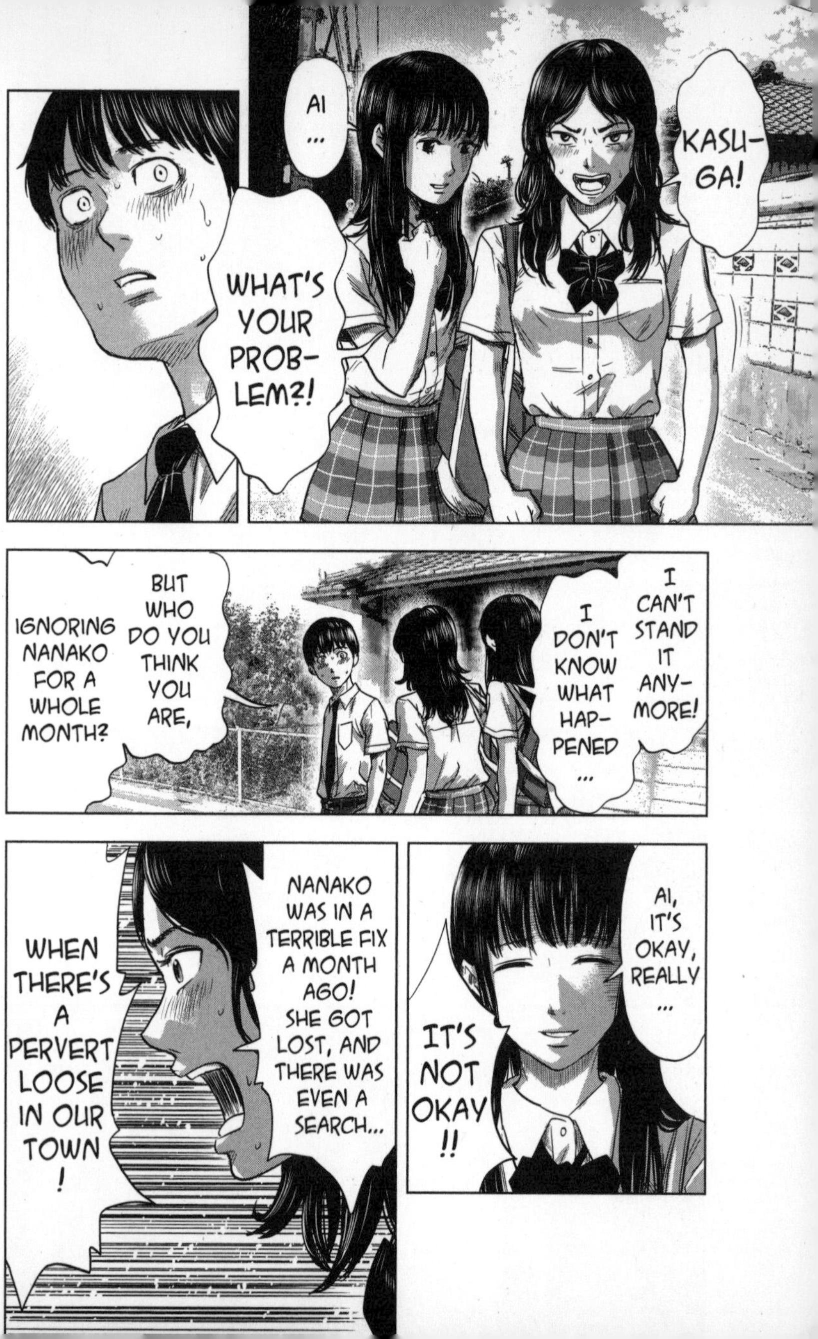
KASU-GA!
AI ...
WHAT'S YOUR PROB-LEM?!
I CAN'T STAND IT ANY-MORE!
I DON'T KNOW WHAT HAP-PENED ...
BUT WHO DO YOU THINK YOU ARE,
IGNORING NANAKO FOR A WHOLE MONTH?
AI, IT'S OKAY, REALLY ...
IT'S NOT OKAY !!
NANAKO WAS IN A TERRIBLE FIX A MONTH AGO! SHE GOT LOST, AND THERE WAS EVEN A SEARCH...
WHEN THERE'S A PERVERT LOOSE IN OUR TOWN !

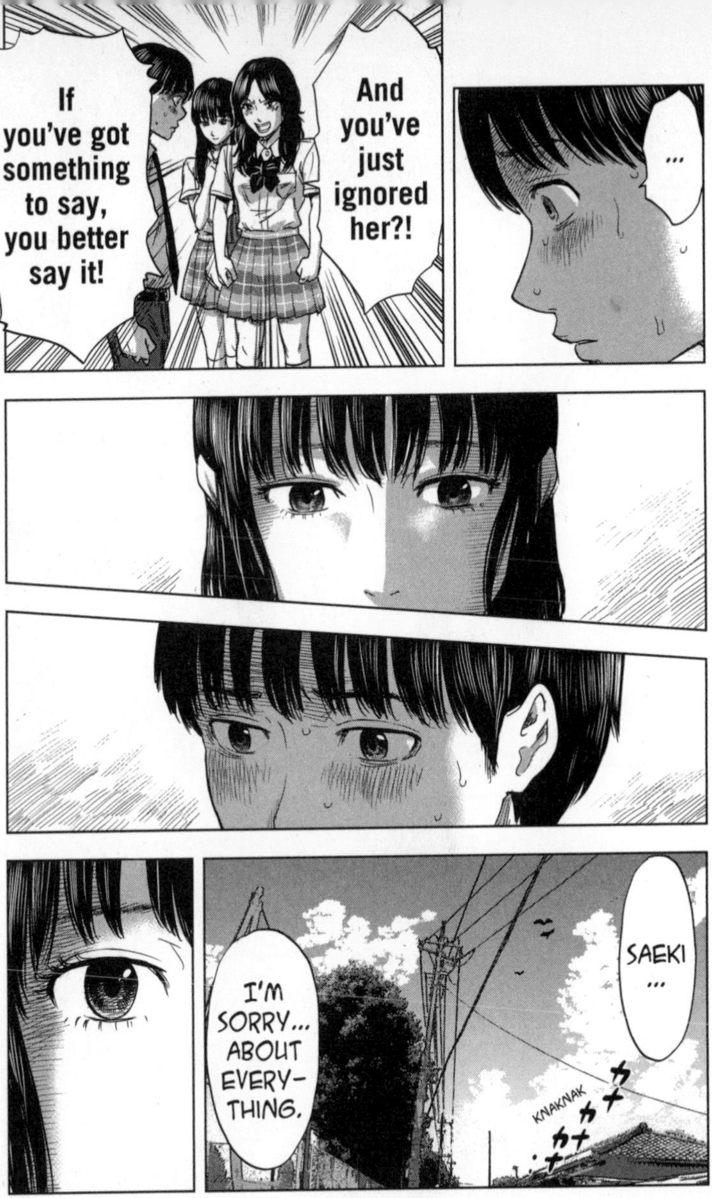
...
And you've just ignored her?!
If you've got something to say, you better say it!
SAEKI...
I'M SORRY... ABOUT EVERYTHING.
KNAKNAK

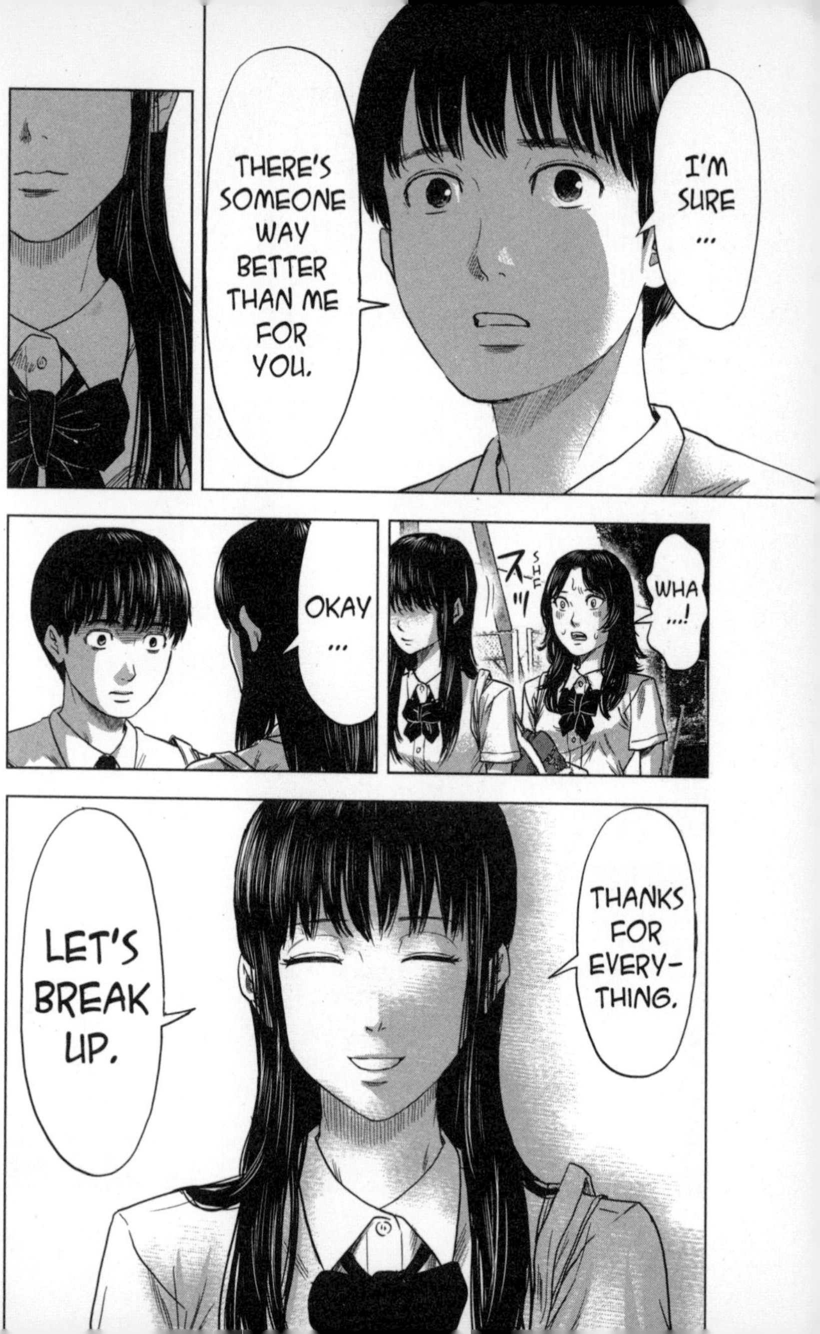
I'M SURE ...
THERE'S SOMEONE WAY BETTER THAN ME FOR YOU.
スッ
SHF
WHA ...!
OKAY ...
THANKS FOR EVERY-THING.
LET'S BREAK UP.

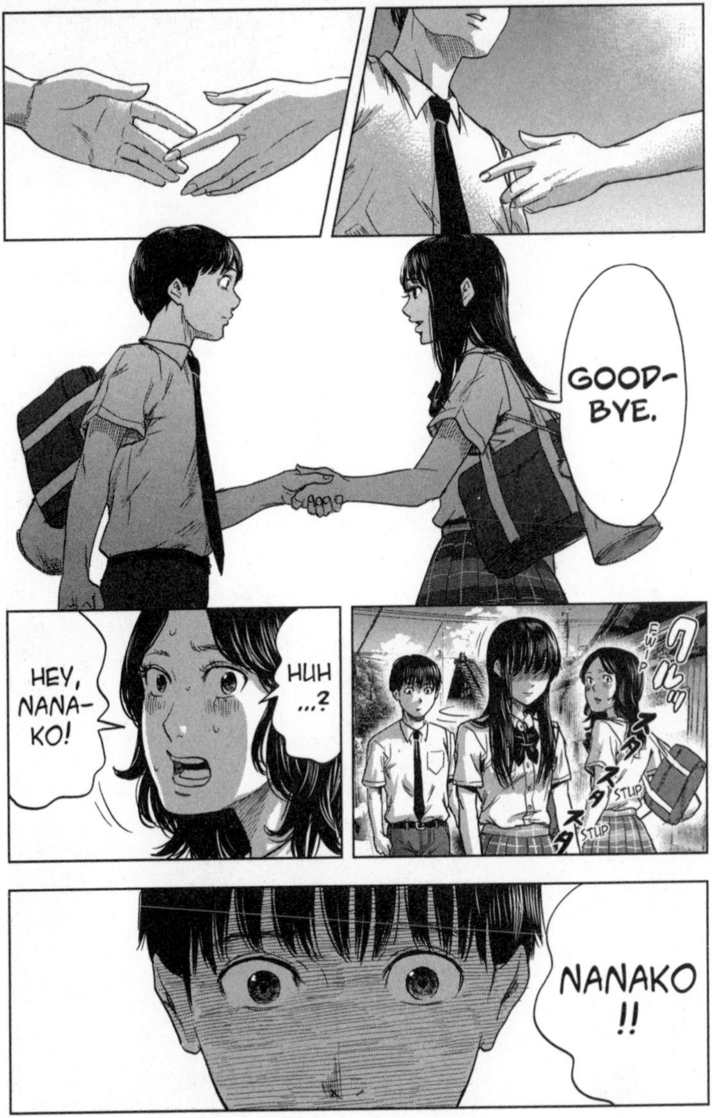
GOOD-BYE.
クルッ
FWIP
スタスタ
STUP
スタ
STUP
HUH ...?
HEY, NANA-KO!
NANAKO !!

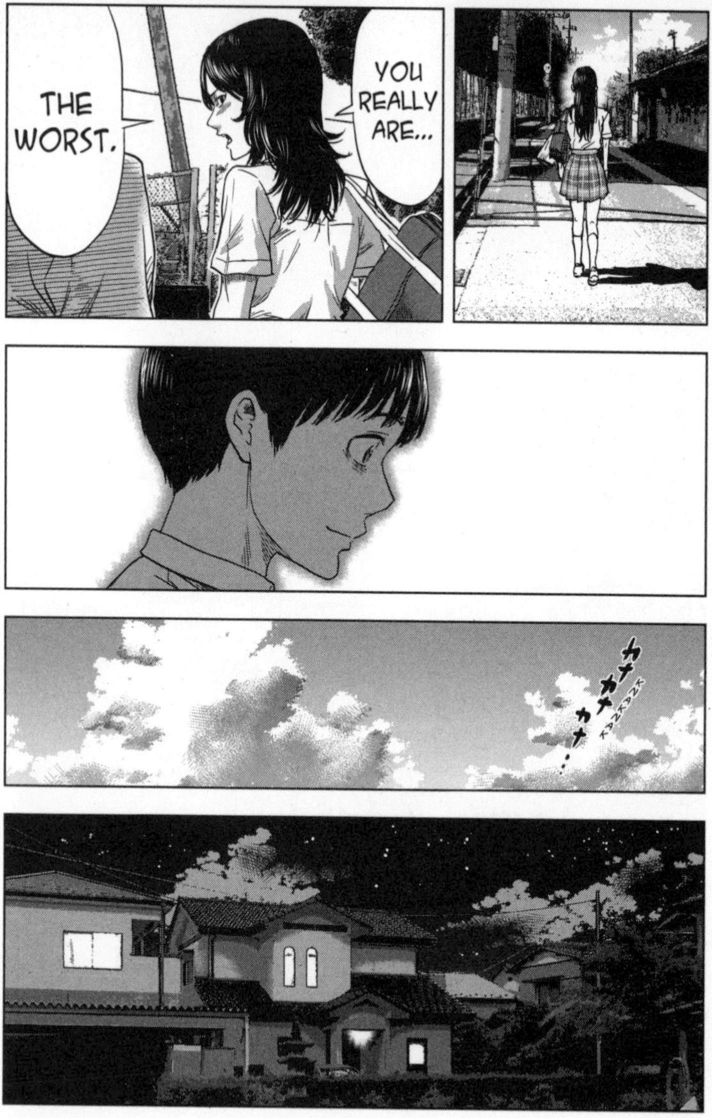
YOU REALLY ARE...
THE WORST.
カナカナカナ…
KANKANK

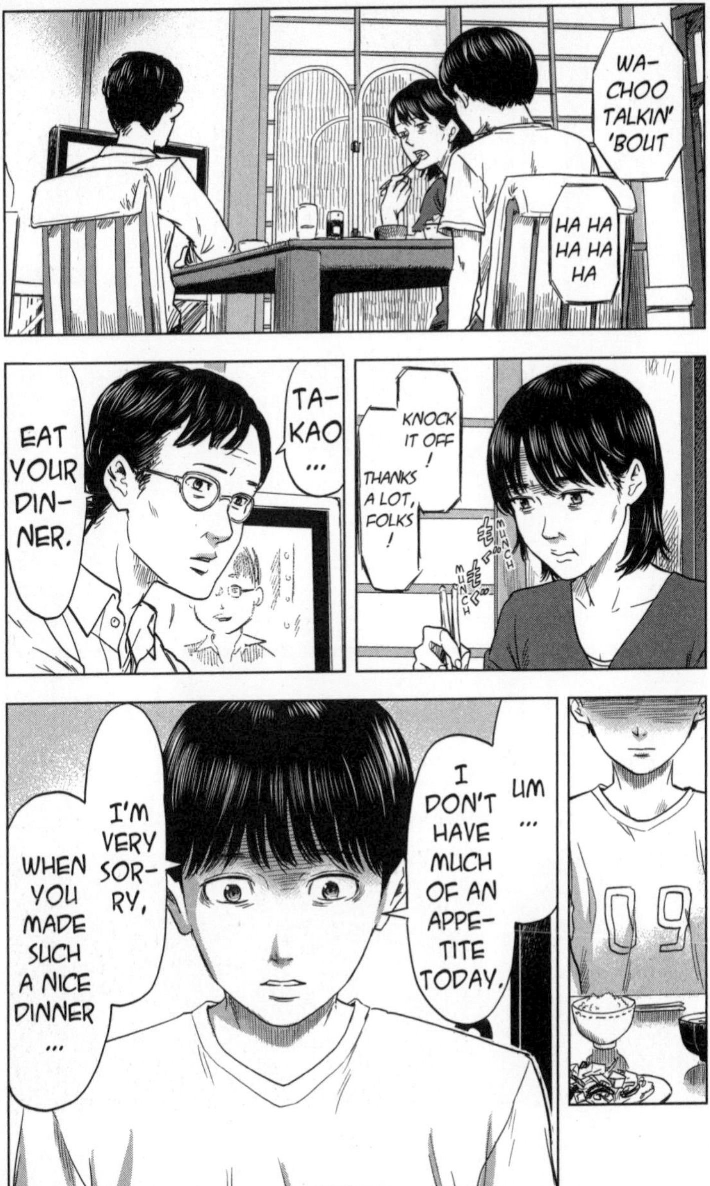
WA-CHOO TALKIN' 'BOUT
HA HA HA HA HA
KNOCK IT OFF!
THANKS A LOT, FOLKS!
MUNCH
MUNCH
TA-KAO ...
EAT YOUR DIN-NER.
UM ...
I DON'T HAVE MUCH OF AN APPE-TITE TODAY.
I'M VERY SOR-RY,
WHEN YOU MADE SUCH A NICE DINNER ...

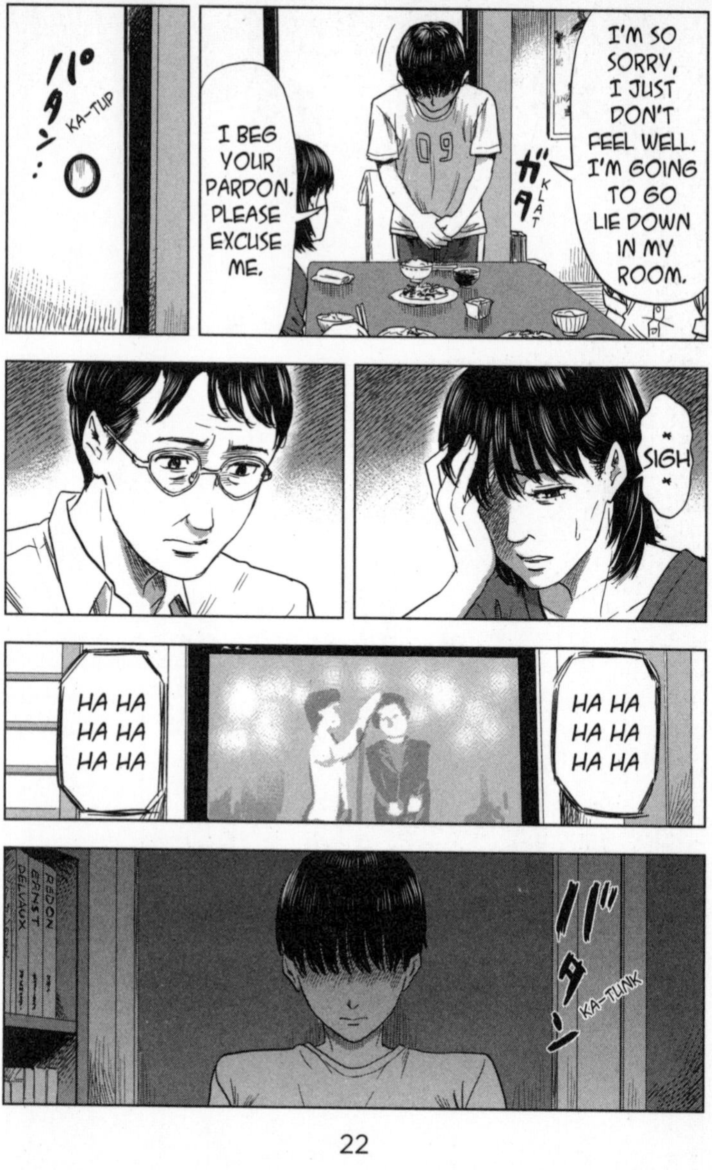
I'M SO SORRY, I JUST DON'T FEEL WELL. I'M GOING TO GO LIE DOWN IN MY ROOM.
ガタ KLAT
I BEG YOUR PARDON. PLEASE EXCUSE ME.
パタン… KA-TUP
SIGH
HA HA HA HA HA HA
HA HA HA HA HA HA
バタン KA-TUNK
REDON
ERNST
DELVAUX

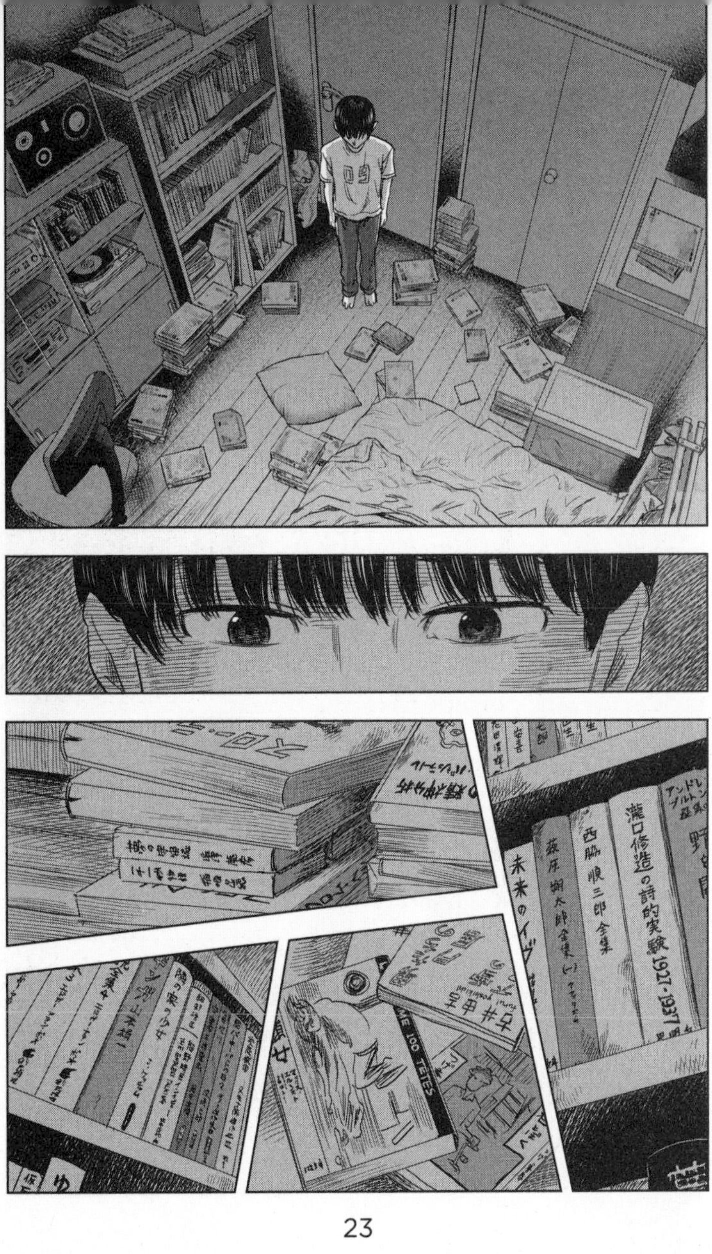
アンドレ・ブルトン
瀧口修造の詩的実験 1927・1937
西脇順三郎全集
萩原朔太郎全集 (一)
未来のイヴ
ME 100 TETES

UNG ...
* BARF *
びちゃ SPLAT
HUR-RRG-GH...
びちゃ SPLAT
びちゃ
HUFF
HUFF
HUFF
フラ… WOBBLE
ドサッ FLUMP
IT WAS FOR THE BEST...

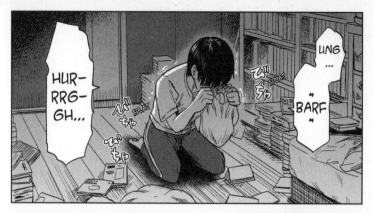

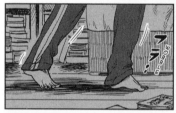

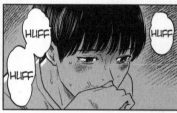

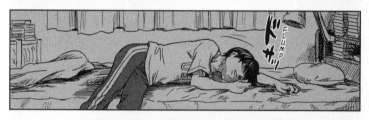

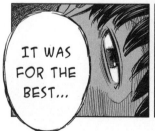

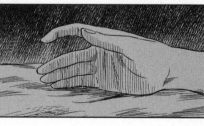

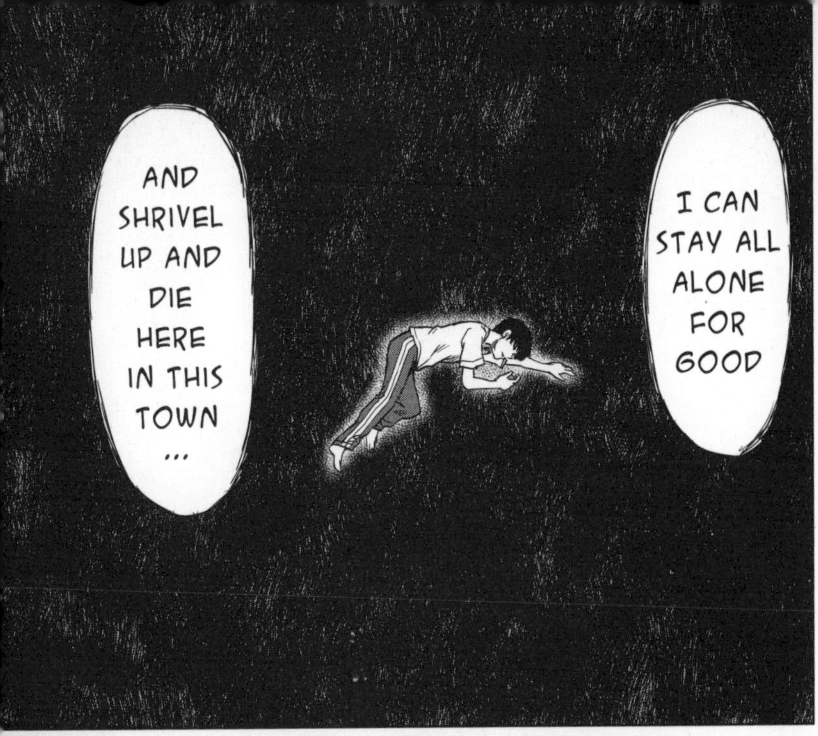
I CAN STAY ALL ALONE FOR GOOD
AND SHRIVEL UP AND DIE HERE IN THIS TOWN ...
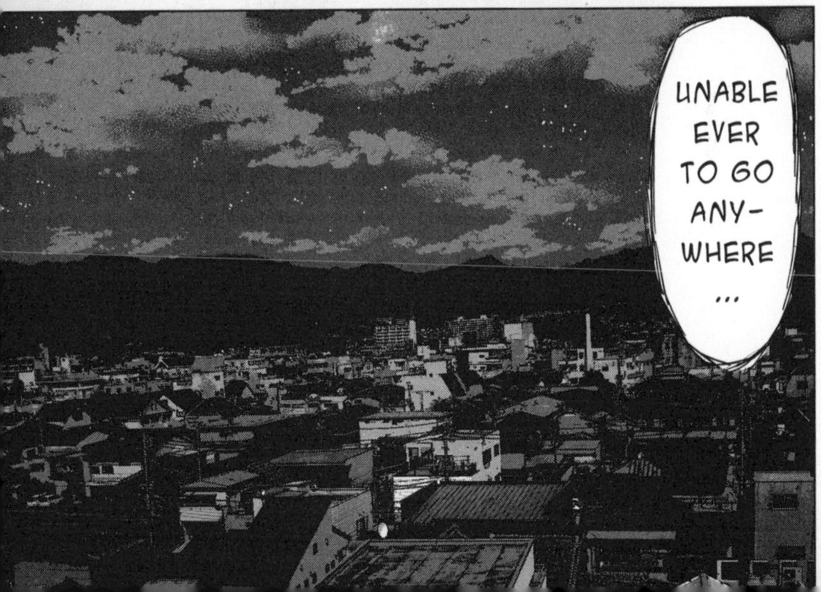
UNABLE EVER TO GO ANY-WHERE ...

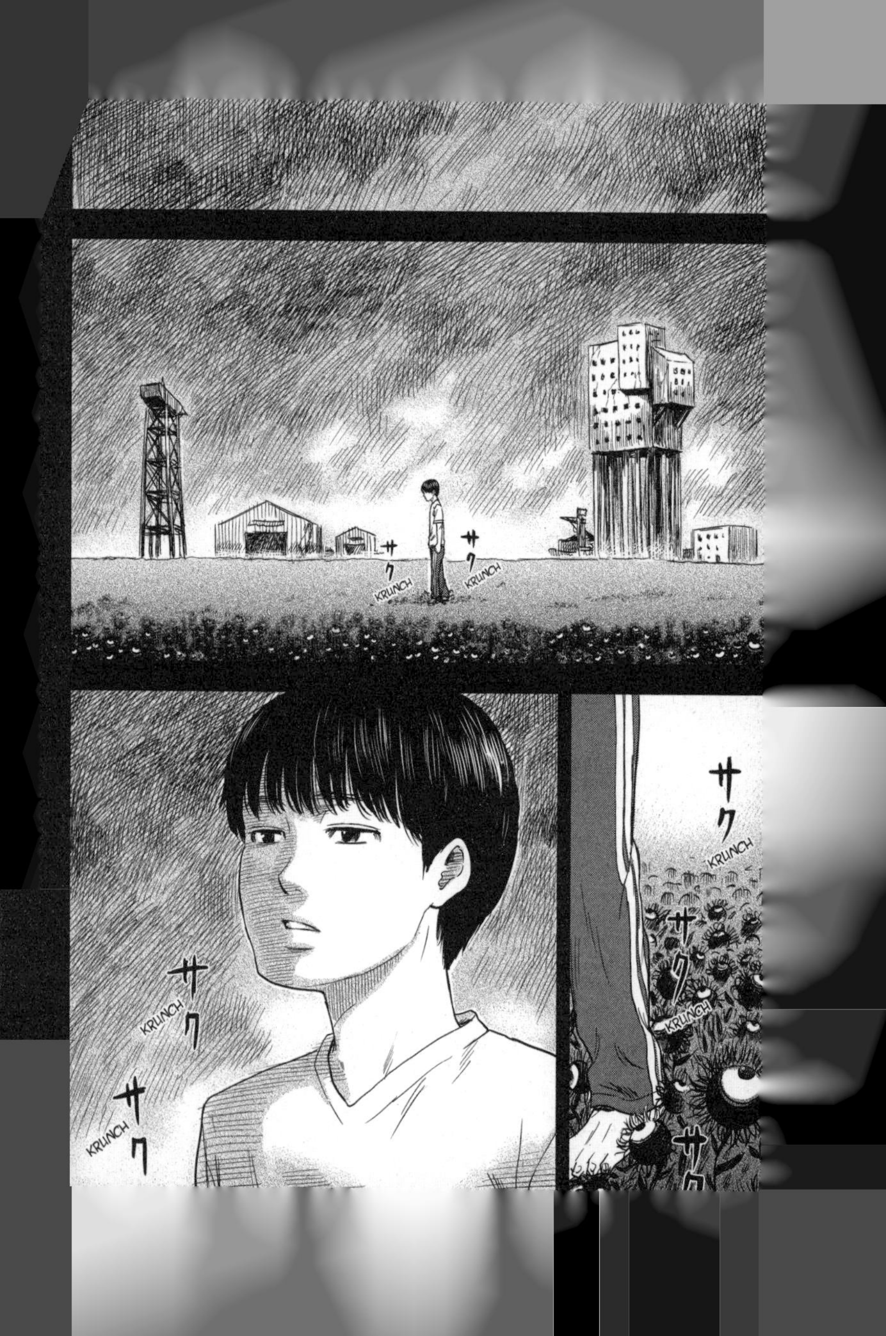
サク
KRUNCH
サク
KRUNCH
サク
KRUNCH
サク
KRUNCH
サ
サク
KRUNCH
サク
KRUNCH

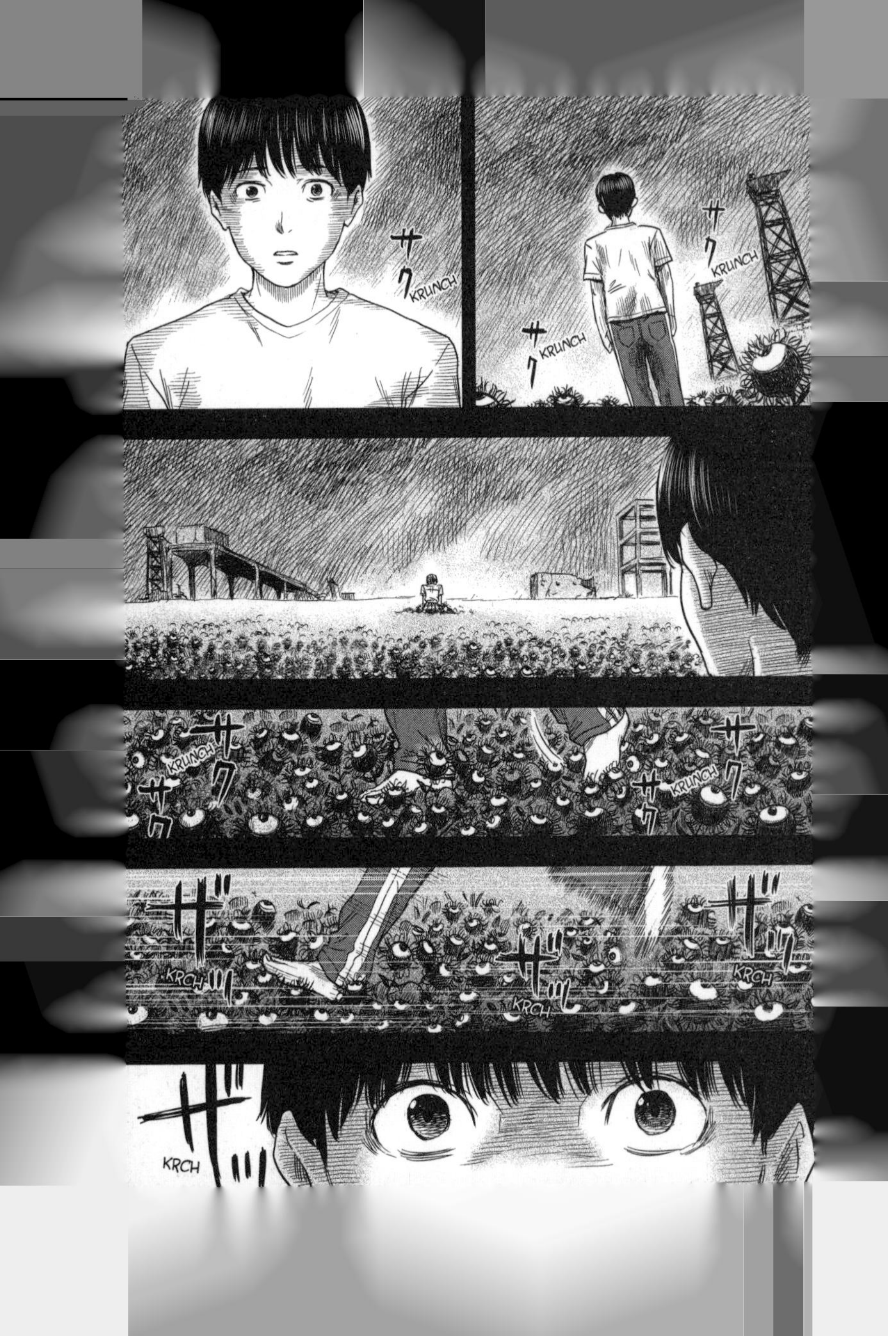
サク
KRUNCH
サク
KRUNCH
サク
KRUNCH
サク
KRUNCH
サク
KRUNCH
サク
ザッ
KRCH
ザッ
KRCH
ザッ
KRCH
ザッ
KRCH

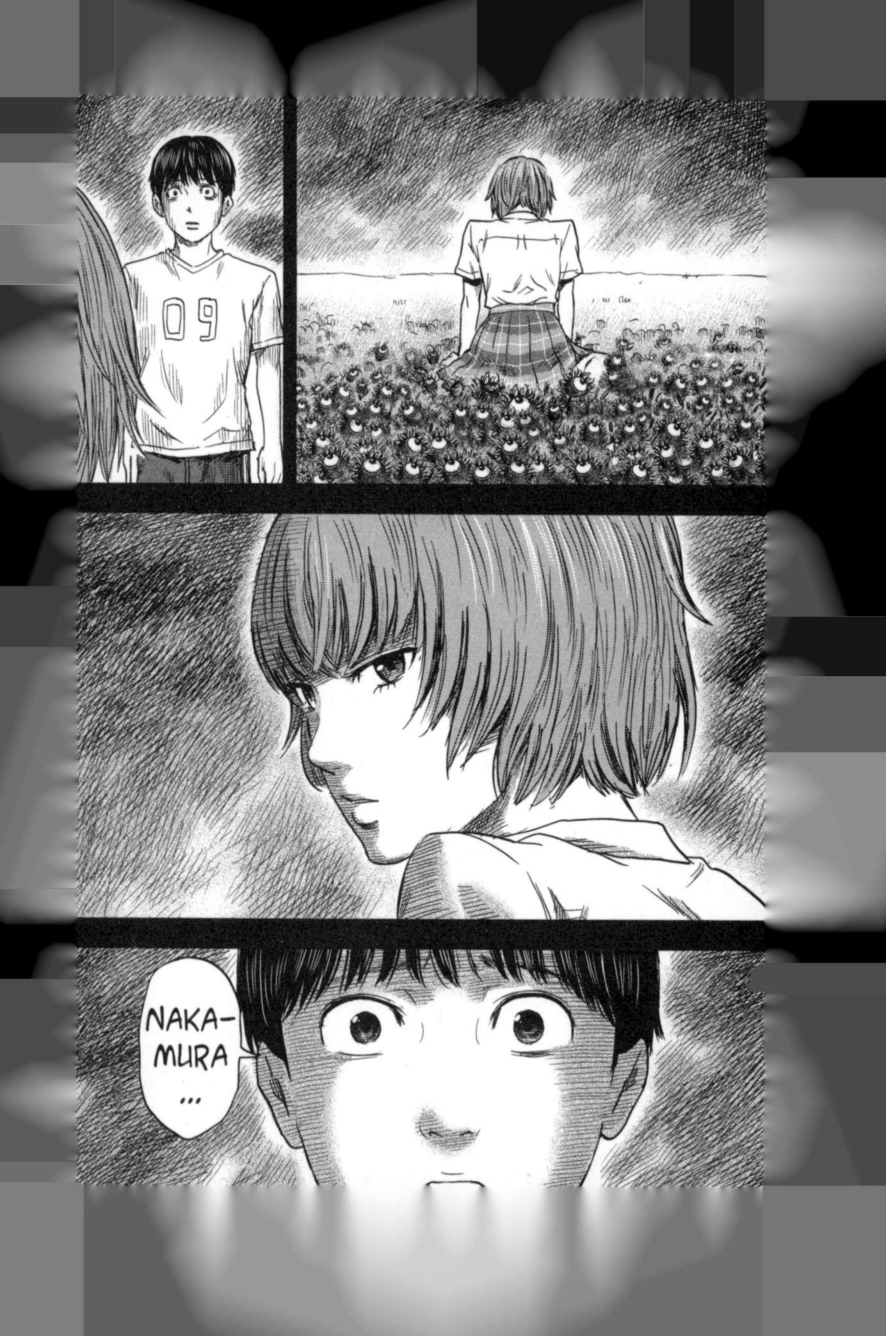
NAKA-MURA...

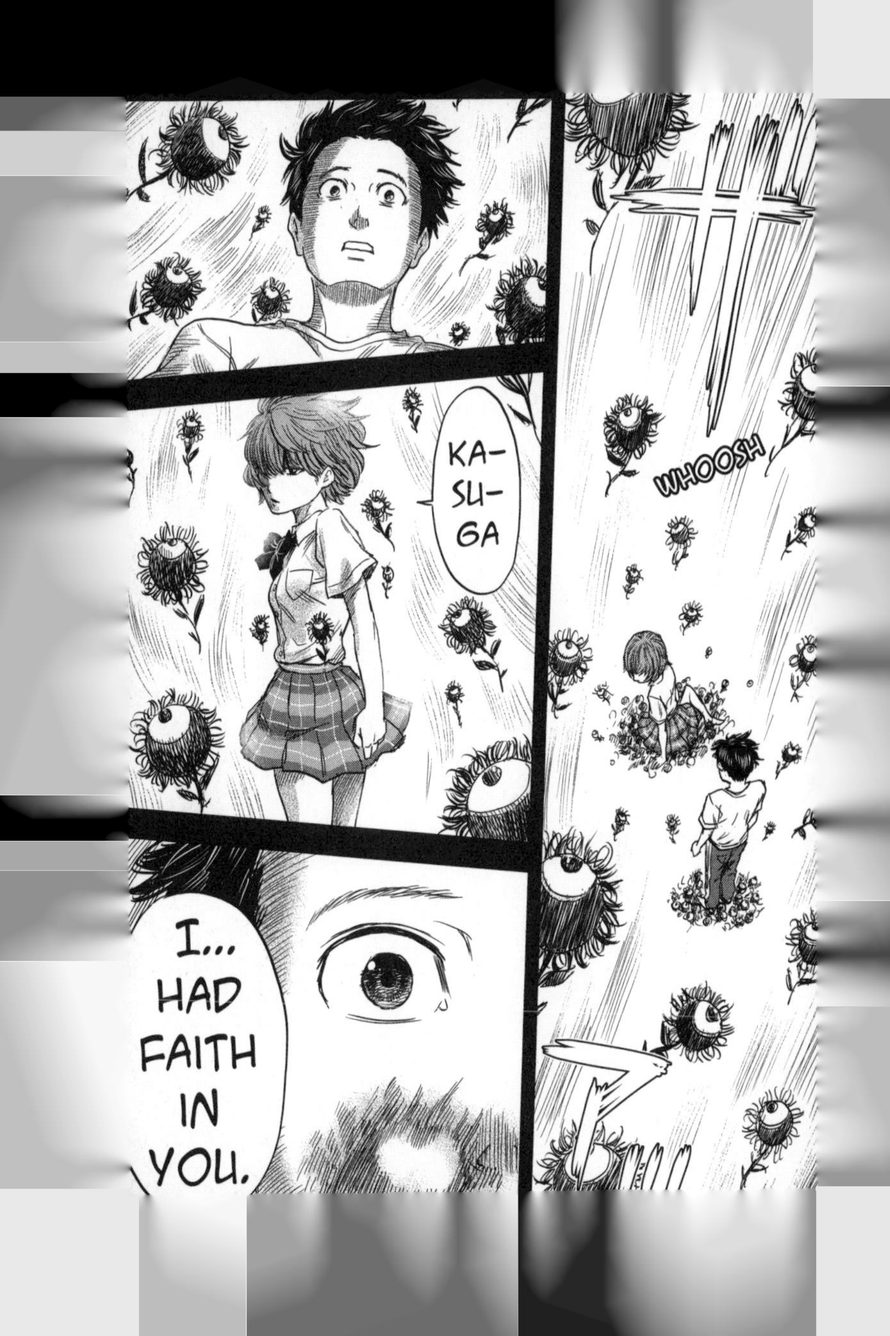
WHOOSH
KA-SU-GA
I... HAD FAITH IN YOU.

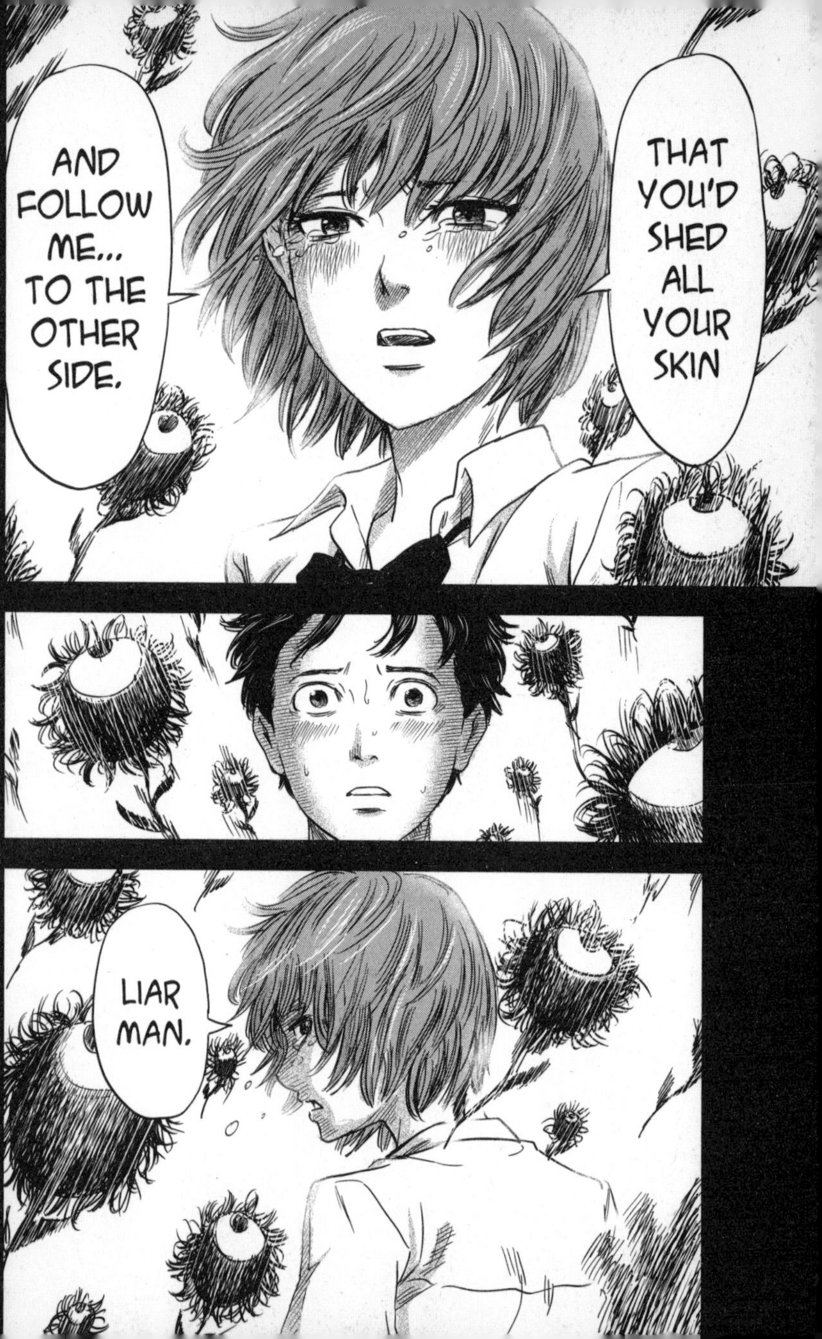
THAT YOU'D SHED ALL YOUR SKIN
AND FOLLOW ME... TO THE OTHER SIDE.
LIAR MAN.

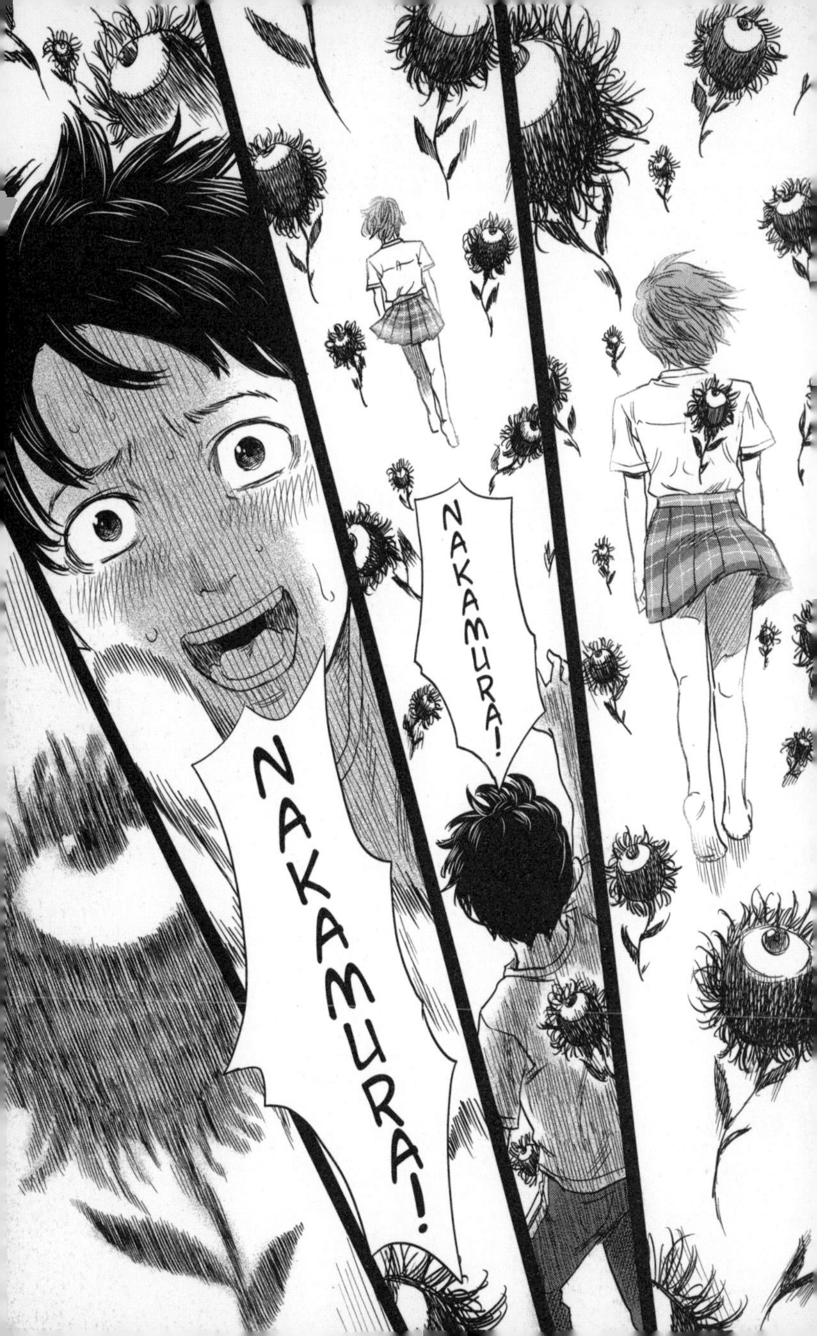
NAKAMURA!
NAKAMURA!

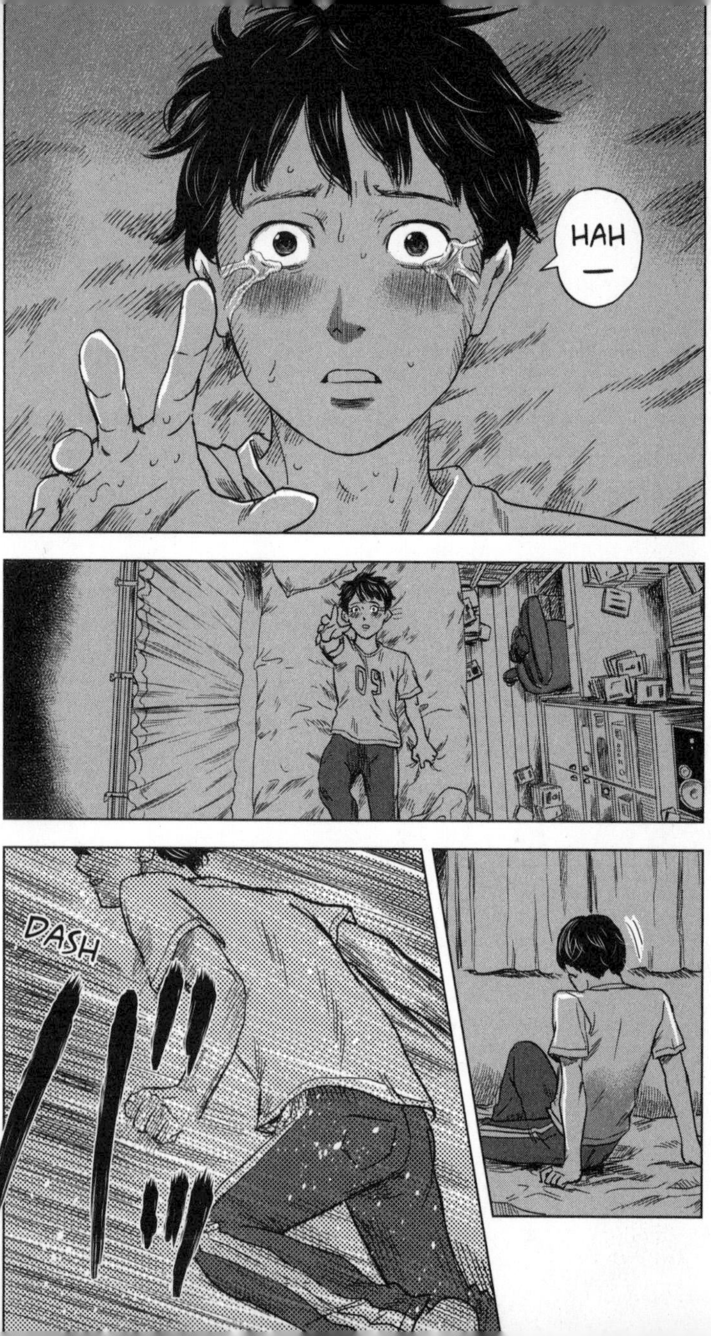
HAH —
DASH

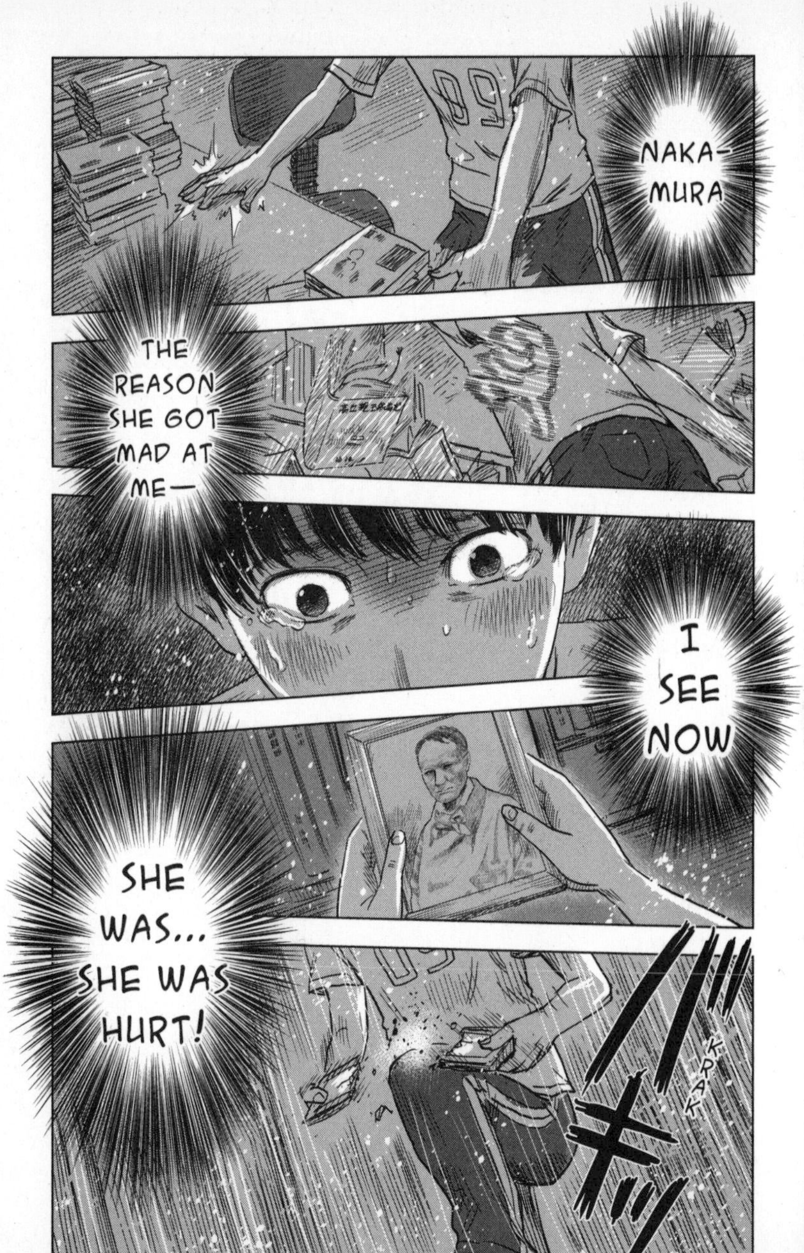

NAKA-MURA
THE REASON SHE GOT MAD AT ME—
I SEE NOW
SHE WAS... SHE WAS HURT!
KRAK

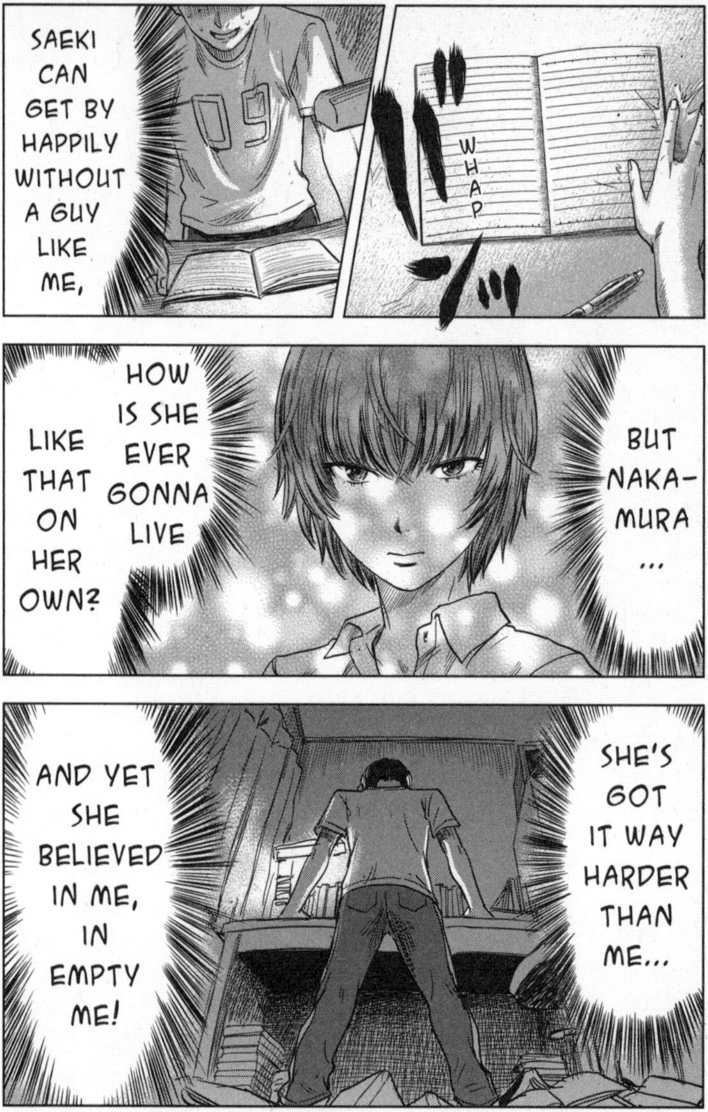
WHAP
SAEKI CAN GET BY HAPPILY WITHOUT A GUY LIKE ME,
BUT NAKA-MURA ...
HOW IS SHE EVER GONNA LIVE
LIKE THAT ON HER OWN?
SHE'S GOT IT WAY HARDER THAN ME...
AND YET SHE BELIEVED IN ME, IN EMPTY ME!

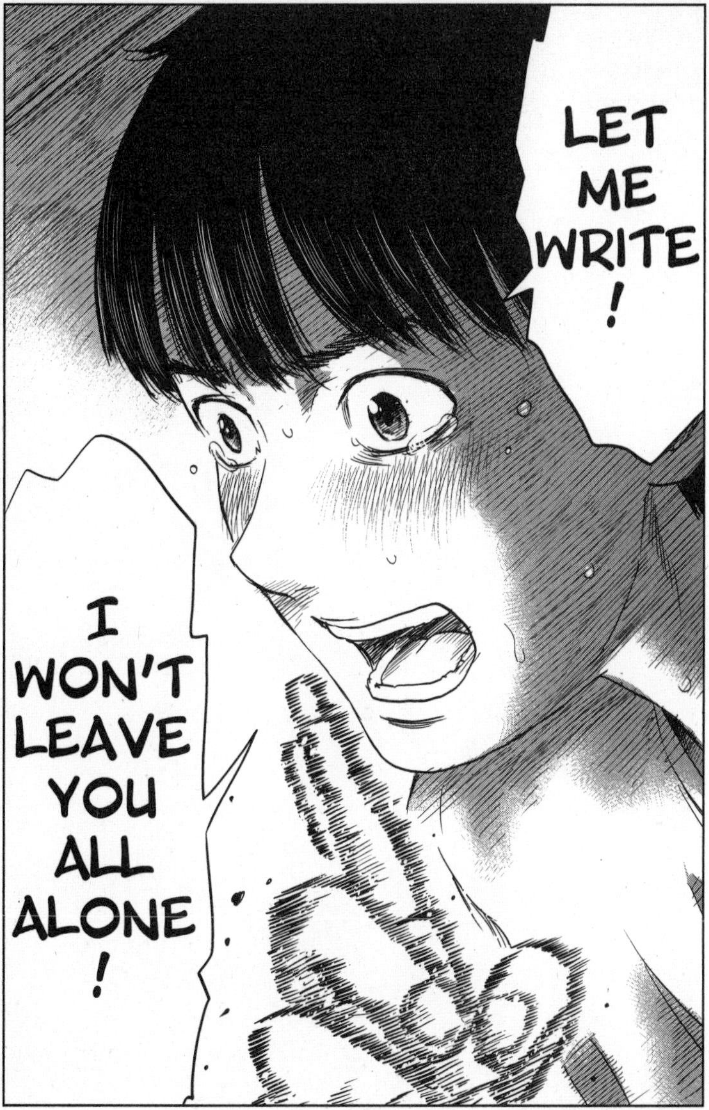
LET ME WRITE!
I WON'T LEAVE YOU ALL ALONE!

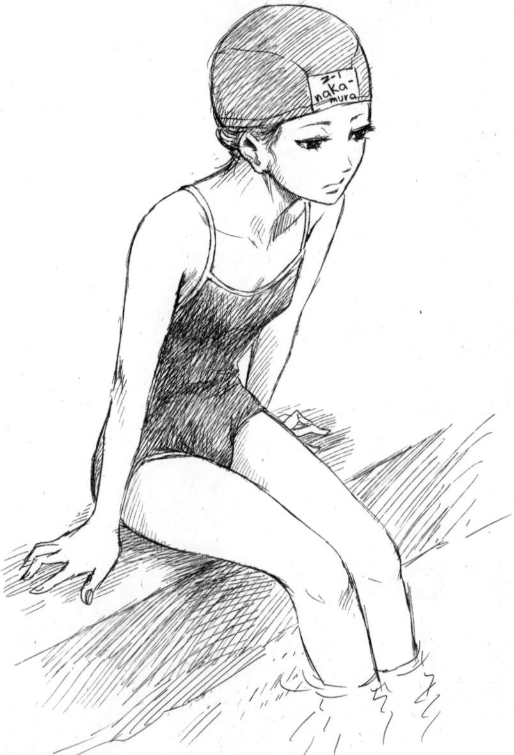
2-1
naka-
mura

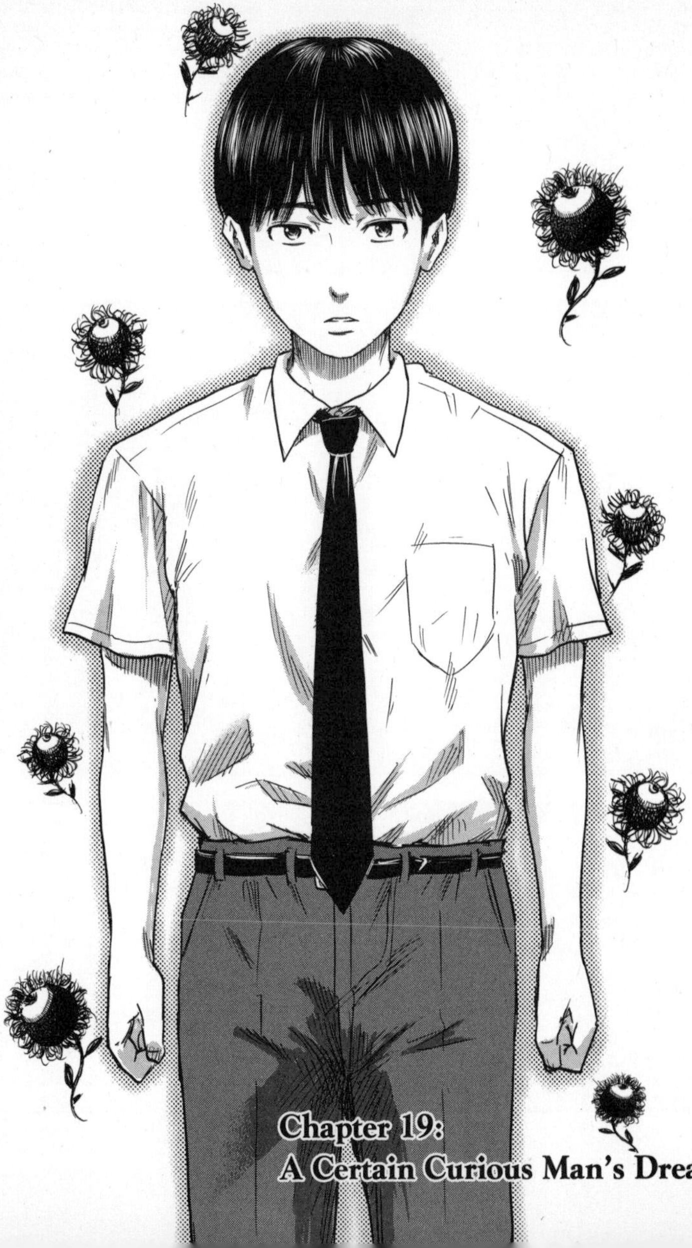

Chapter 19:
A Certain Curious Man's Dream

チュン
CHIRP
チュン
CHIRP
チュン
CHIRP
チュン
CHIRP
コト‥
TUPP

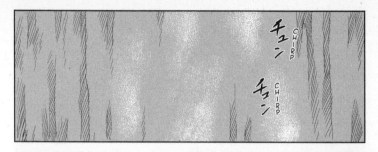

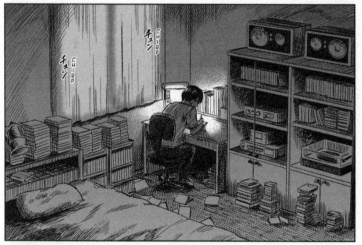

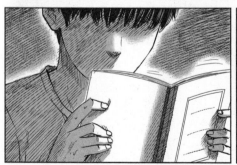

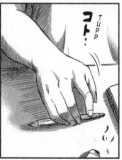

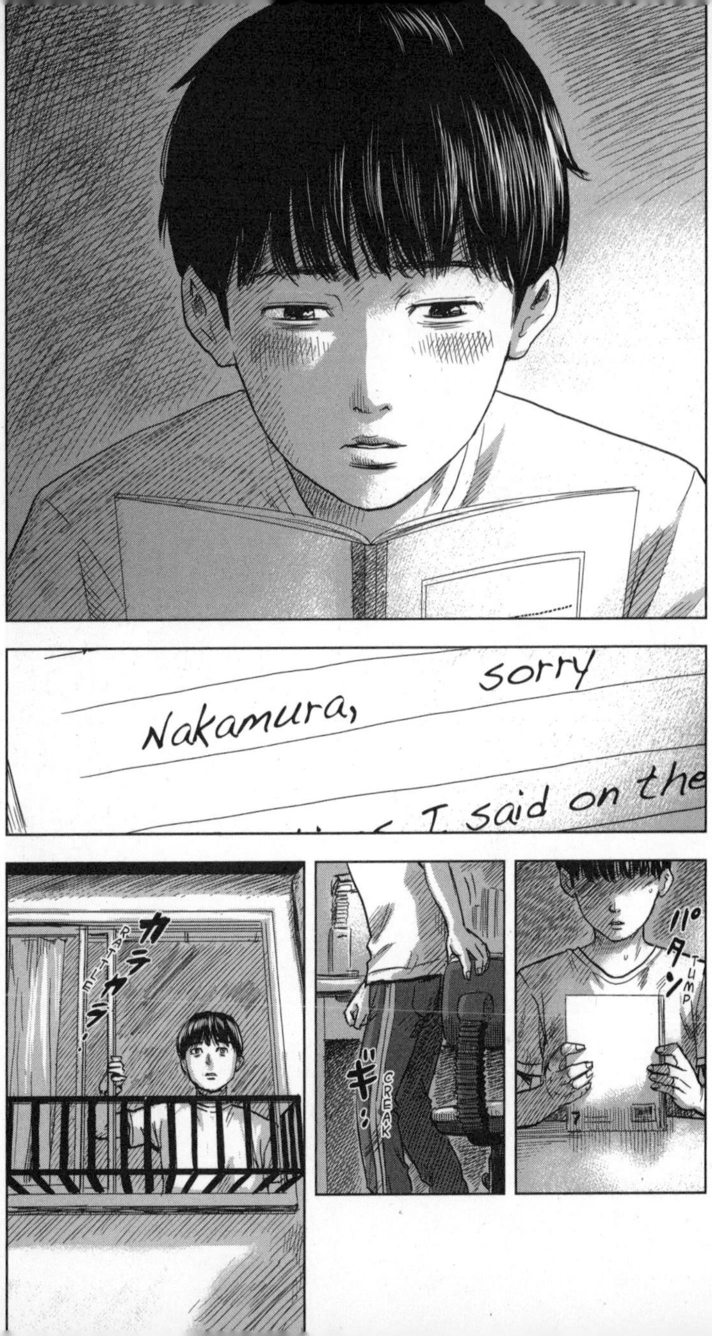
Nakamura, sorry
I said on the
パタン
TUMP
ギ…
CREAK
カラカラ…
RATTLE

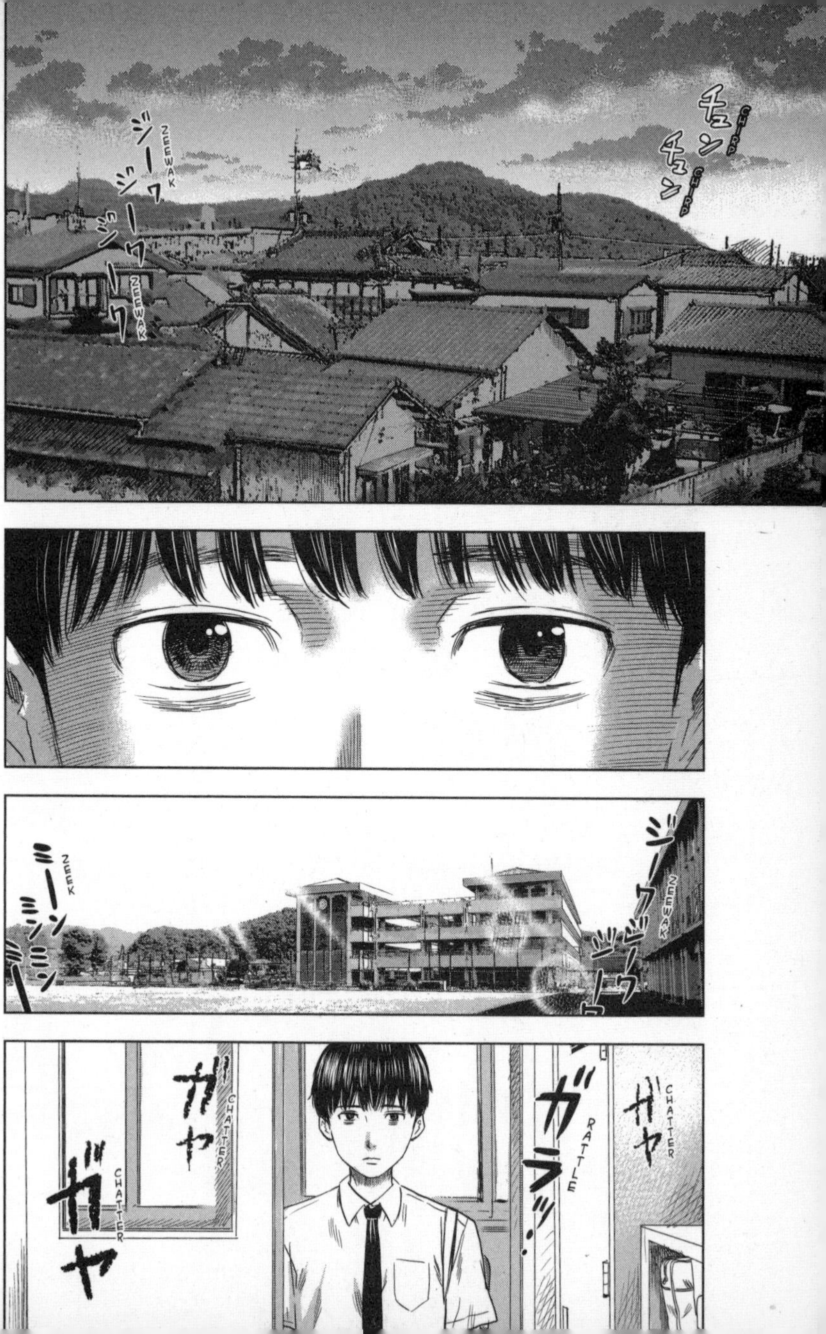
チュン
CHIRP
チュン
CHIRP
ジーワ
ZEEWAK
ZEEWAK
ZEEWAK
ミーン
ZEEK
ガヤ
CHATTER
ガラッ
RATTLE
ガヤ
CHATTER
ガヤ
CHATTER

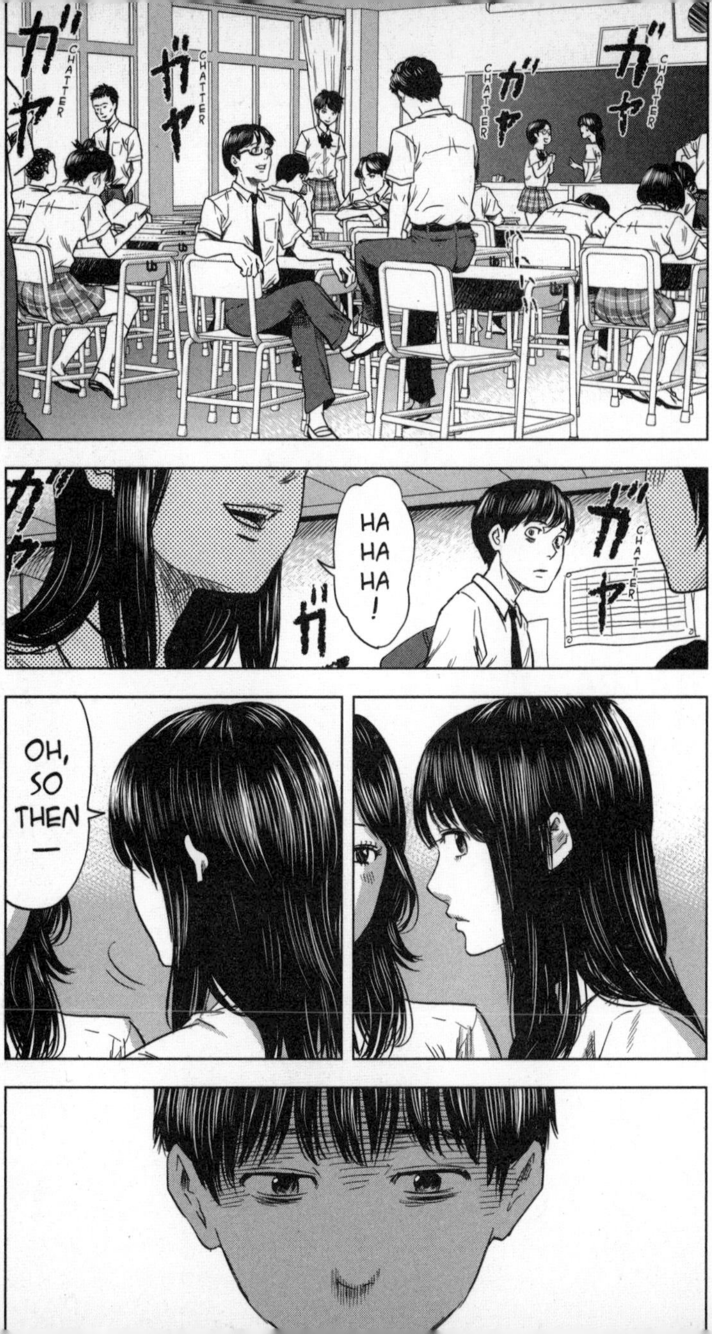
ガヤ
CHATTER
ガヤ
CHATTER
ガヤ
CHATTER
ガヤ
CHATTER
ガヤ
CHATTER
HA HA HA!
OH, SO THEN —

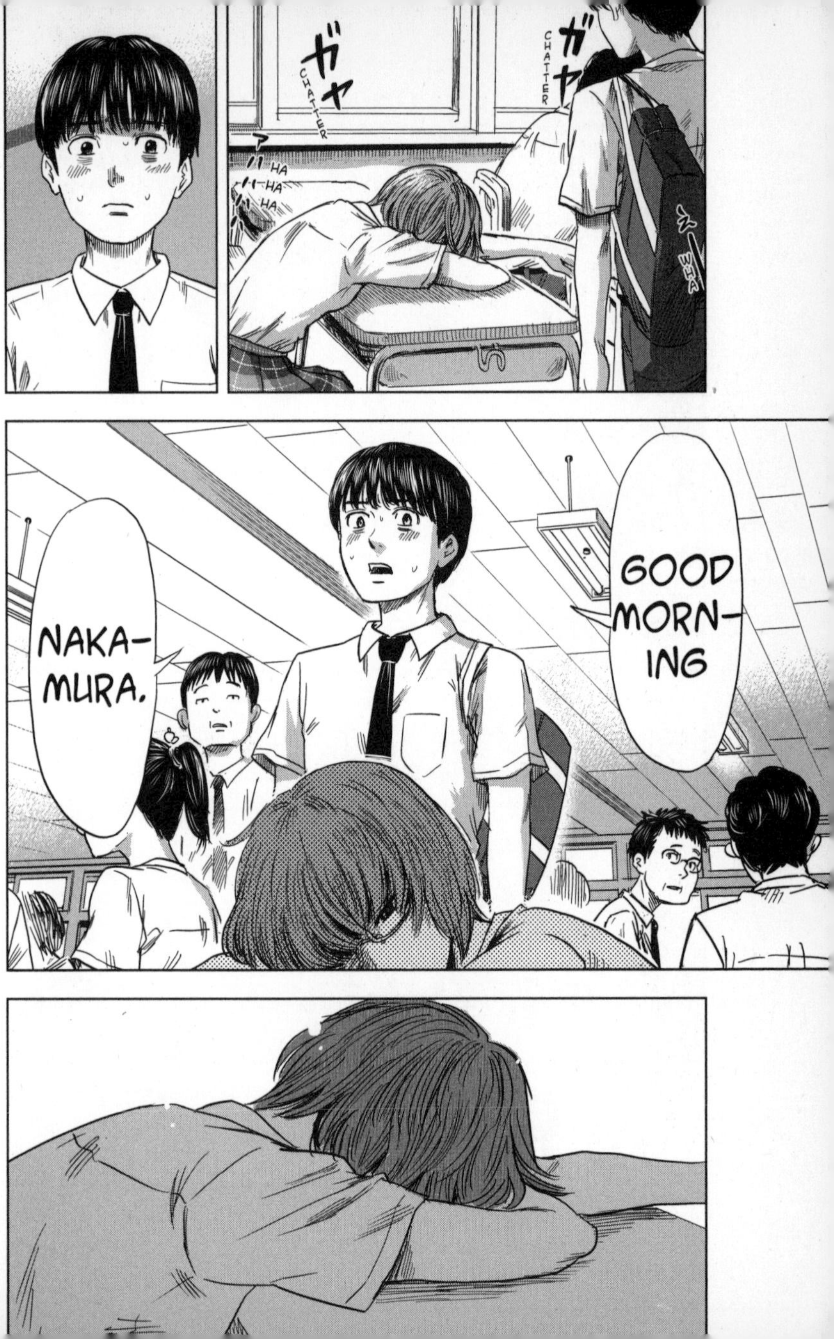
ガヤ CHATTER
ガヤ CHATTER
え WHA
アハハハ HA HA HA
GOOD MORNING
NAKAMURA.

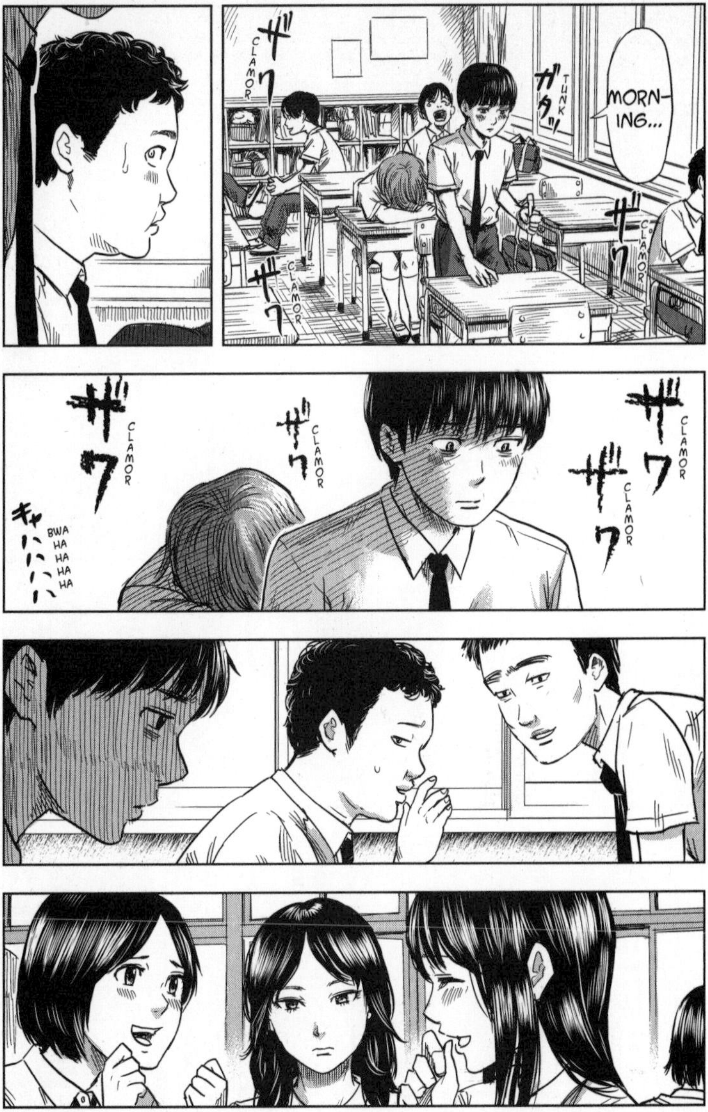
MORNING...
ザワ CLAMOR
ガタッ TUNK
ザワ CLAMOR
ザワ CLAMOR
ザワ CLAMOR
ザワ CLAMOR
ザワ CLAMOR
ザワ CLAMOR
キャハハハハ BWA HA HA HA HA

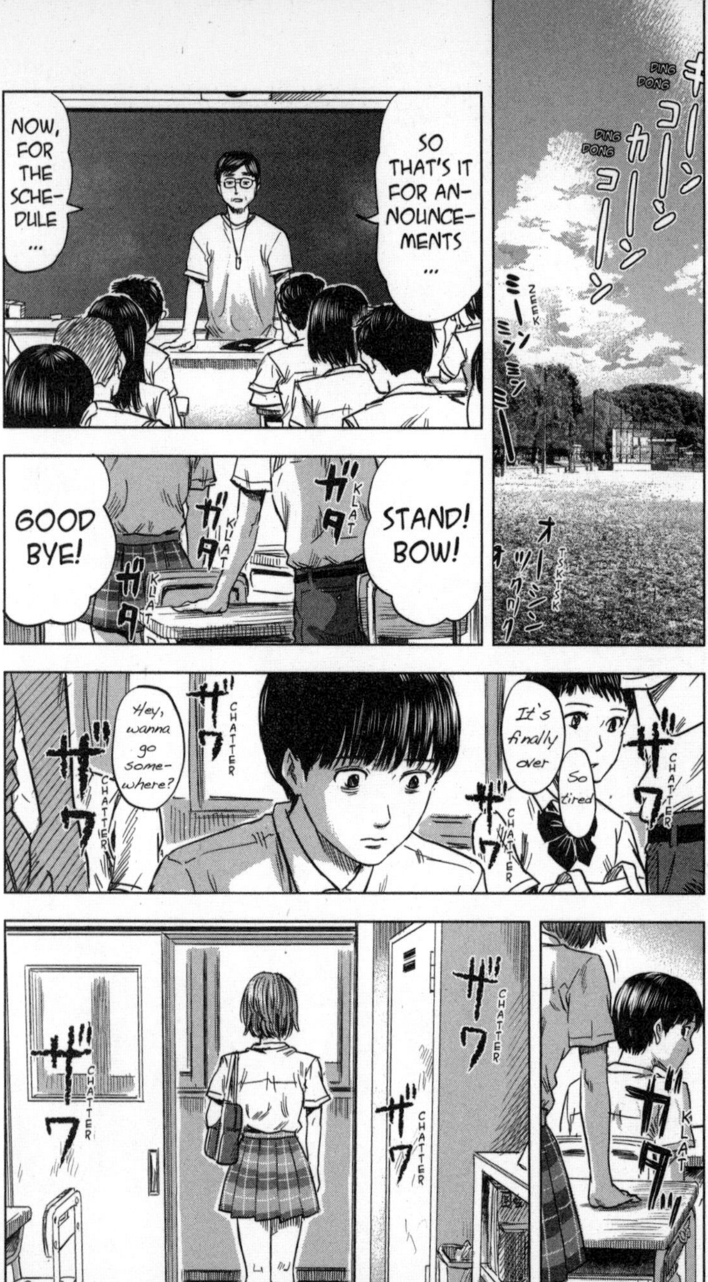
DING DONG
DING DONG
ZEEK
TSKTSK
SO THAT'S IT FOR AN-NOUNCE-MENTS ...
NOW, FOR THE SCHE-DULE ...
STAND! BOW!
KLAT
KLAT
KLAT
GOOD BYE!
CHATTER
It's finally over
So tired
CHATTER
CHATTER
Hey, wanna go some-where?
CHATTER
KLAT
CHATTER
CHATTER
CHATTER

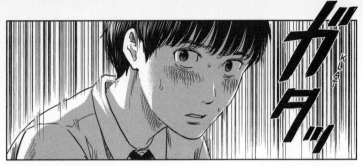

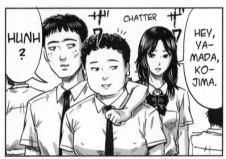

ガタッ
KLAT
たっ TUP
たっ TUP
たっ TUP
HEY, YA-MADA, KO-JIMA.
ザワ
CHATTER
ザワ
HUNH?
WHAT'S GOING ON WITH KASUGA?
HE'S BEEN ACTING WEIRDER THAN USUAL LATELY.
HUH?
HOW THE HELL SHOULD WE KNOW?
YOU'RE HIS FRIENDS, AREN'T YOU?
WHAT'S UP WITH HIM?! TELL ME!

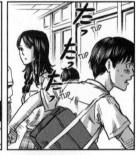

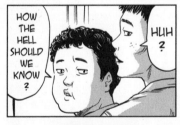

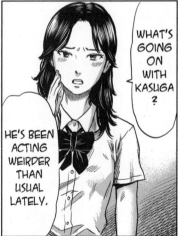

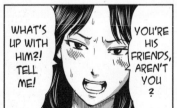

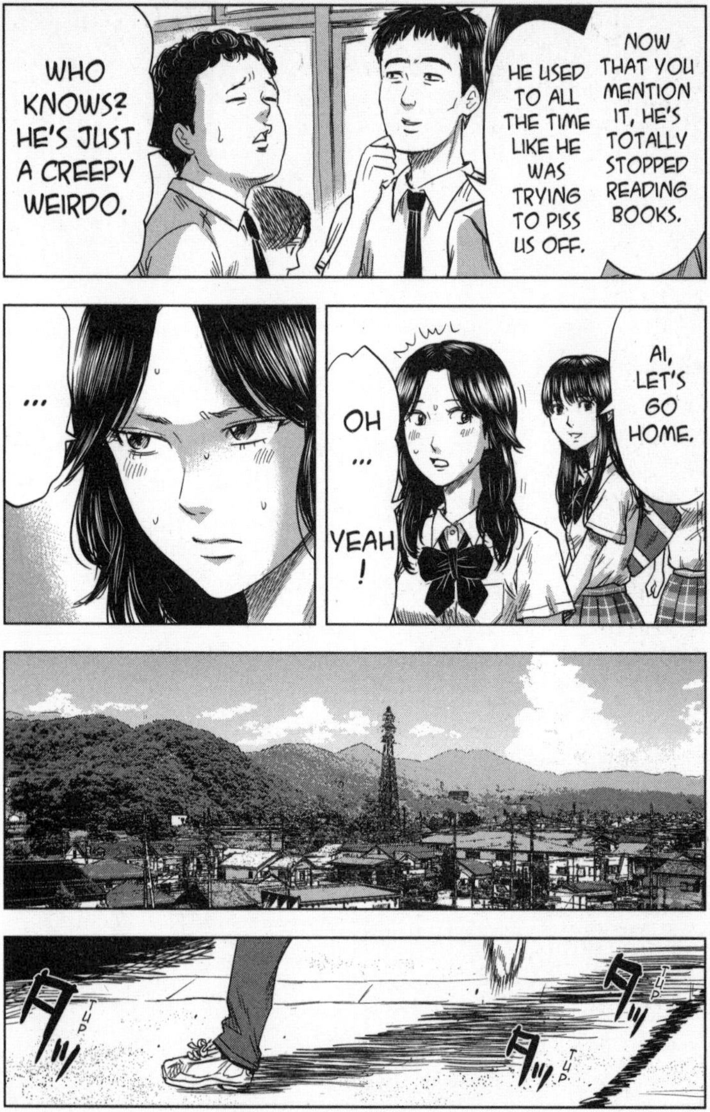
NOW THAT YOU MENTION IT, HE'S TOTALLY STOPPED READING BOOKS.
HE USED TO ALL THE TIME LIKE HE WAS TRYING TO PISS US OFF.
WHO KNOWS? HE'S JUST A CREEPY WEIRDO.
AI, LET'S GO HOME.
OH ... YEAH!
...
タッ TUP
タッ TUP
タッ TUP

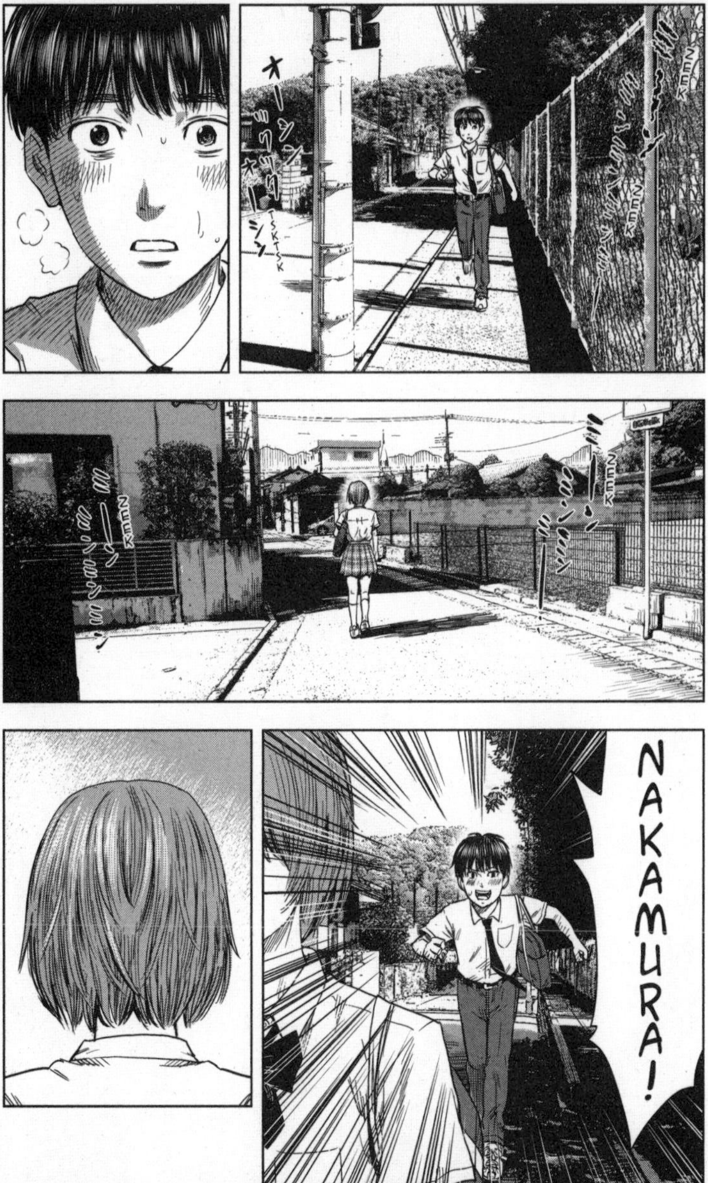
ZEEK
ZEEK
TSKTSK
ZEEK
ZEEK
NAKAMURA!

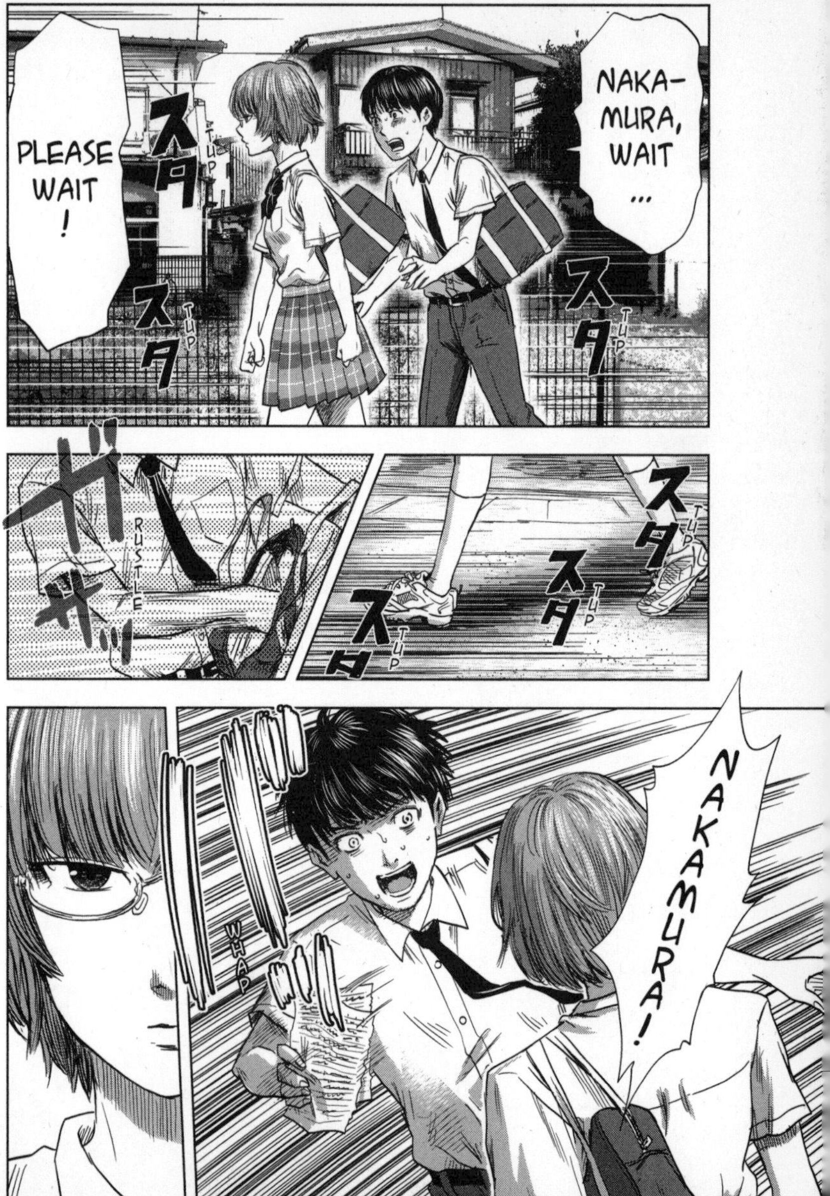
NAKA-MURA, WAIT ...
PLEASE WAIT !
スタ TUP
スタ TUP
スタ TUP
スタ TUP
スタ TUP
スタ TUP
ガサ RUSTLE
NAKAMURA!
WHAP

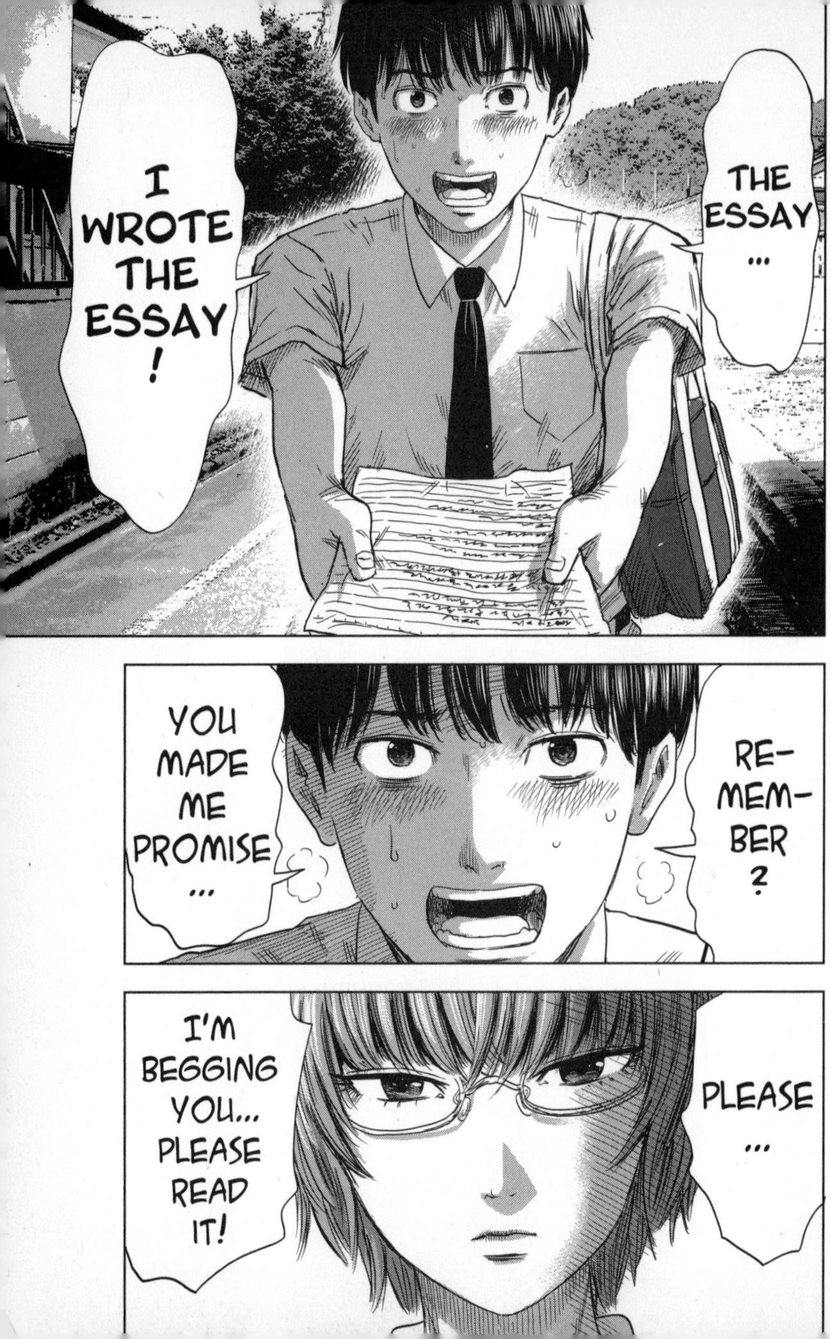
THE ESSAY ...
I WROTE THE ESSAY!
RE-MEM-BER?
YOU MADE ME PROMISE ...
PLEASE ...
I'M BEGGING YOU... PLEASE READ IT!

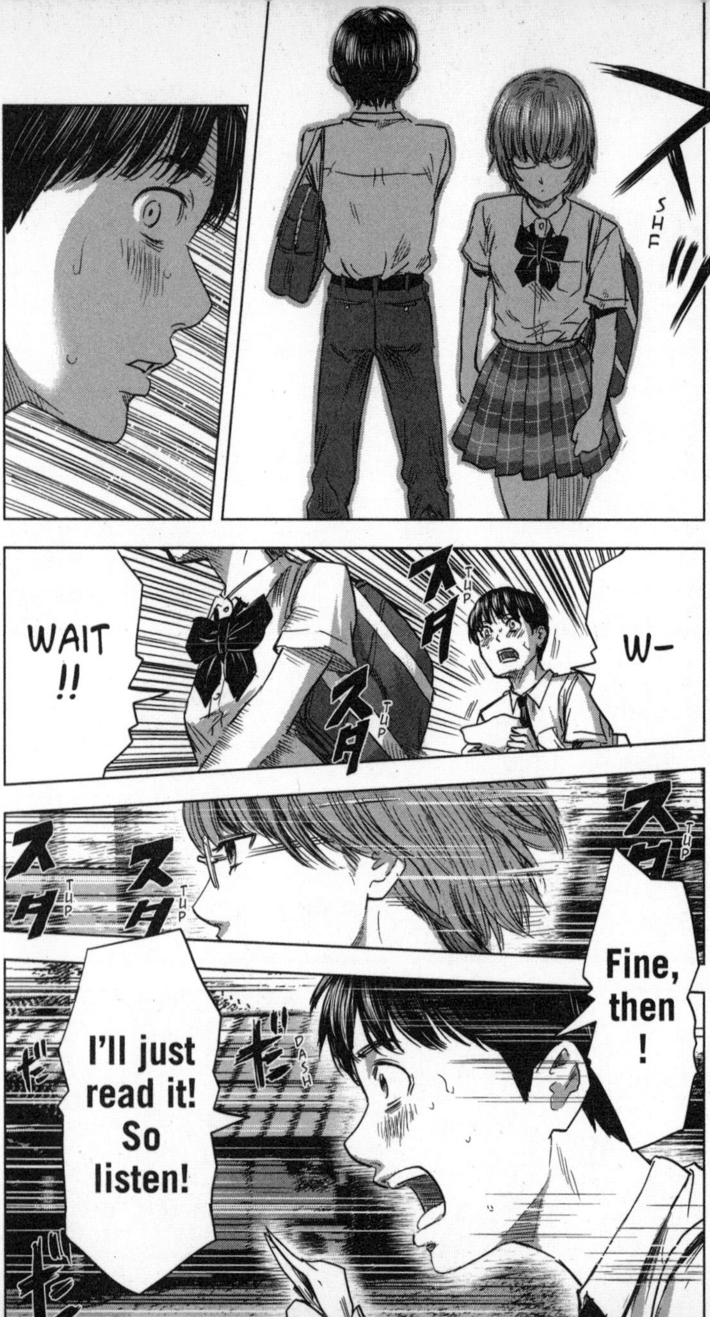
SHF
W-
TUP
TUP
WAIT !!
TUP
TUP
TUP
Fine, then !
DASH
I'll just read it! So listen!

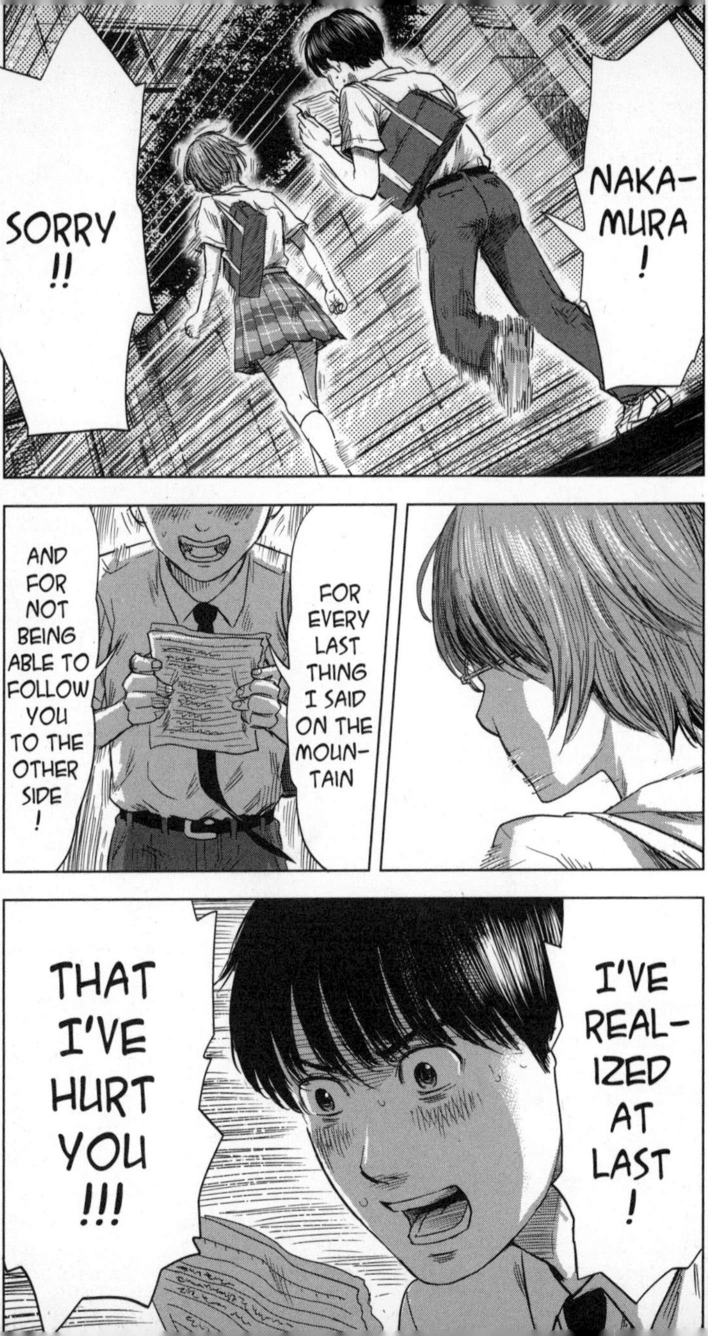
NAKA-MURA!
SORRY!!
FOR EVERY LAST THING I SAID ON THE MOUN-TAIN
AND FOR NOT BEING ABLE TO FOLLOW YOU TO THE OTHER SIDE!
I'VE REAL-IZED AT LAST!
THAT I'VE HURT YOU!!!

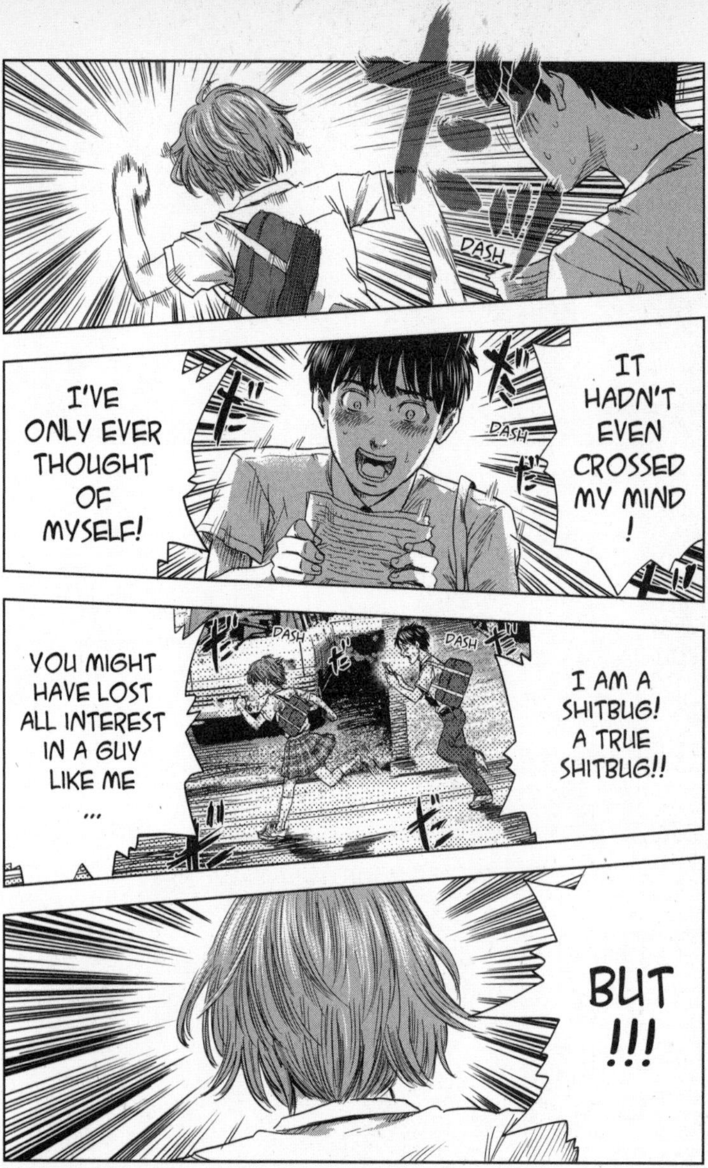
DASH
IT HADN'T EVEN CROSSED MY MIND!
DASH
I'VE ONLY EVER THOUGHT OF MYSELF!
I AM A SHITBUG! A TRUE SHITBUG!!
DASH
DASH
YOU MIGHT HAVE LOST ALL INTEREST IN A GUY LIKE ME ...
BUT!!!

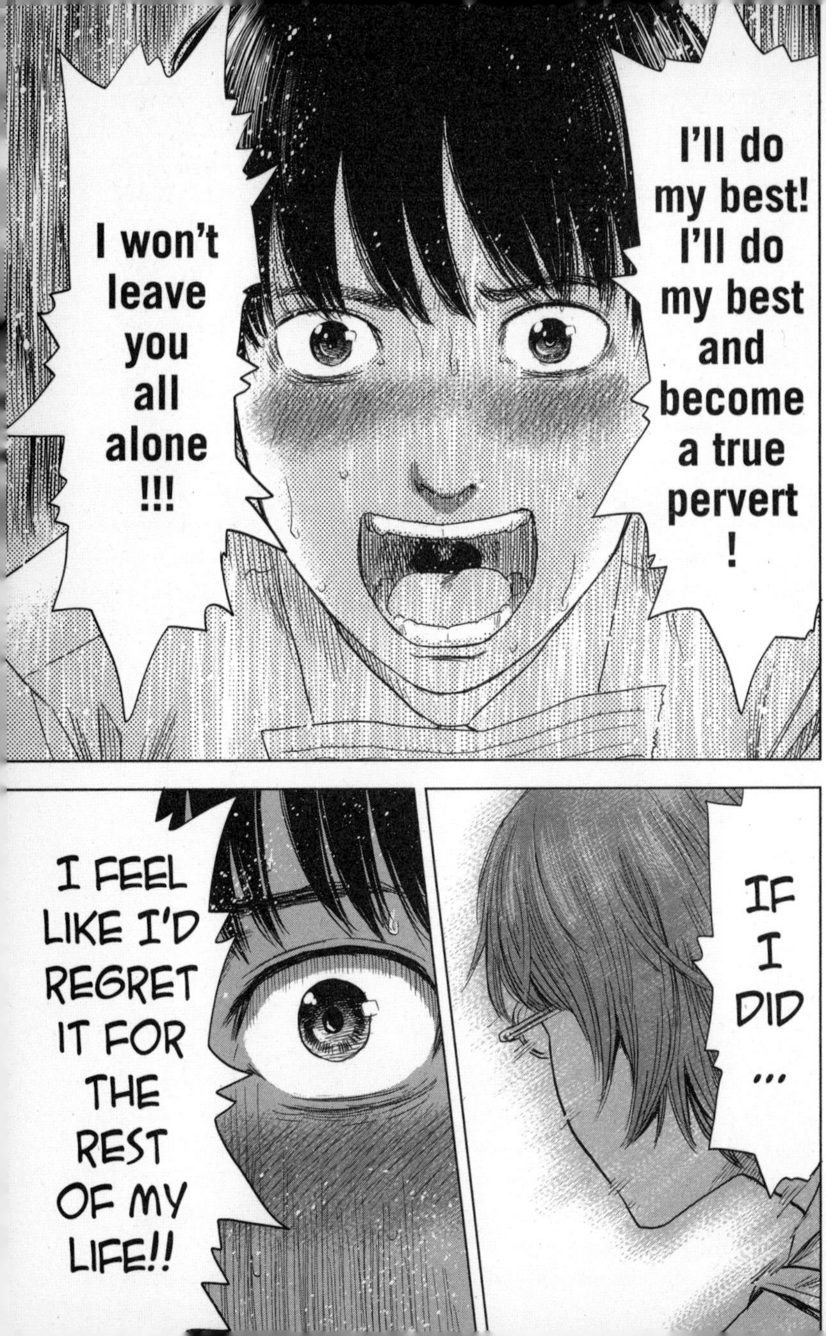
I'll do my best! I'll do my best and become a true pervert!
I won't leave you all alone!!!
IF I DID...
I FEEL LIKE I'D REGRET IT FOR THE REST OF MY LIFE!!

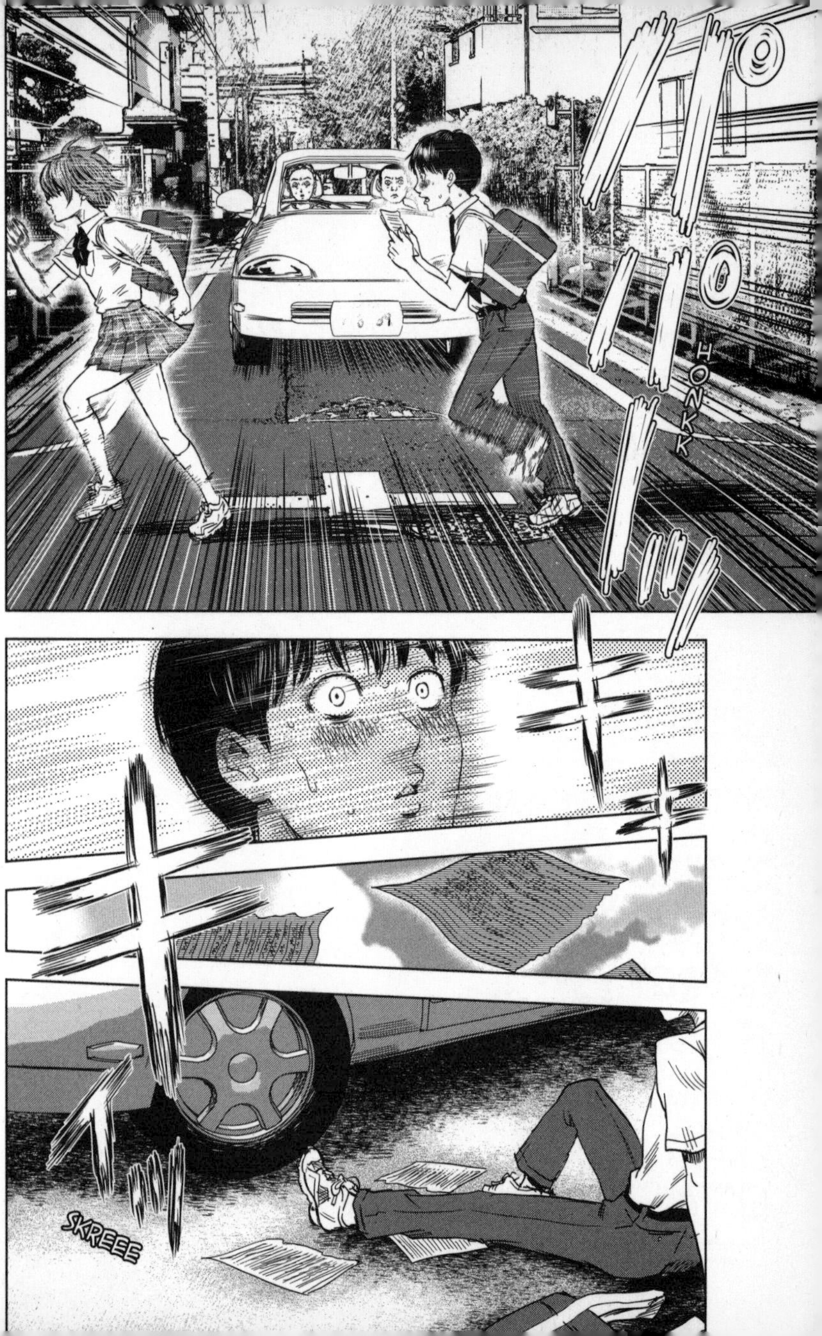
HONKK
SKREEE

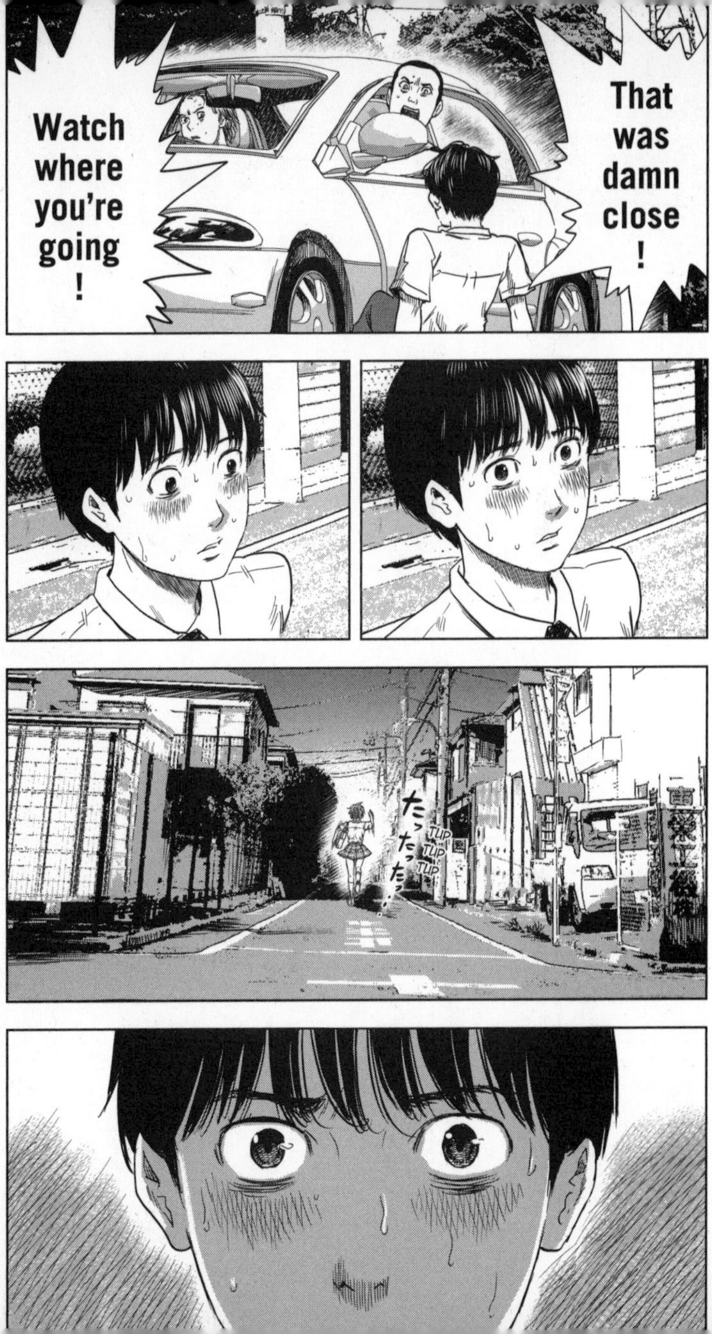
That was damn close!
Watch where you're going!
たったった
TUP TUP TUP

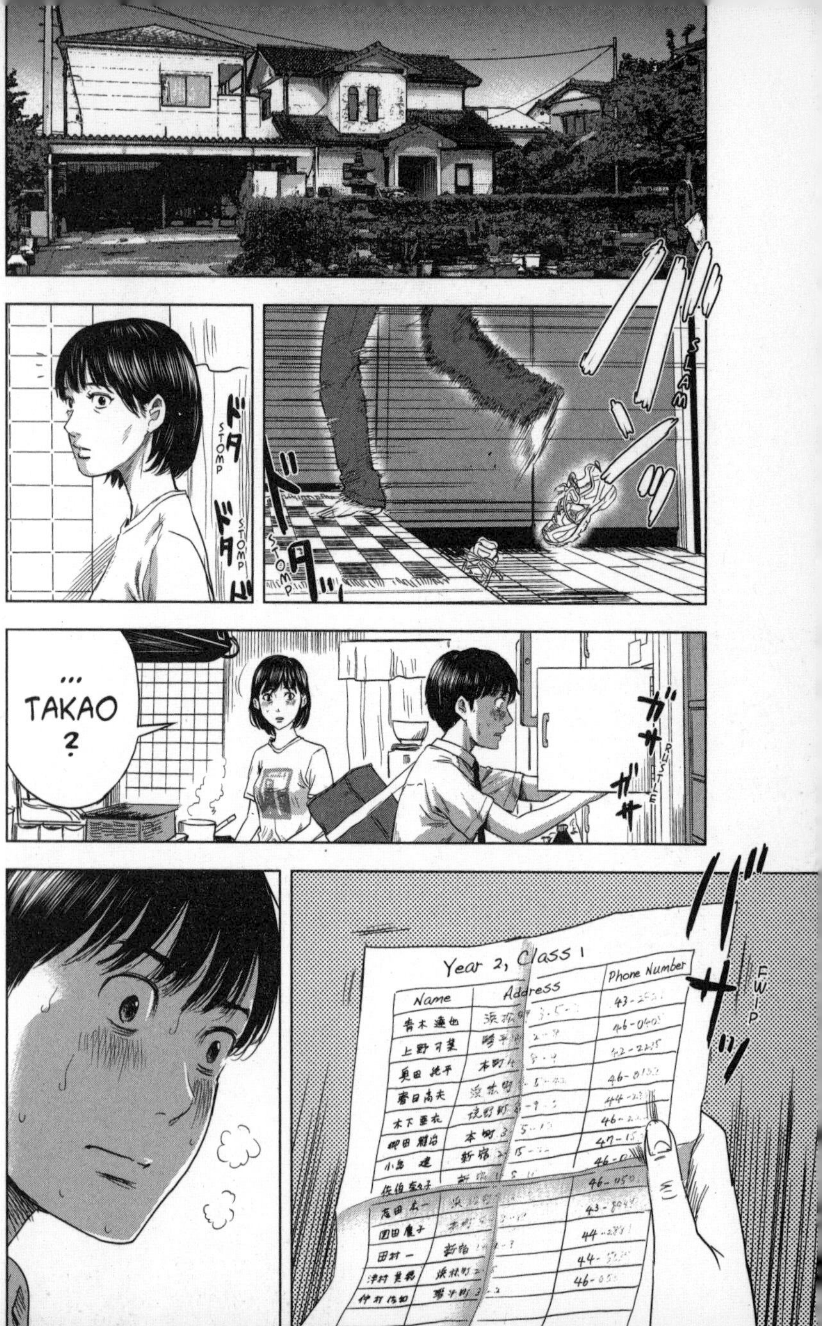
SLAM
STOMP
STOMP
STOMP
... TAKAO ?
RUSTLE
FWIP
Year 2, Class 1
Name
Address
Phone Number

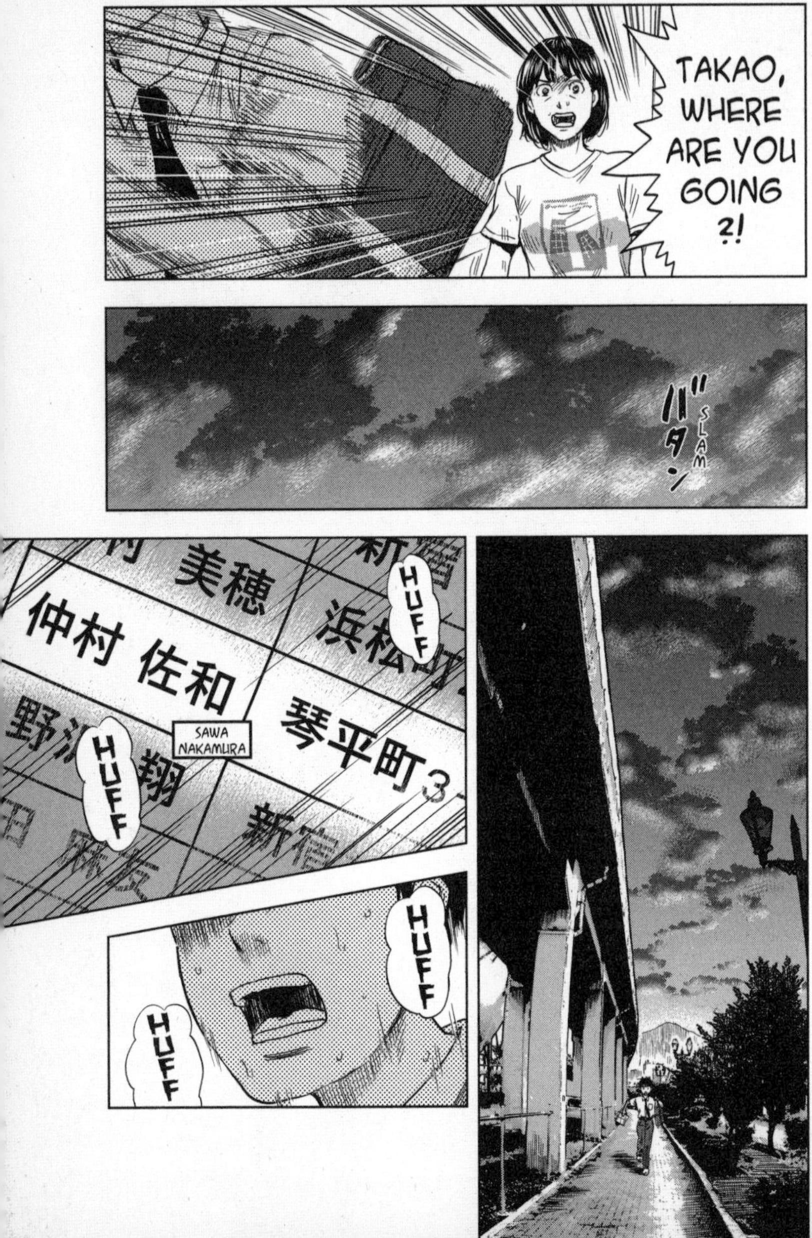

TAKAO, WHERE ARE YOU GOING ?!
バタン
SLAM
HUFF
美穂
仲村 佐和
琴平町3
新宿
SAWA NAKAMURA
HUFF
HUFF
HUFF

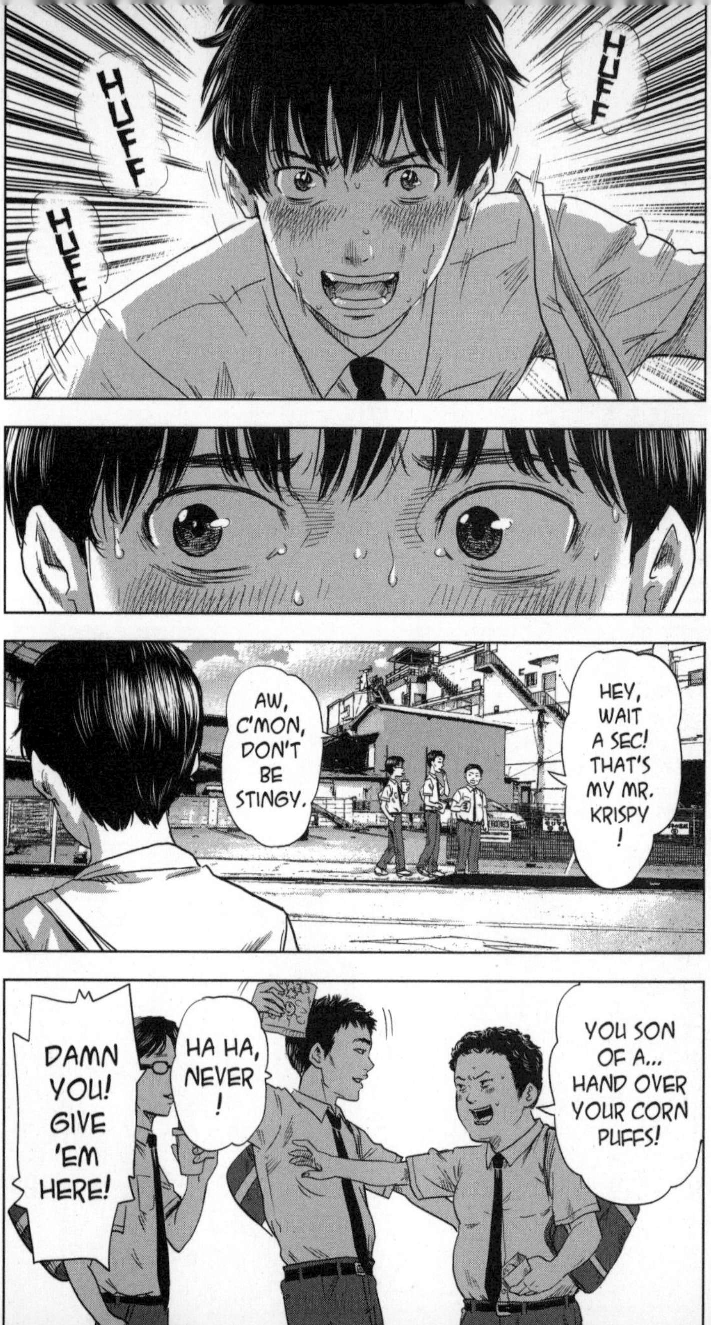

HUFF
HUFF
HUFF
HEY, WAIT A SEC! THAT'S MY MR. KRISPY!
AW, C'MON, DON'T BE STINGY.
YOU SON OF A... HAND OVER YOUR CORN PUFFS!
HA HA, NEVER!
DAMN YOU! GIVE 'EM HERE!

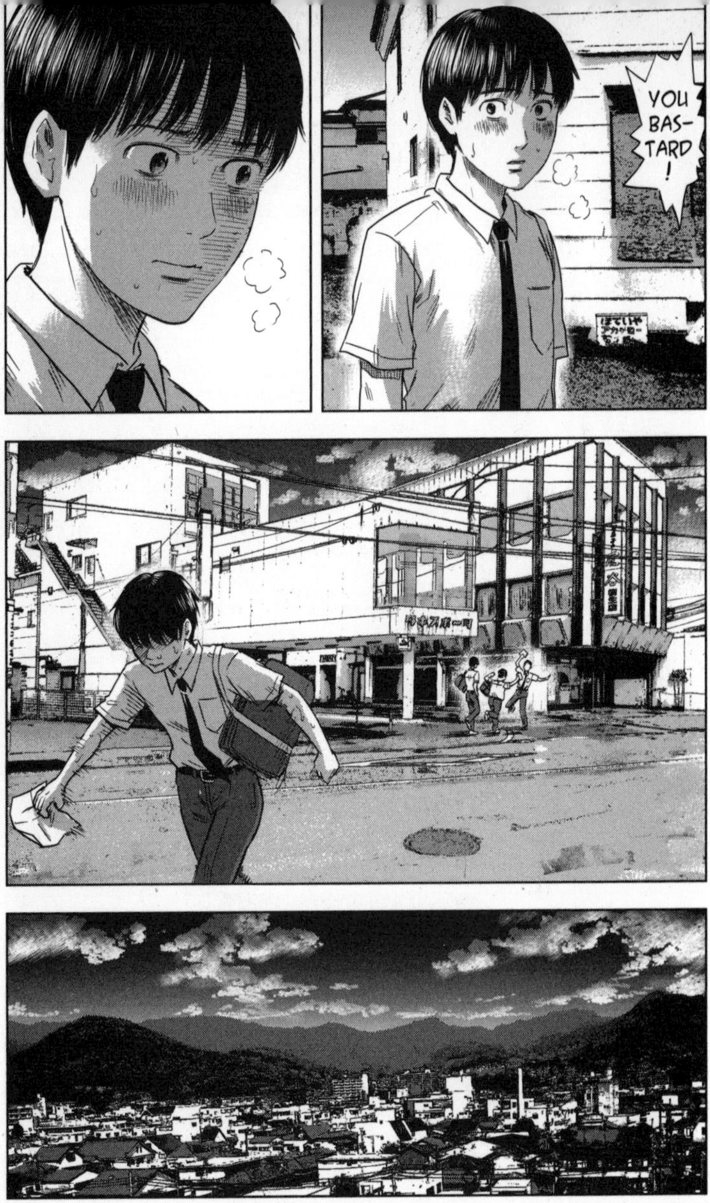
YOU BAS- TARD !

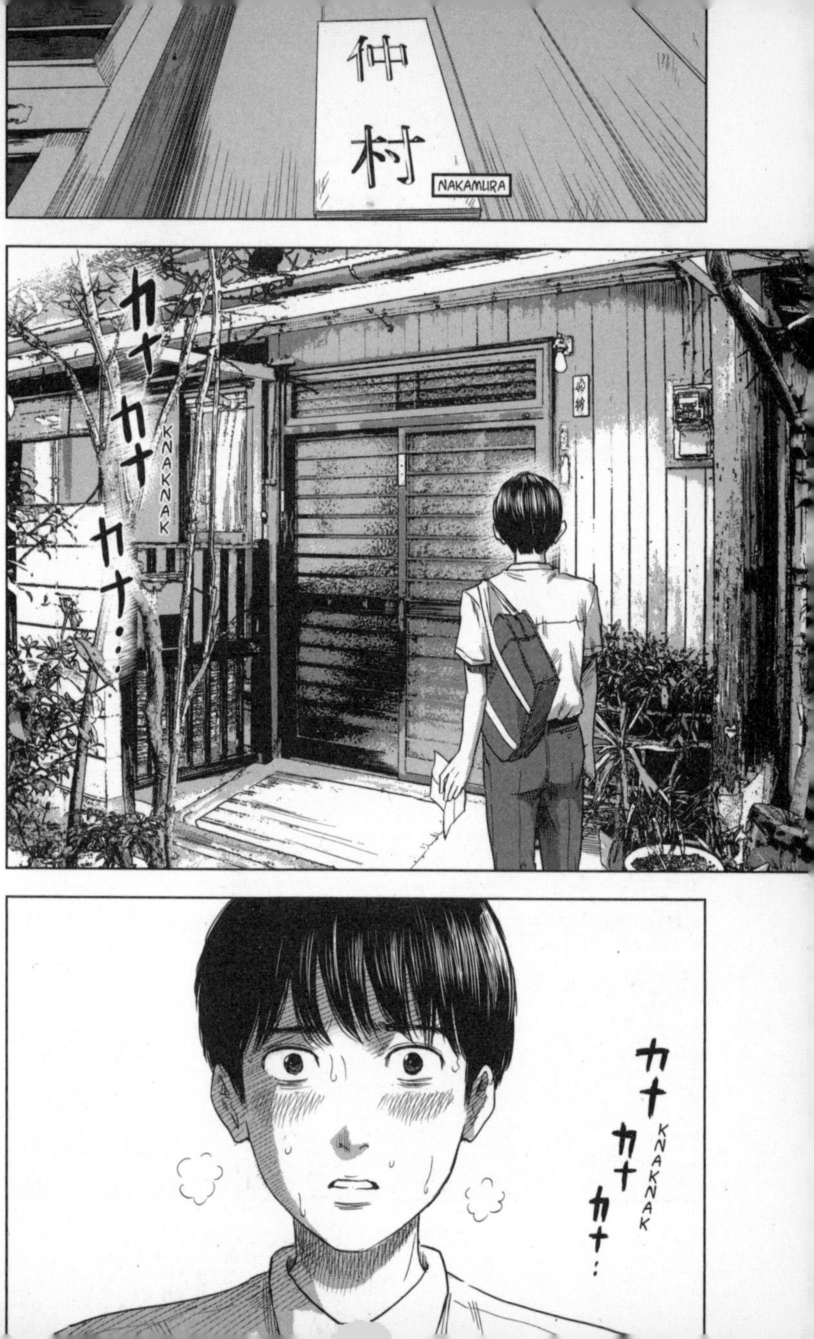
仲村
NAKAMURA
カナ
カナ
カナ…
KNAKNAK
カナ
カナ
カナ!
KNAKNAK

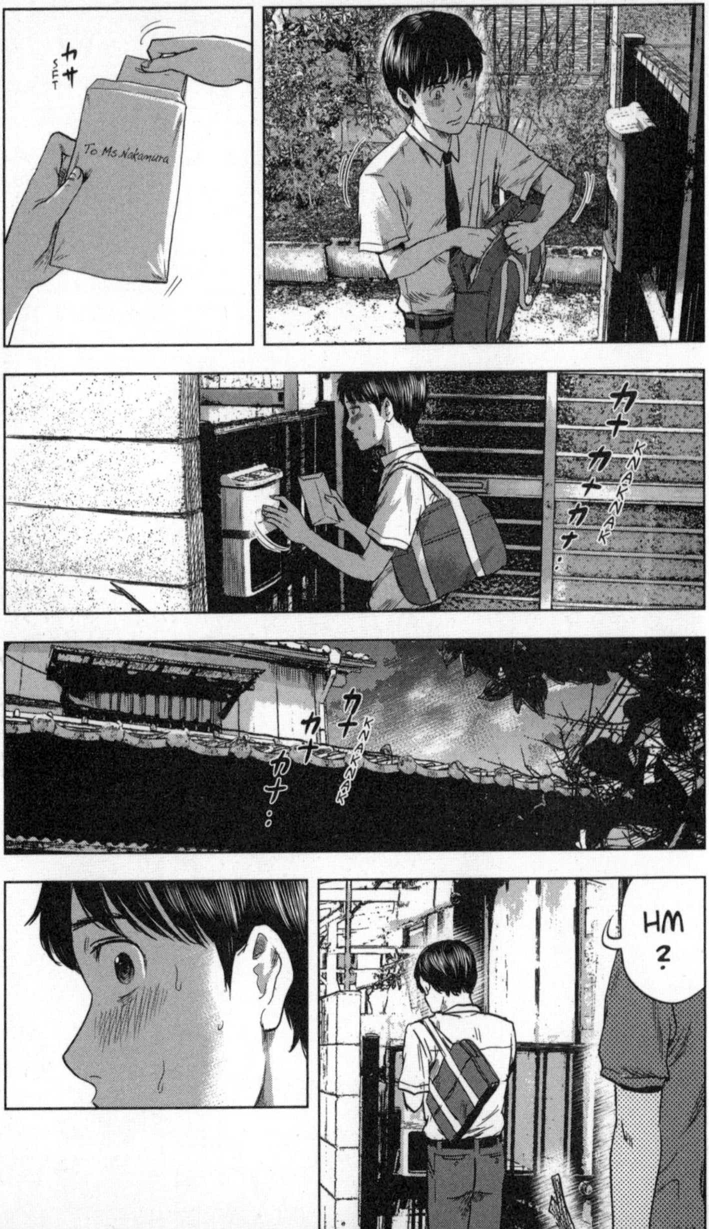

カサ
SET
To Ms. Nakamura
カナカナカナ..
KNAKNAK
カナカナカナ..
KNAKNAK
HM ?

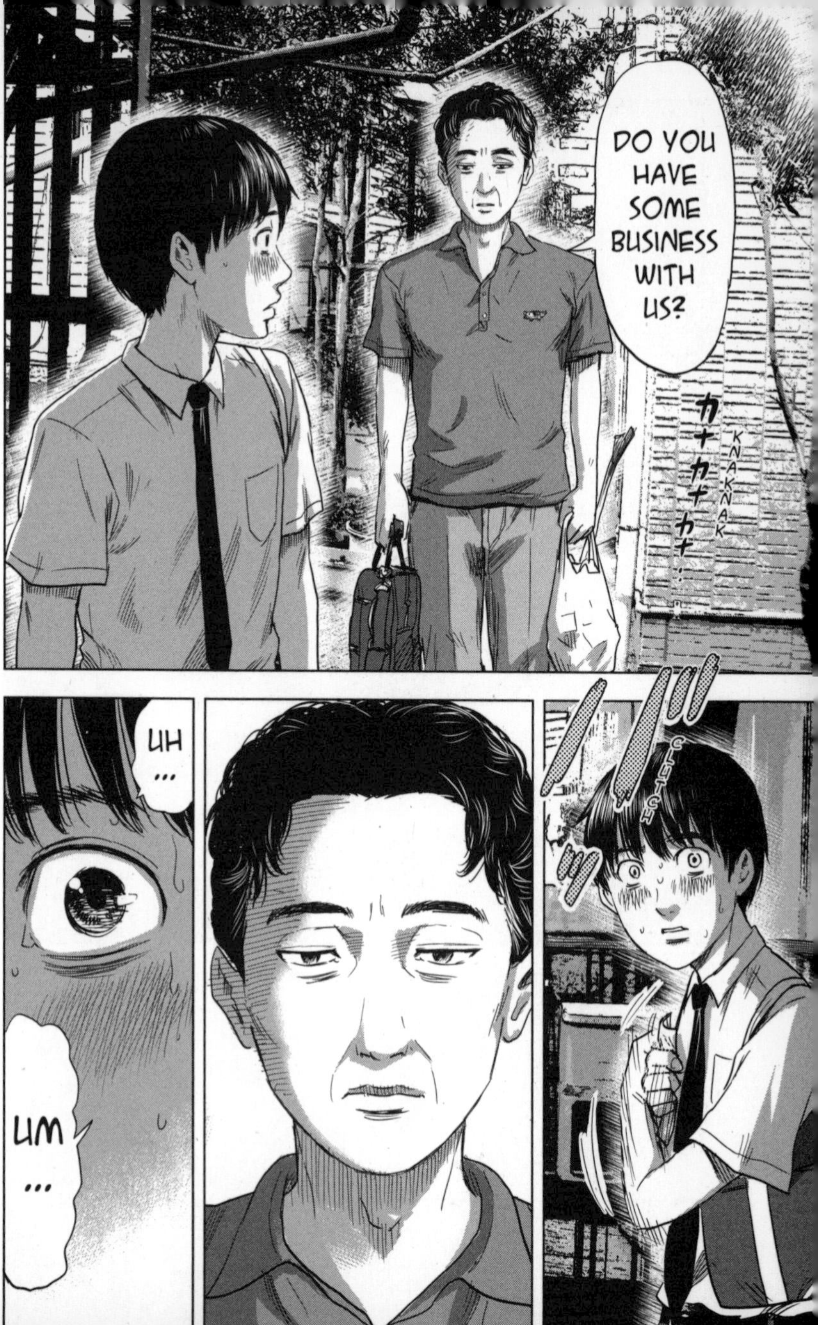
DO YOU HAVE SOME BUSINESS WITH US?
カナカナカナ…
KNAKNAK
CLUTCH
UH ...
UM ...

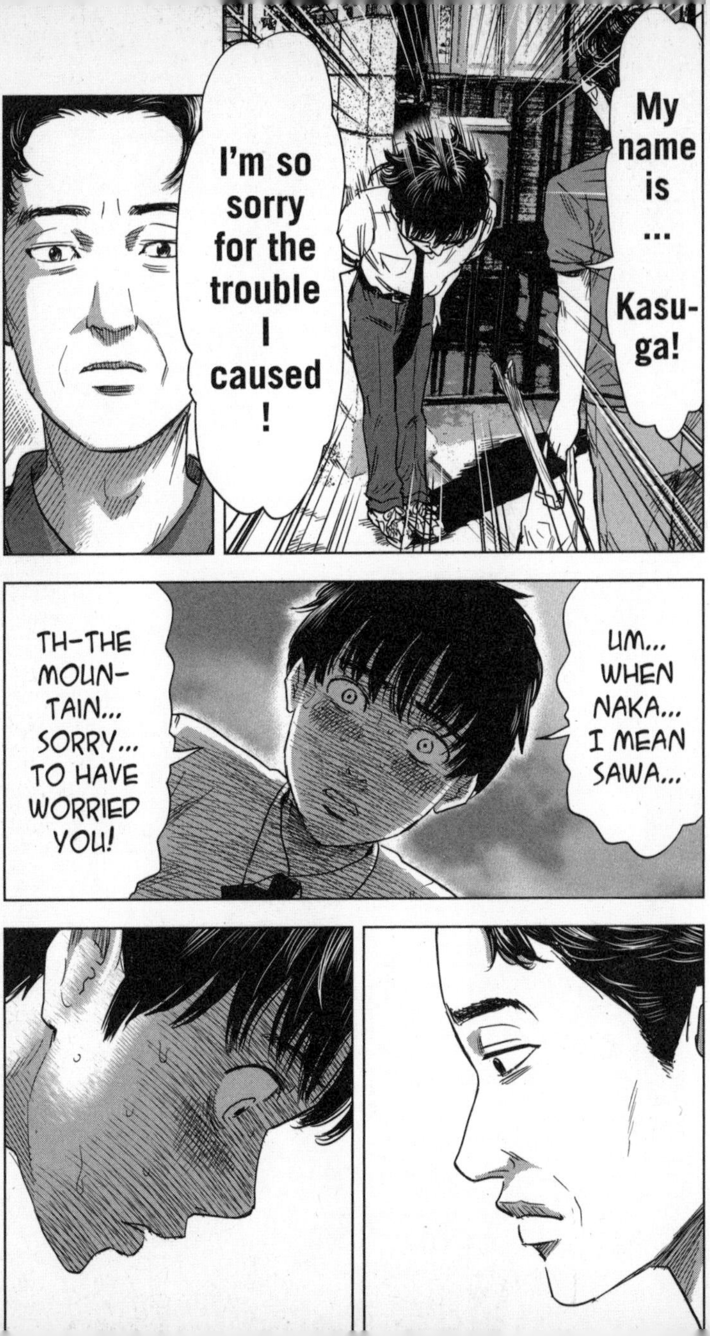
My name is ... Kasuga!
I'm so sorry for the trouble I caused!
UM... WHEN NAKA... I MEAN SAWA...
TH-THE MOUNTAIN... SORRY... TO HAVE WORRIED YOU!

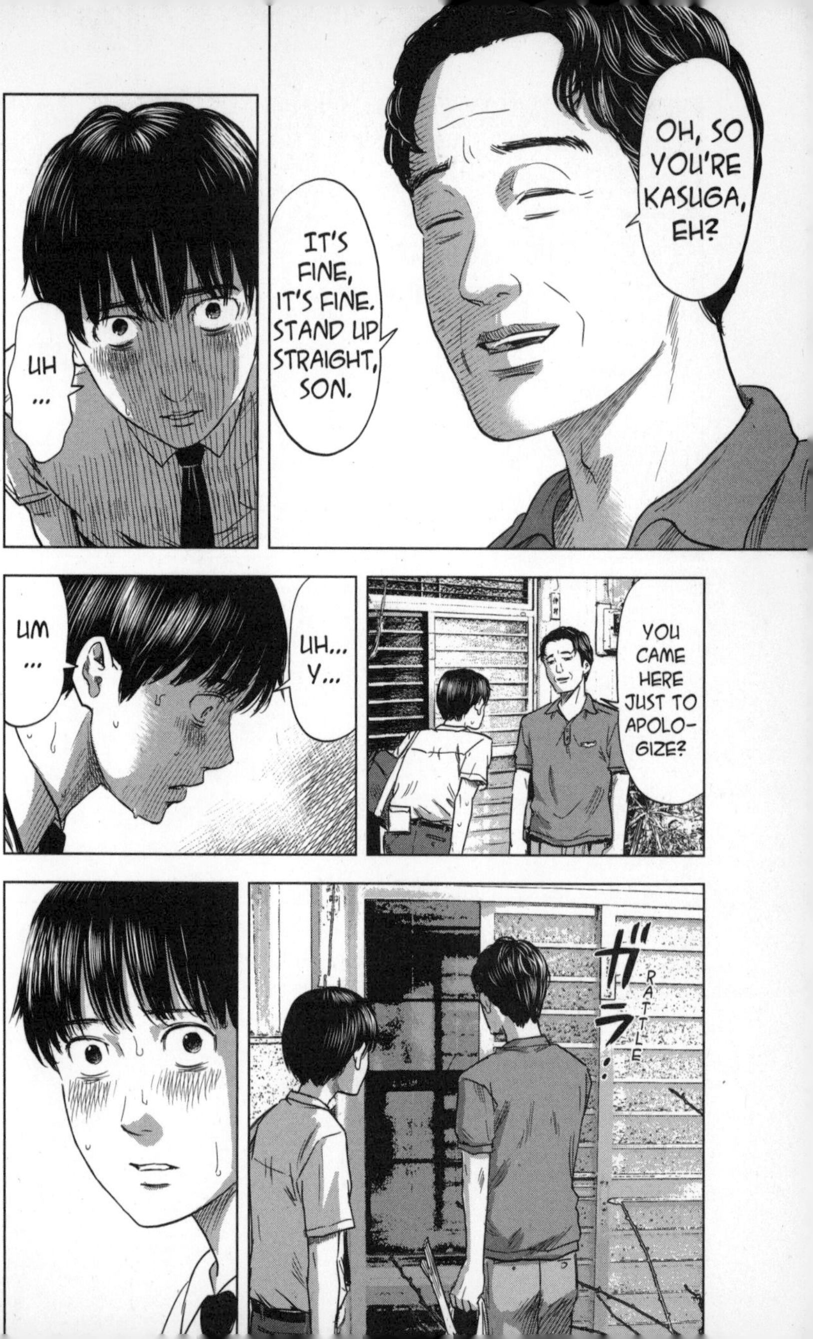
OH, SO YOU'RE KASUGA, EH?
IT'S FINE, IT'S FINE. STAND UP STRAIGHT, SON.
UH ...
YOU CAME HERE JUST TO APOLOGIZE?
UH... Y...
UM ...
ガラ
RATTLE

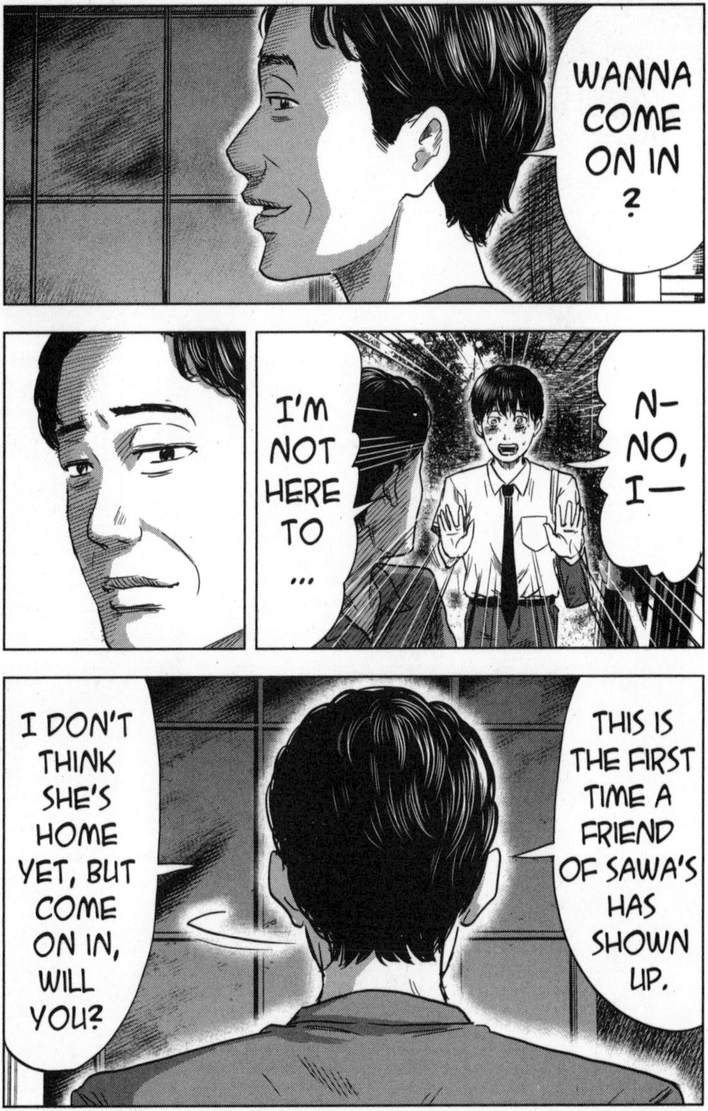
WANNA COME ON IN?
N-NO, I—
I'M NOT HERE TO ...
THIS IS THE FIRST TIME A FRIEND OF SAWA'S HAS SHOWN UP.
I DON'T THINK SHE'S HOME YET, BUT COME ON IN, WILL YOU?

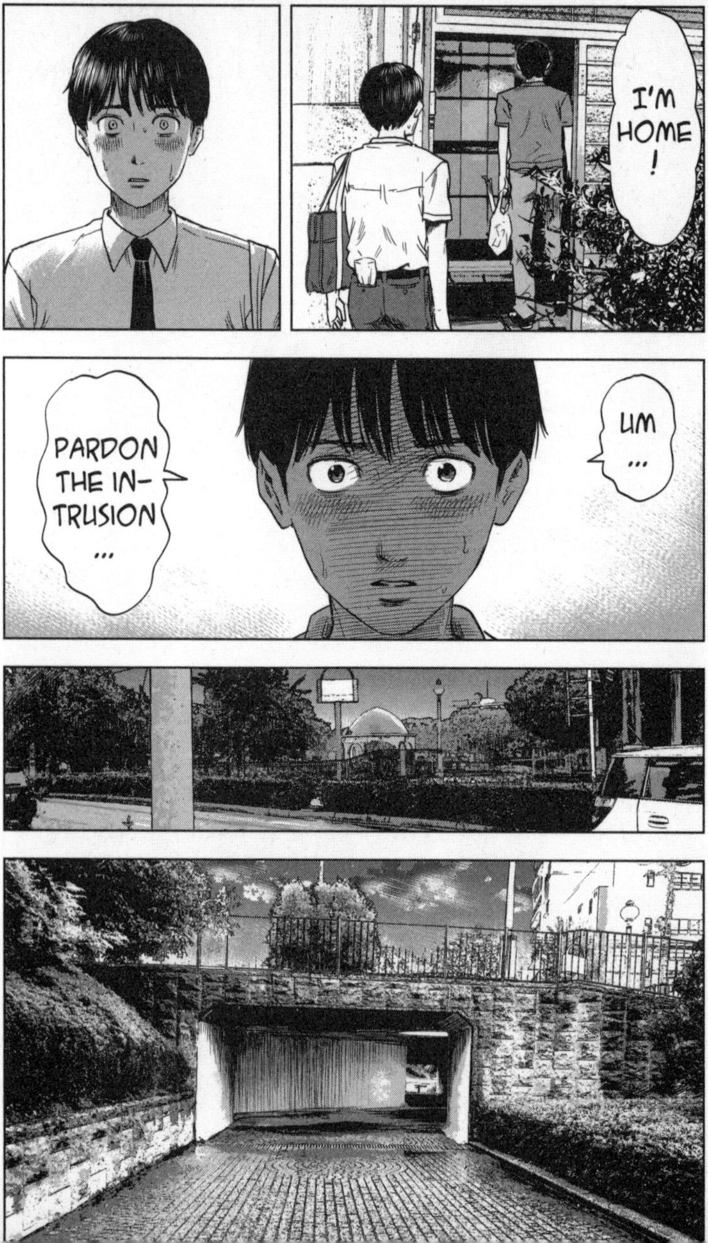
I'M HOME!
UM...
PARDON THE IN-TRUSION...

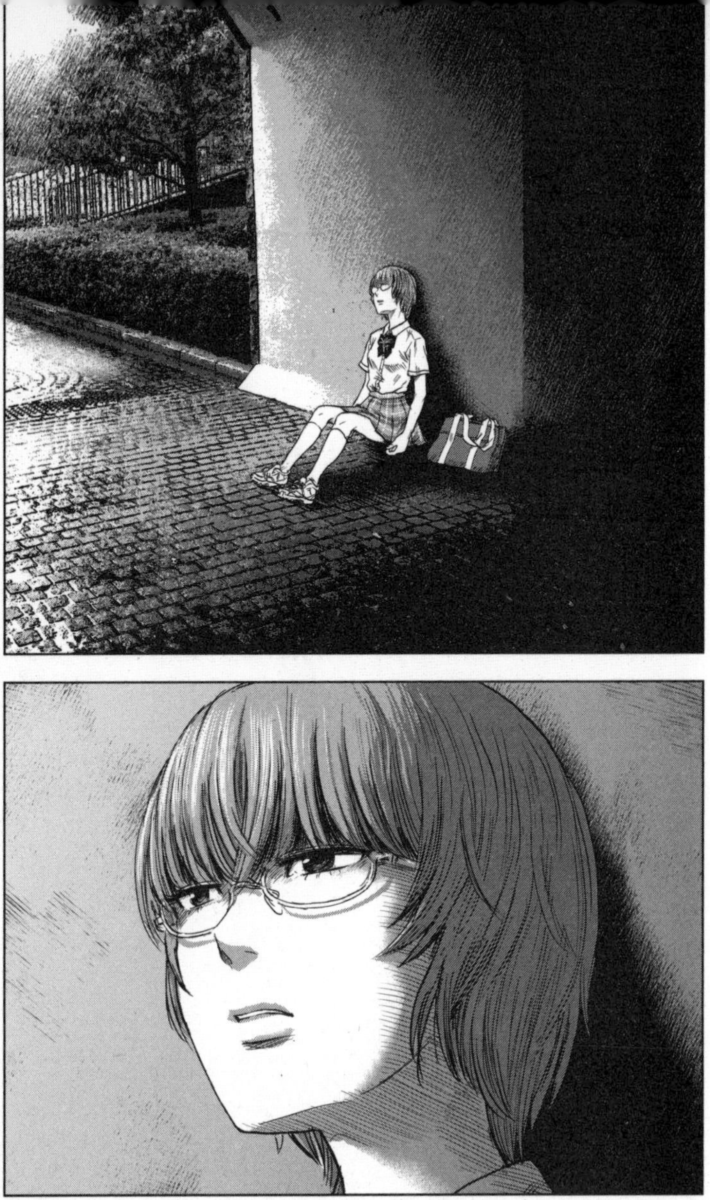

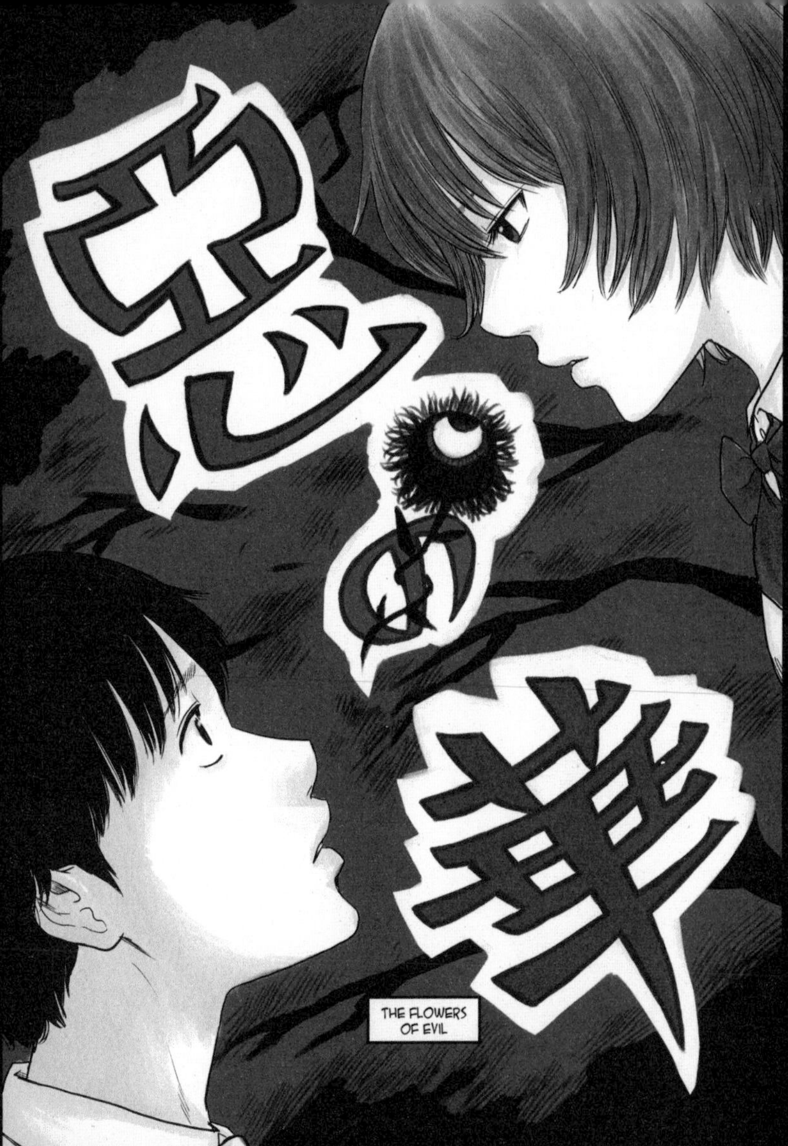
悪の華
THE FLOWERS OF EVIL

The Flowers
of Evil

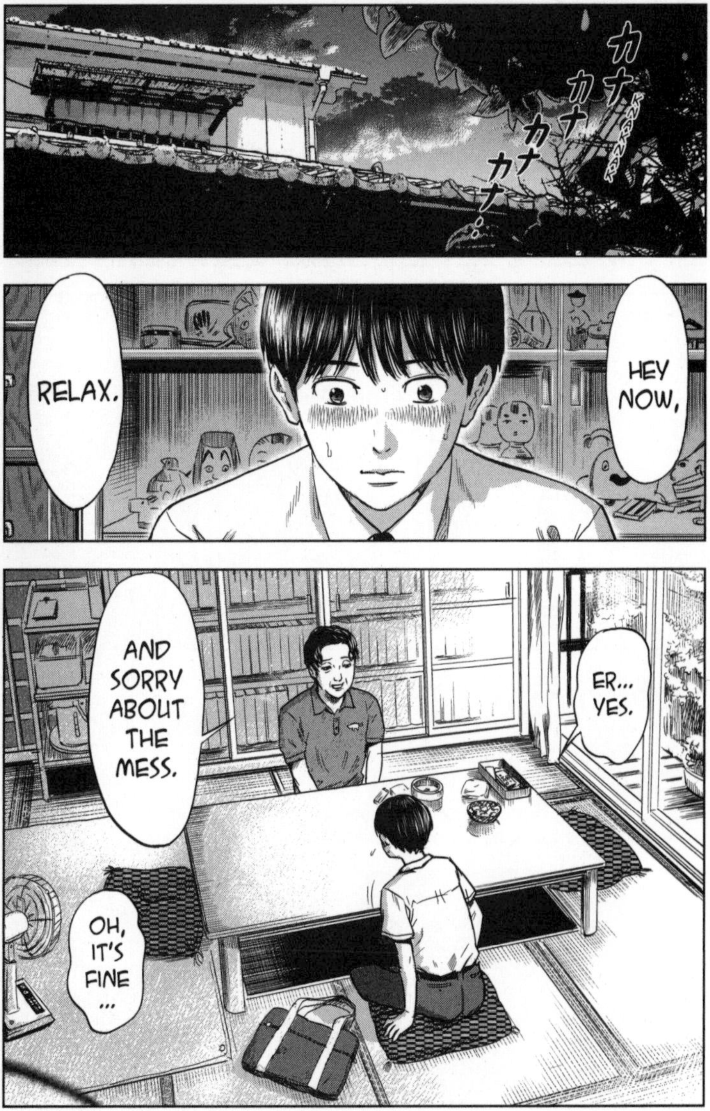
カナカナカナカナ…
KANAKANA
HEY NOW,
RELAX.
ER... YES.
AND SORRY ABOUT THE MESS.
OH, IT'S FINE ...

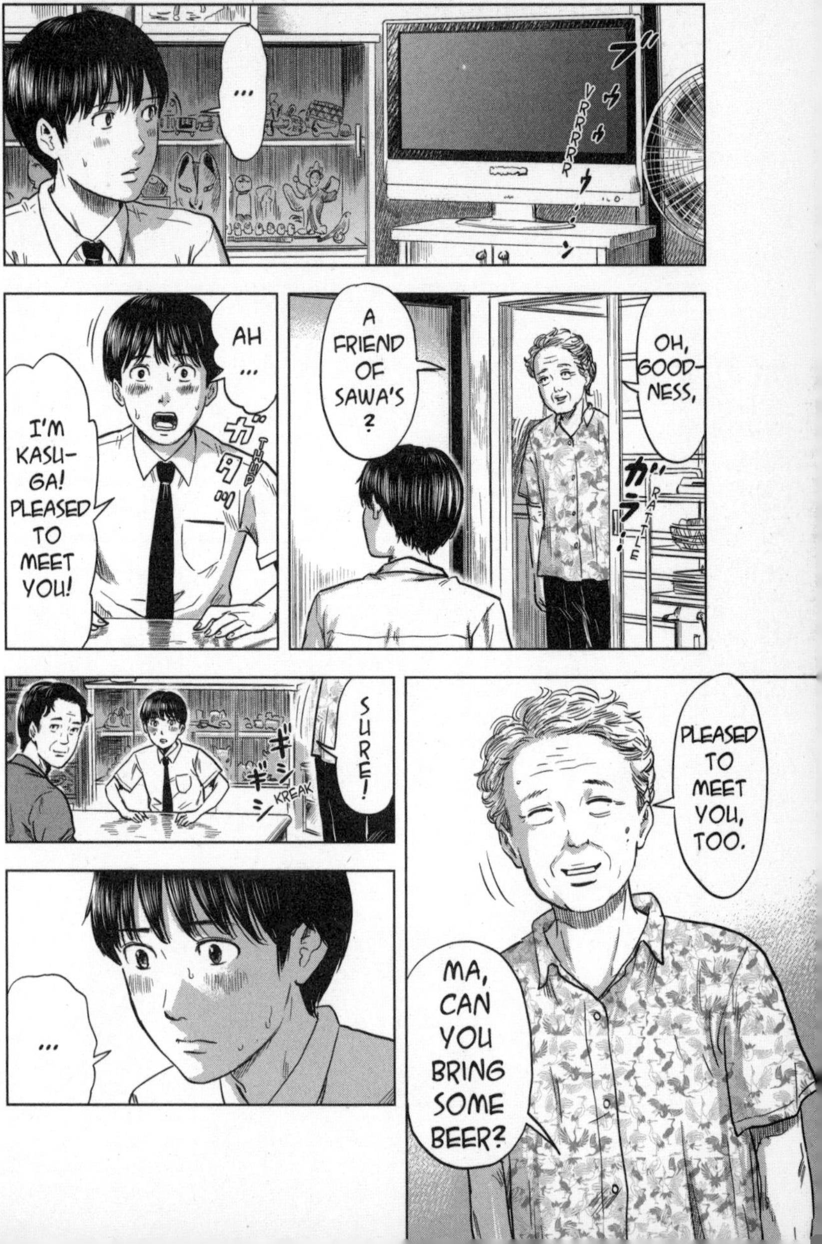
...
VRRRRR
OH, GOODNESS,
RATTLE
A FRIEND OF SAWA'S?
AH ...
THUMP
I'M KASUGA! PLEASED TO MEET YOU!
PLEASED TO MEET YOU, TOO.
MA, CAN YOU BRING SOME BEER?
SURE!
KREAK
...

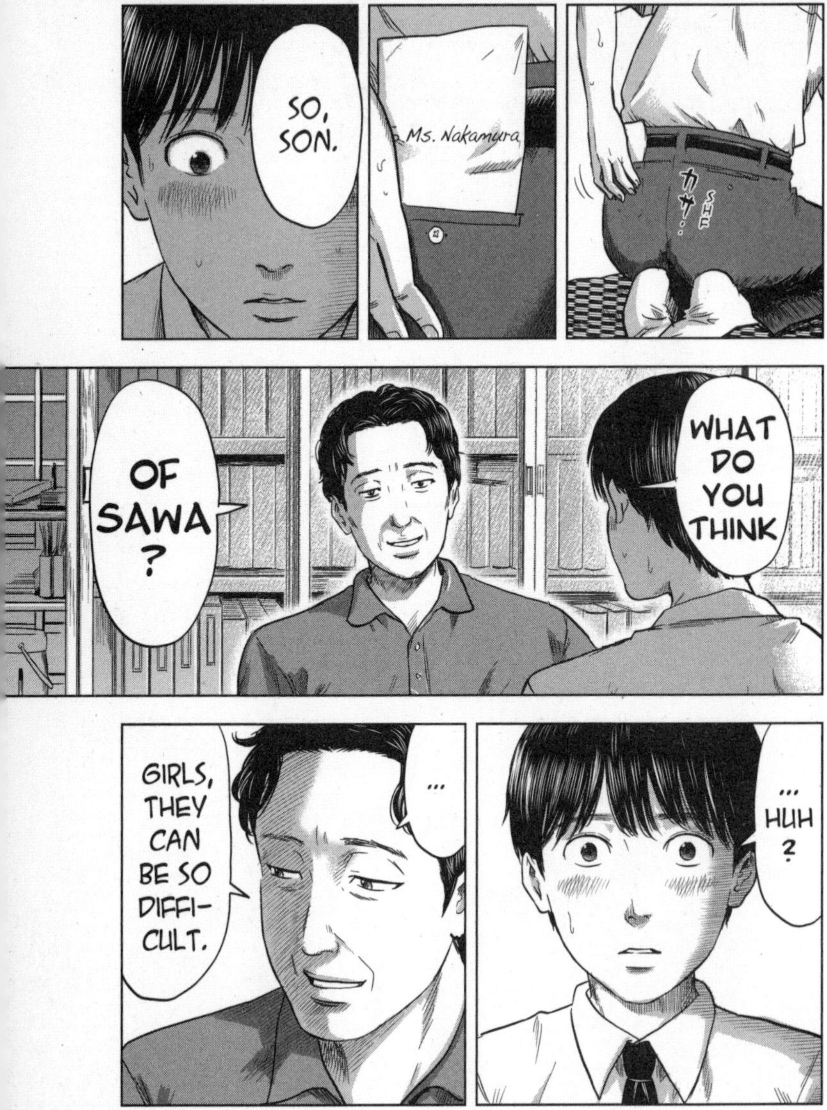
カサ…
SHF
Ms. Nakamura
SO, SON.
WHAT DO YOU THINK
OF SAWA?
... HUH?
...
GIRLS, THEY CAN BE SO DIFFI-CULT.

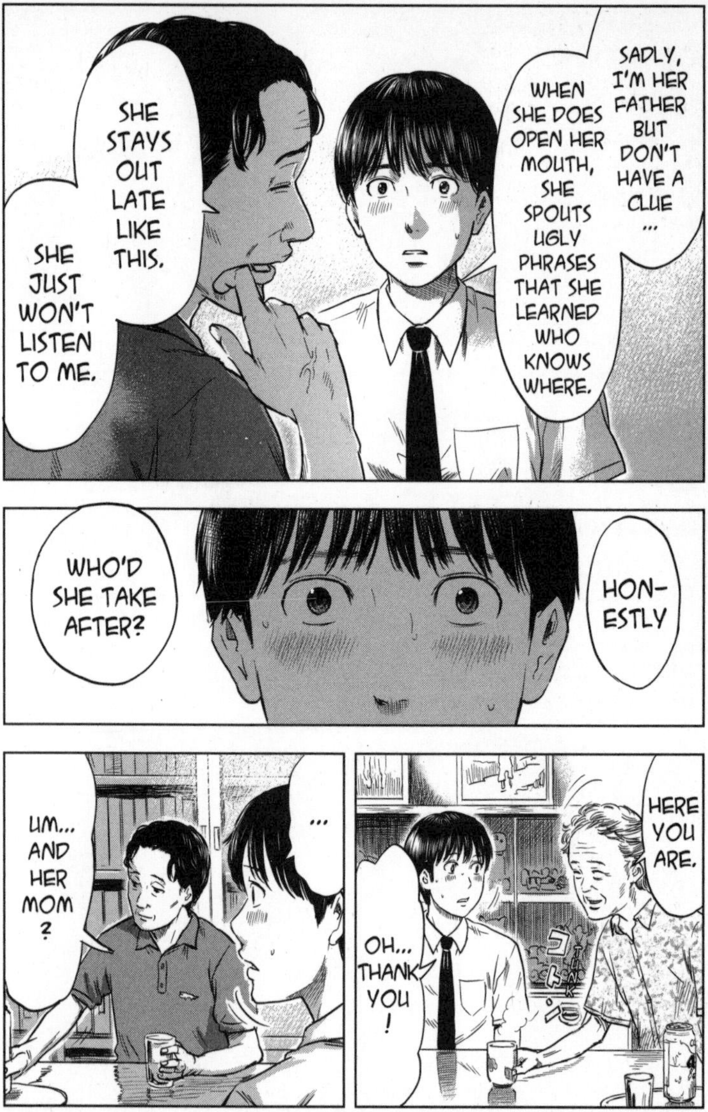
SADLY, I'M HER FATHER BUT DON'T HAVE A CLUE ...
WHEN SHE DOES OPEN HER MOUTH, SHE SPOUTS UGLY PHRASES THAT SHE LEARNED WHO KNOWS WHERE.
SHE STAYS OUT LATE LIKE THIS.
SHE JUST WON'T LISTEN TO ME.
HON-ESTLY
WHO'D SHE TAKE AFTER?
HERE YOU ARE.
TINK
OH... THANK YOU!
...
UM... AND HER MOM?

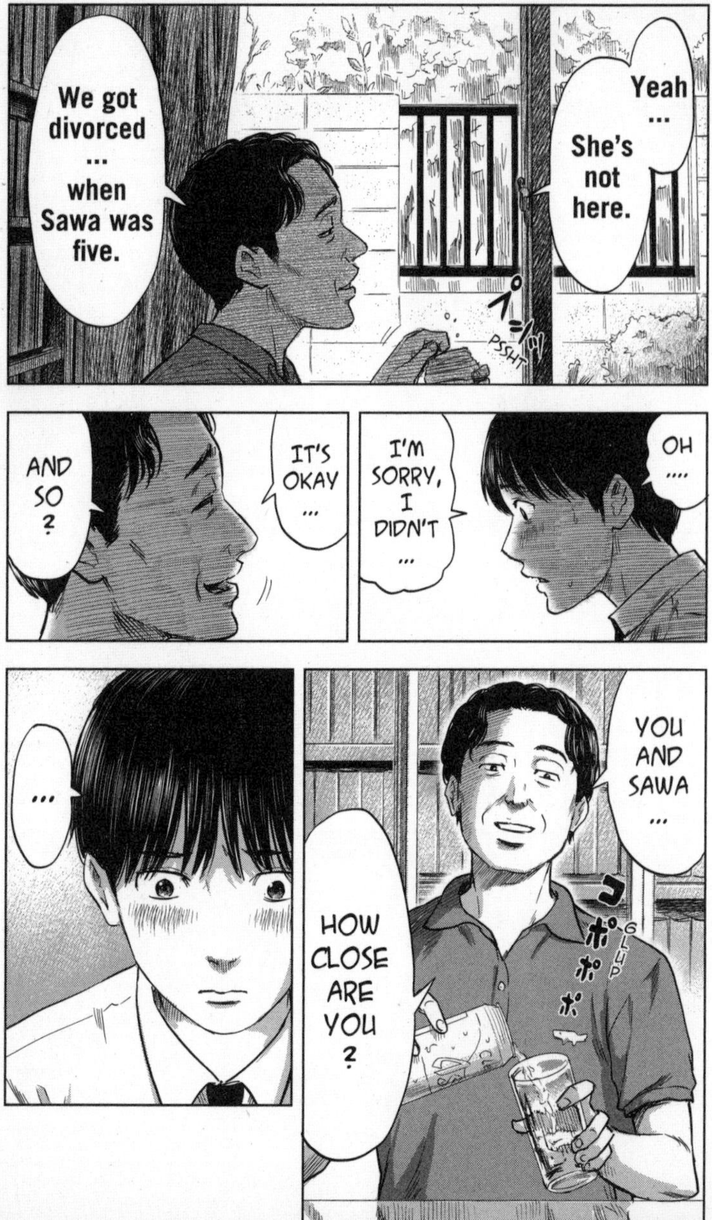
Yeah ... She's not here.
PSSHT
We got divorced ... when Sawa was five.
OH ....
I'M SORRY, I DIDN'T ...
IT'S OKAY ...
AND SO?
YOU AND SAWA ...
GLUP
HOW CLOSE ARE YOU?
...

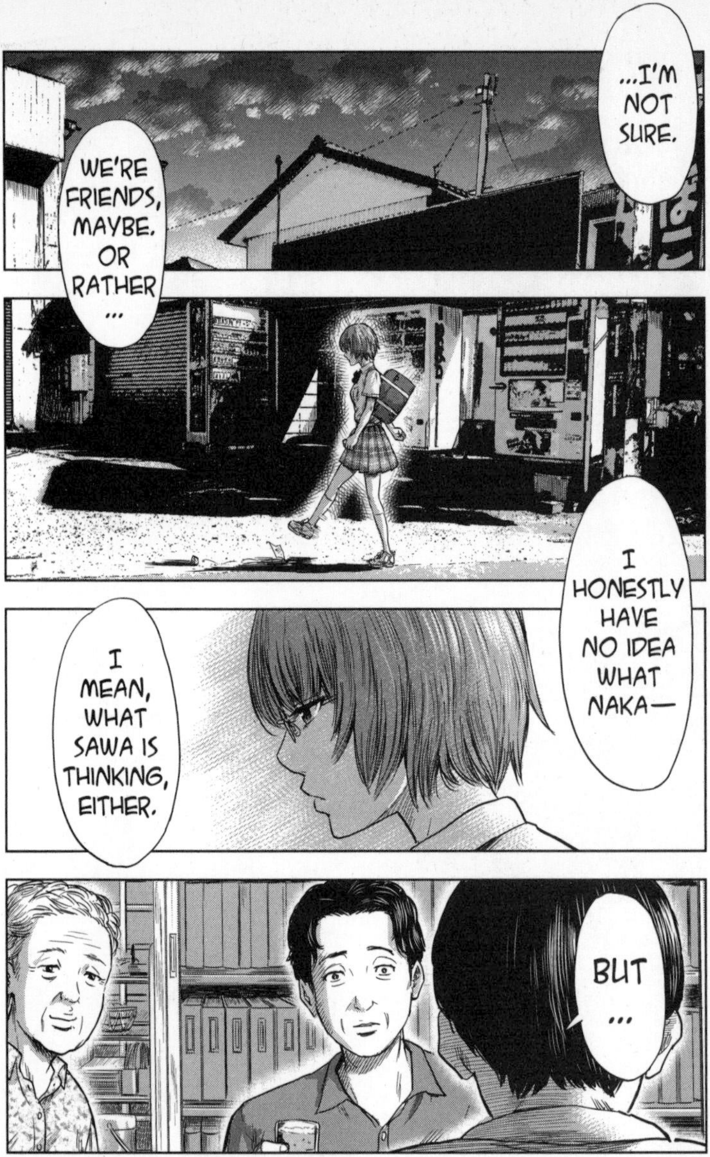
...I'M NOT SURE.
WE'RE FRIENDS, MAYBE. OR RATHER...
I HONESTLY HAVE NO IDEA WHAT NAKA—
I MEAN, WHAT SAWA IS THINKING, EITHER.
BUT...

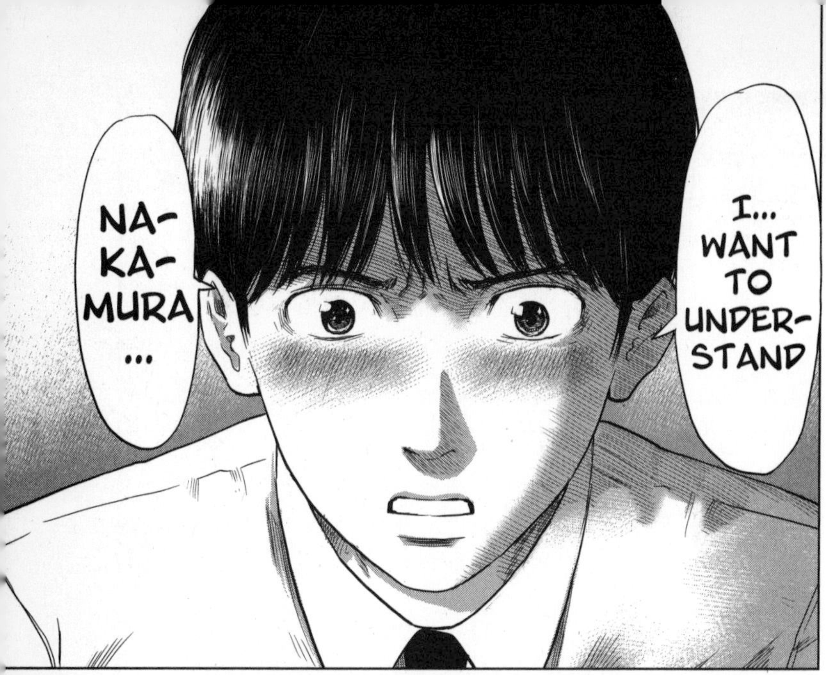
I... WANT TO UNDER-STAND
NA-KA-MURA...
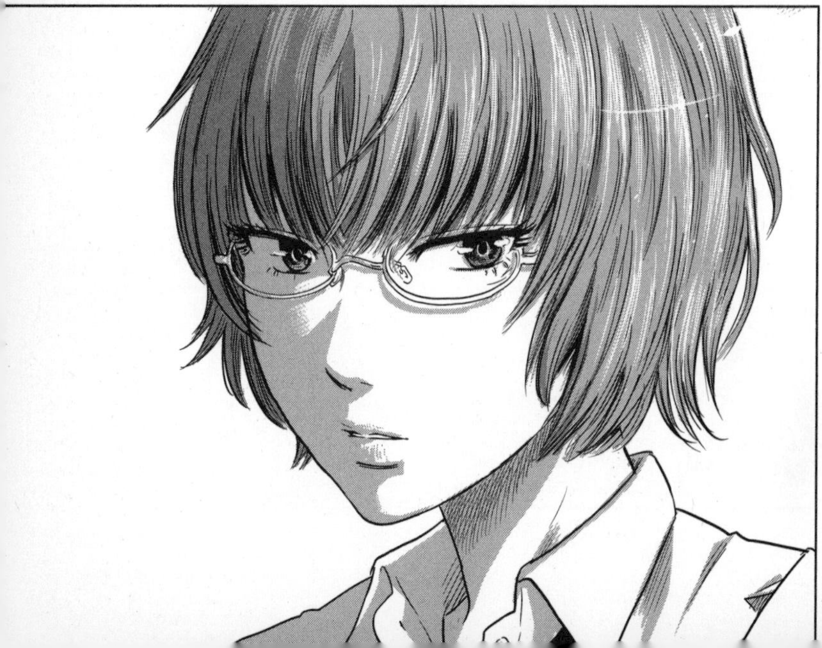

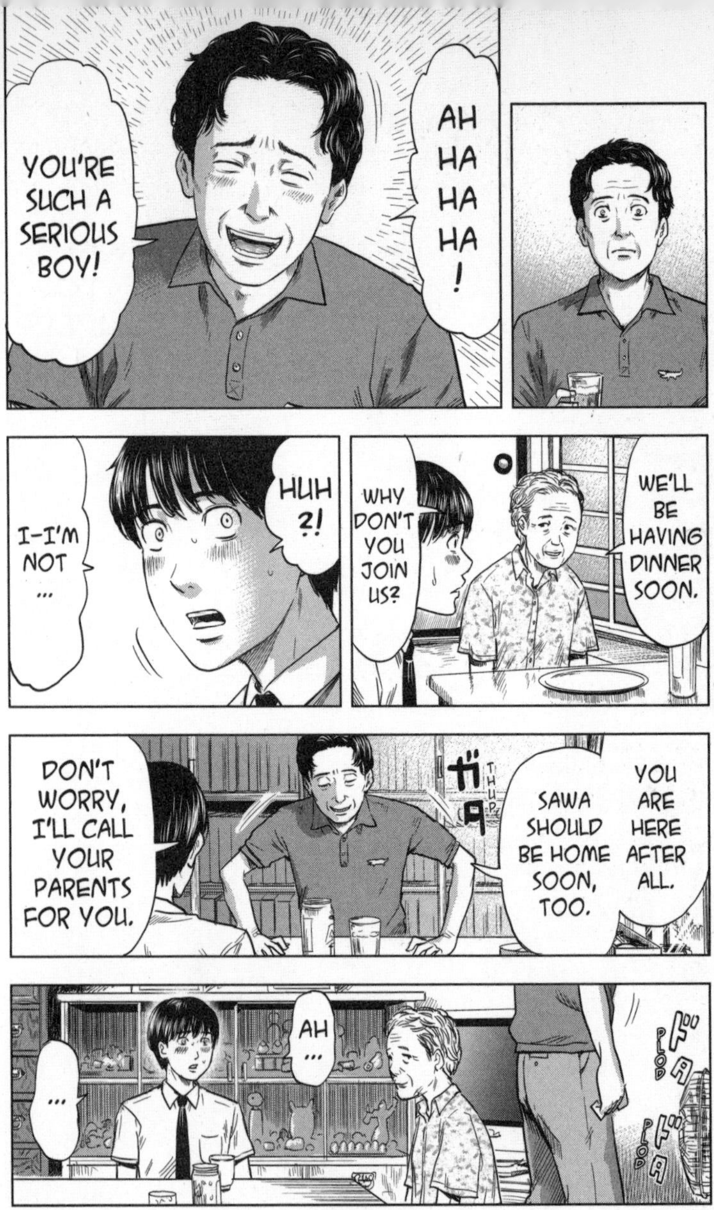
AH HA HA HA!
YOU'RE SUCH A SERIOUS BOY!
WE'LL BE HAVING DINNER SOON.
WHY DON'T YOU JOIN US?
HUH ?!
I-I'M NOT ...
YOU ARE HERE AFTER ALL.
SAWA SHOULD BE HOME SOON, TOO.
THUD
DON'T WORRY, I'LL CALL YOUR PARENTS FOR YOU.
PLOD
PLOD
AH ...
...

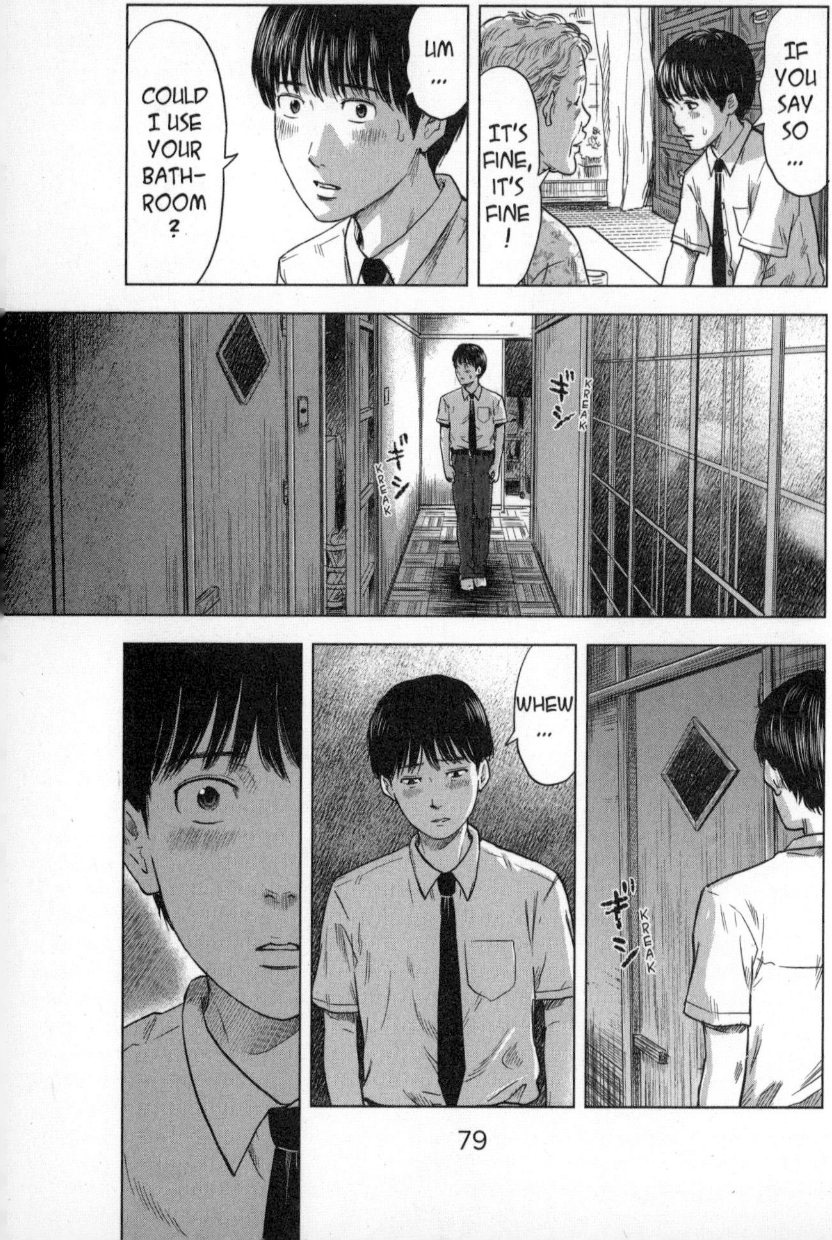
IF YOU SAY SO ...
IT'S FINE, IT'S FINE!
UM ...
COULD I USE YOUR BATH-ROOM?
ギシ KREAK
ギシ KREAK
ギシ KREAK
WHEW ...

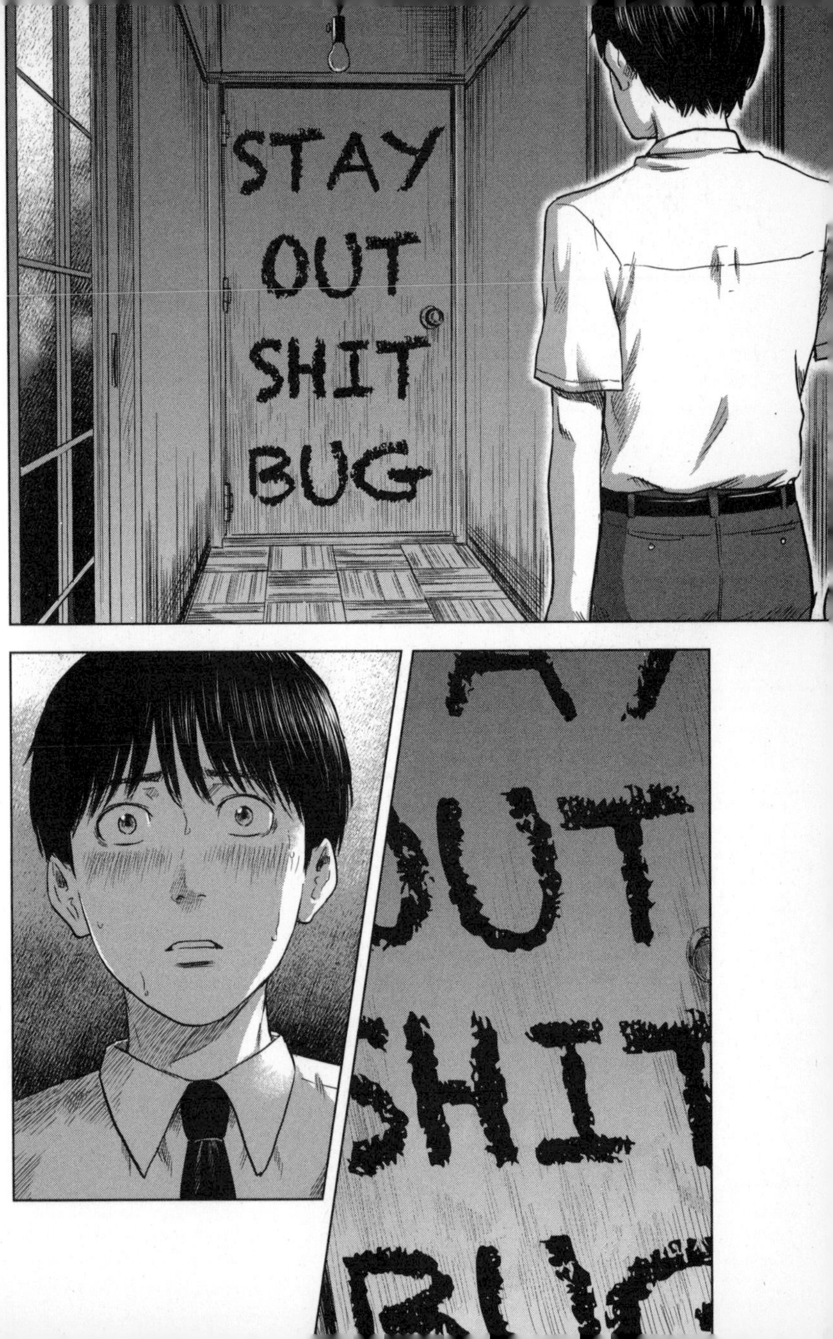
STAY OUT SHIT BUG

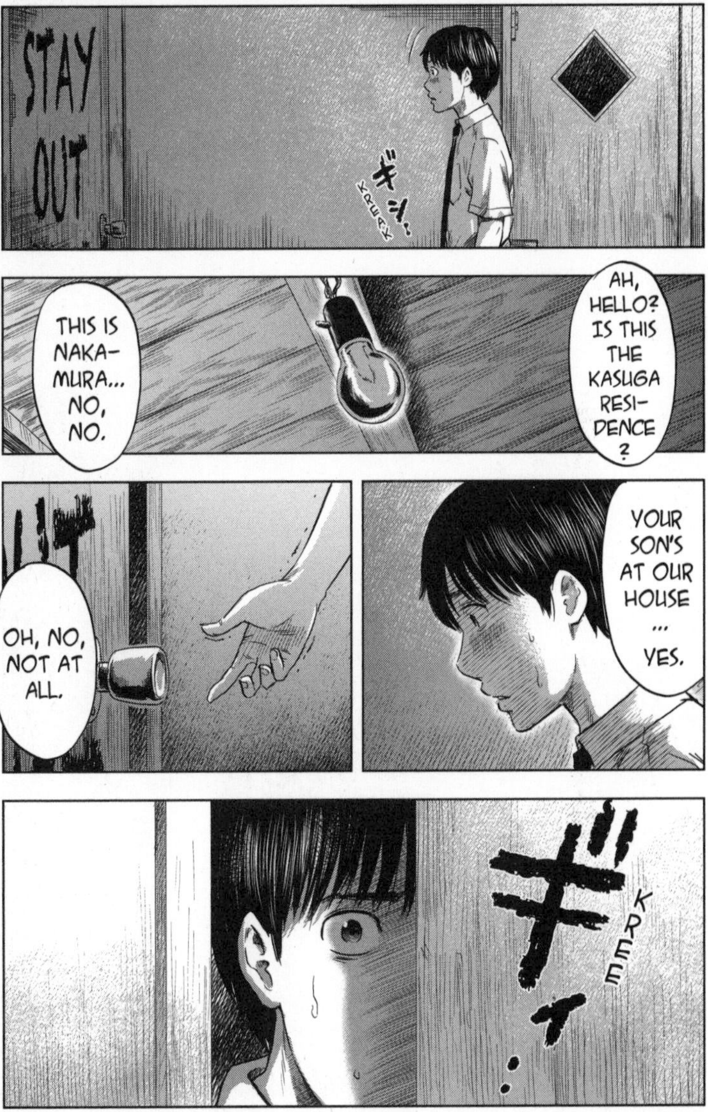
STAY OUT
ギシ
KREAK
AH, HELLO? IS THIS THE KASUGA RESIDENCE?
THIS IS NAKAMURA... NO, NO.
YOUR SON'S AT OUR HOUSE... YES.
OUT
OH, NO, NOT AT ALL.
ギィ
KREE

…トクン
BA-BUMP
トクン
BA-BUMP
トクン
BA-BUMP
トクン
BA-BUMP
トクン
BA-BUMP

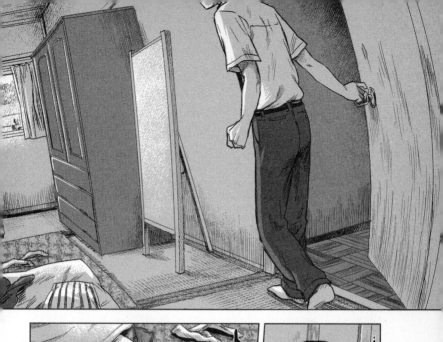

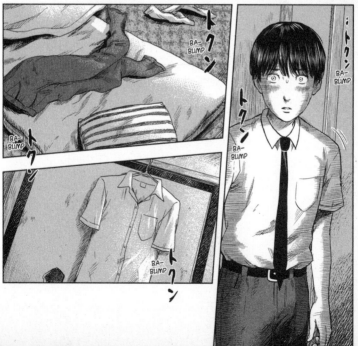

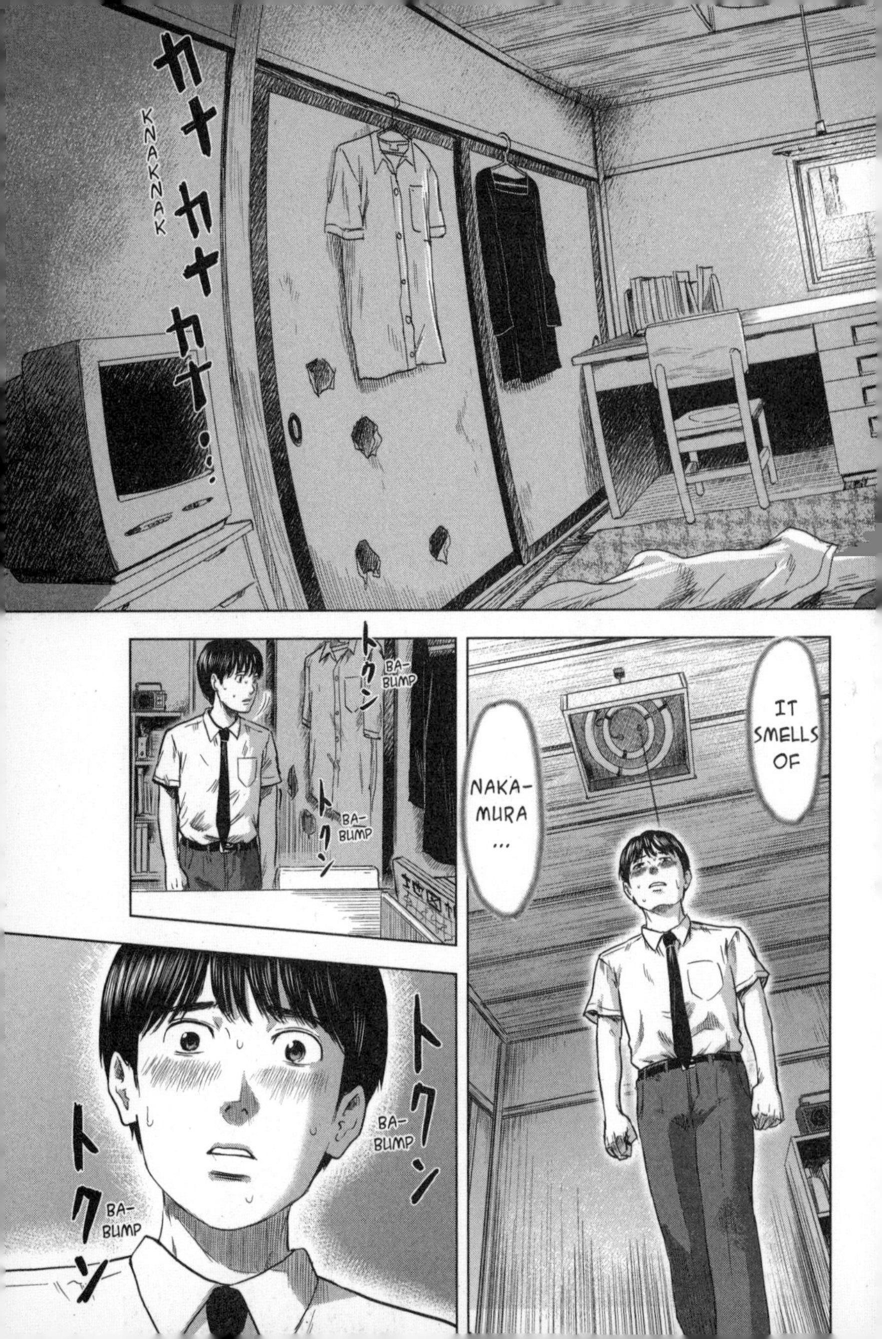

カナカナカナカナ…
KNAKNAK
IT SMELLS OF
NAKA-MURA...
トクン
BA-BUMP
トクン
BA-BUMP
トクン
BA-BUMP
トクン
BA-BUMP

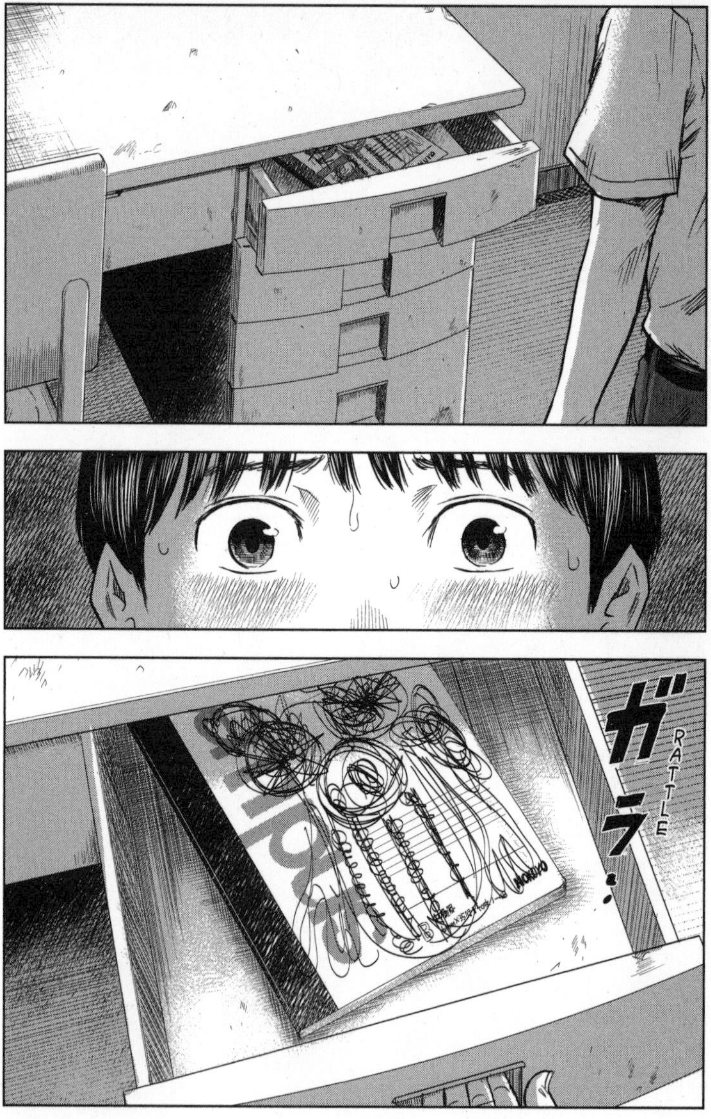
ガラ
RATTLE

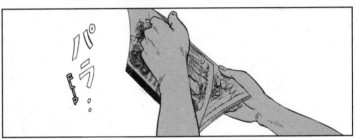

Worthless.

Worthless.
All of them.
Scum. Scum. Scum.
So bored. So bored.
Only shitbugs in
this town.
I can't stand it.

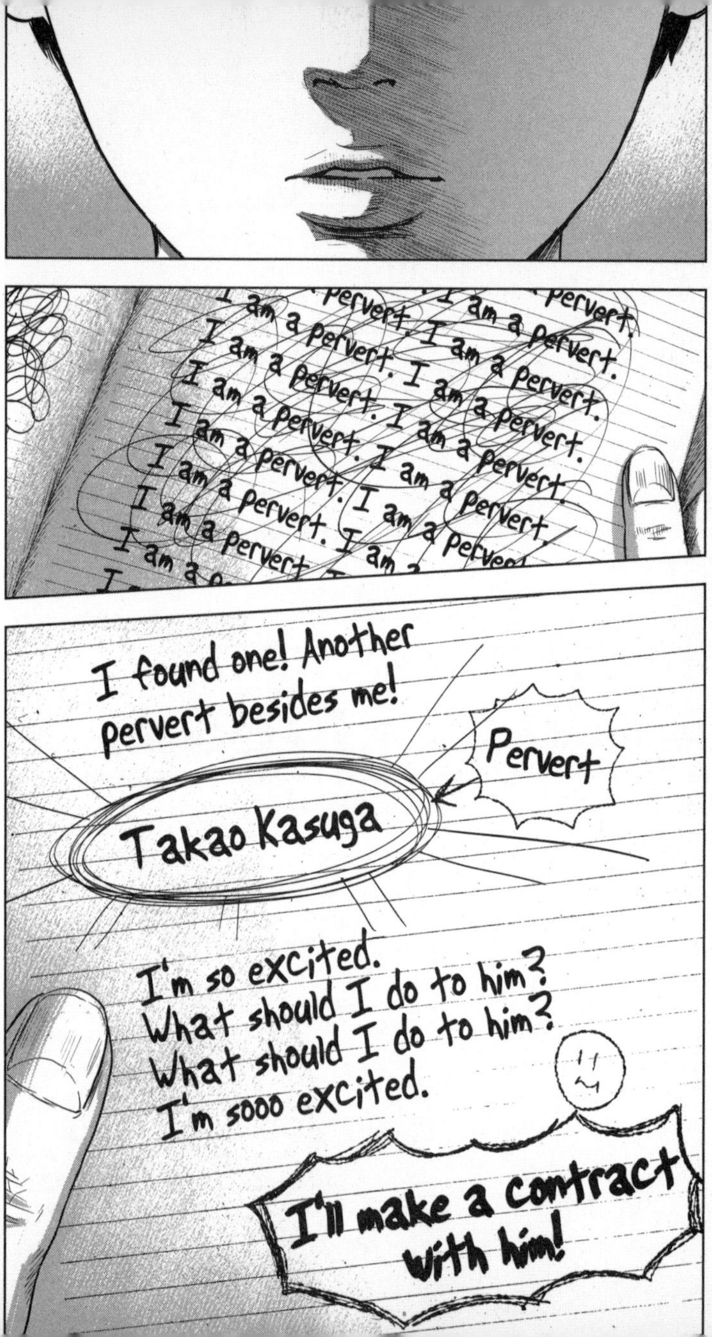
I am a pervert. I am a pervert.
I am a pervert. I am a pervert.
I am a pervert. I am a pervert.
I am a pervert. I am a pervert.
I am a pervert. I am a pervert.
I am a pervert. I am a pervert.
I found one! Another pervert besides me!
Pervert
Takao Kasuga
I'm so excited.
What should I do to him?
What should I do to him?
I'm sooo excited.
I'll make a contract with him!

I made Kasuga wear Nanako Saeki's gym clothes. He looked happy. Kasuga looked happy. He really is a pervert. What a pervert!

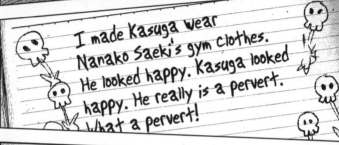

That lame Kasuga went on a date with Nanako Saeki. Well, fine. Kasuga's a pervert. I'll peel everything away.

I turned the classroom into a sea of shitbugs with Kasuga. He hasn't my approval for nothing!

It felt great

ALL ALL ALL ALL ALL ALL

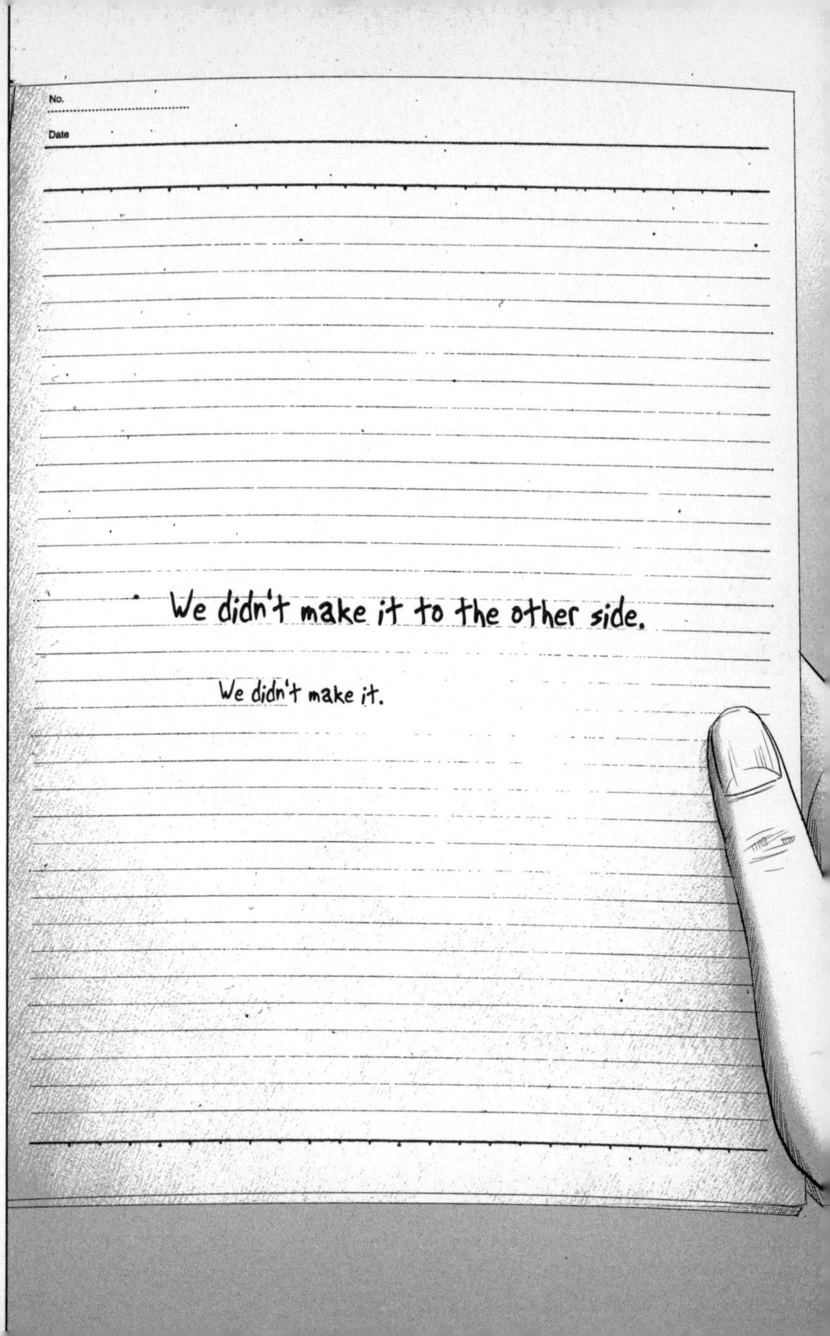
No.
Date
We didn't make it to the other side.
We didn't make it.

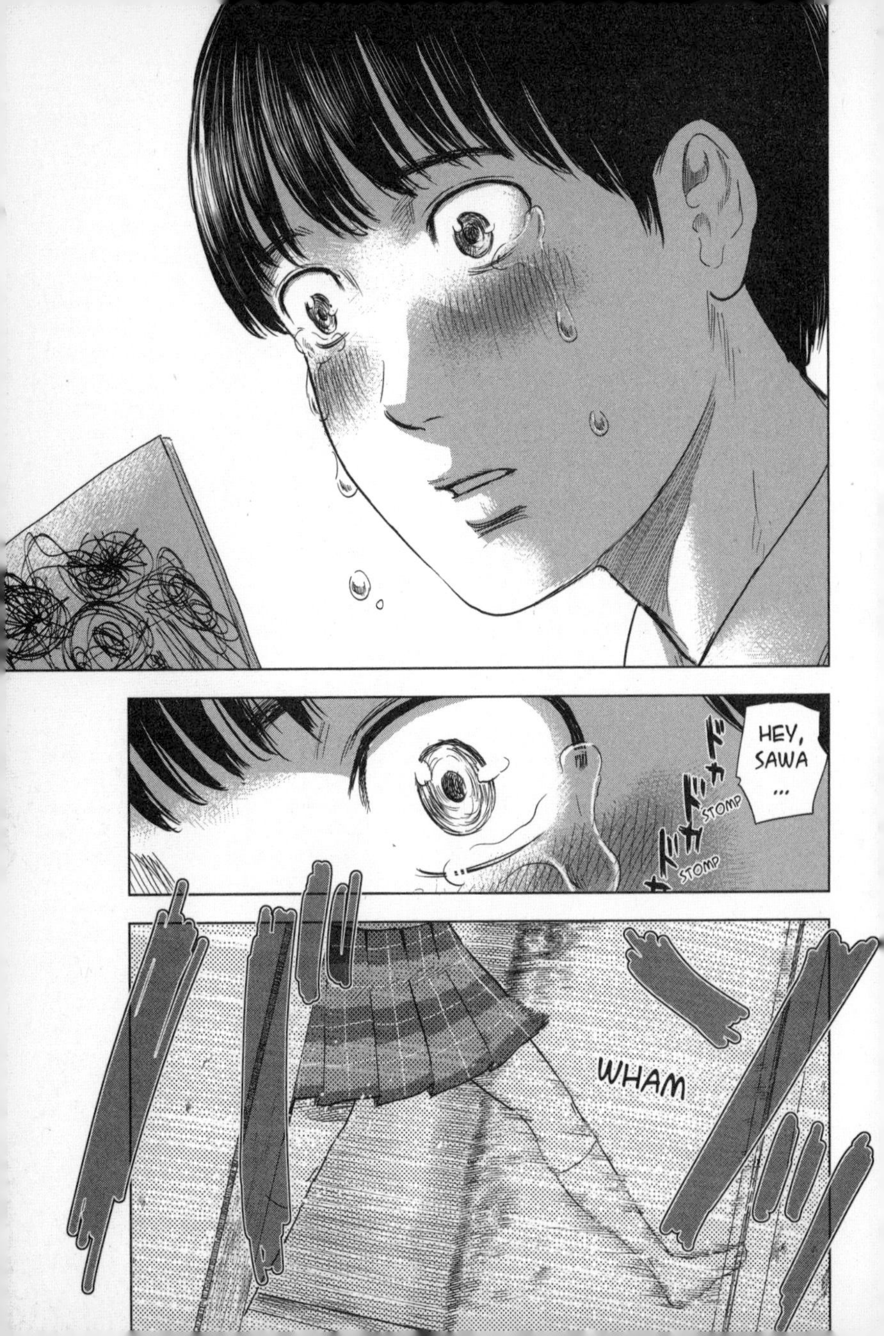
HEY, SAWA ...
STOMP
STOMP
WHAM

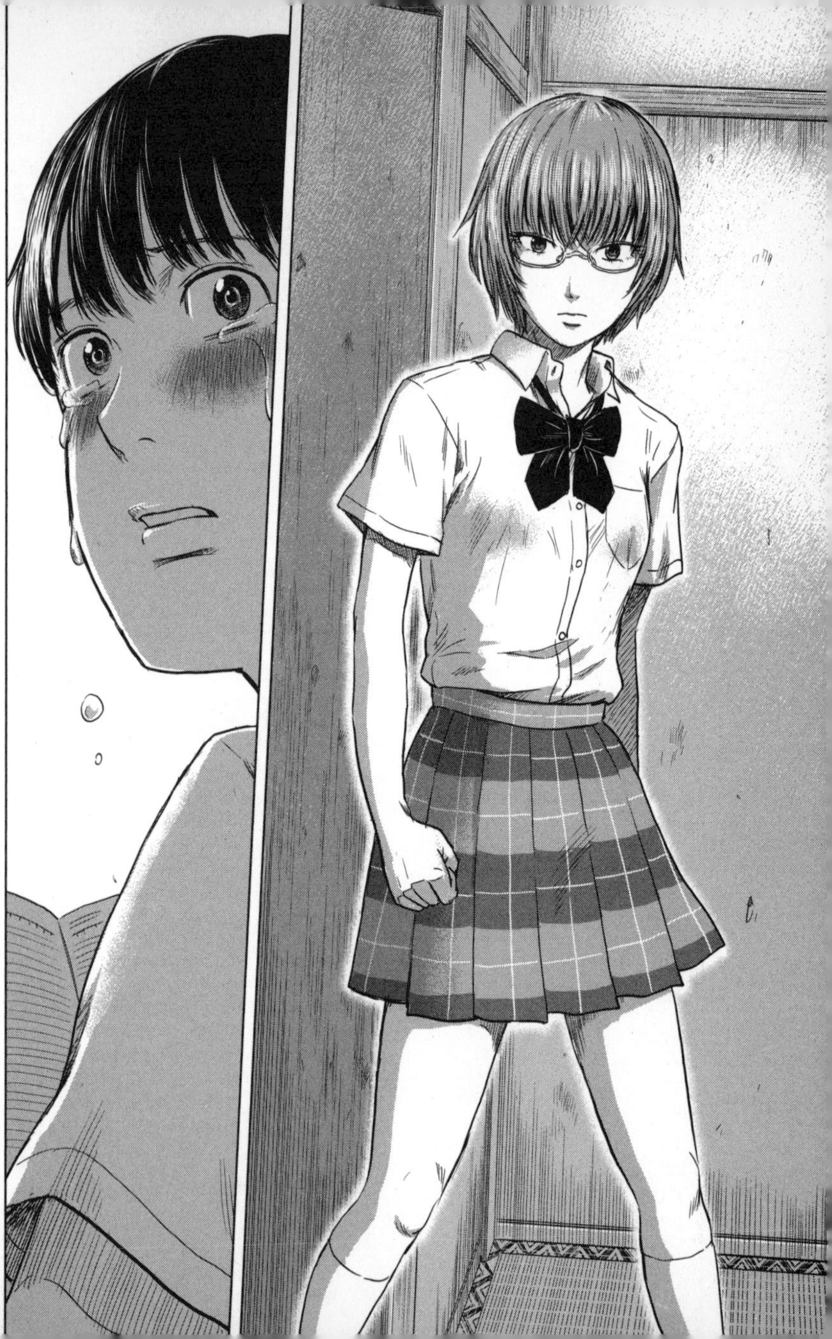

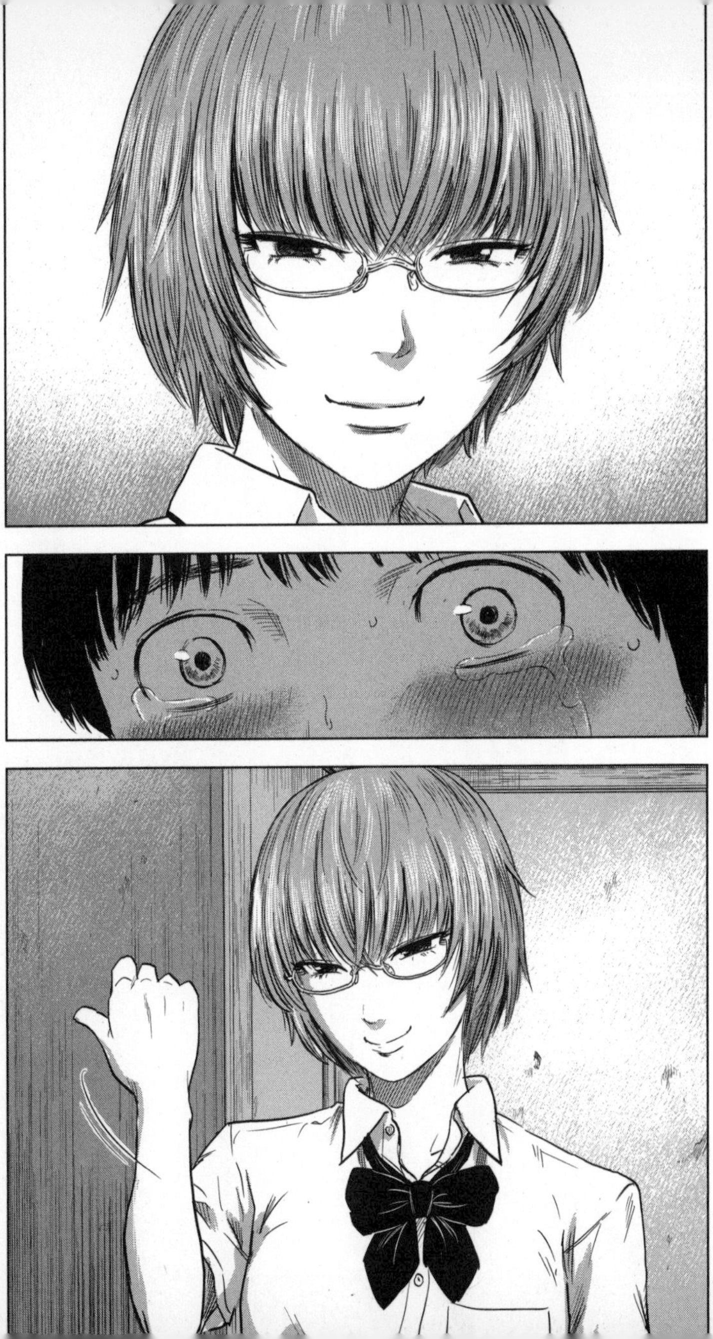

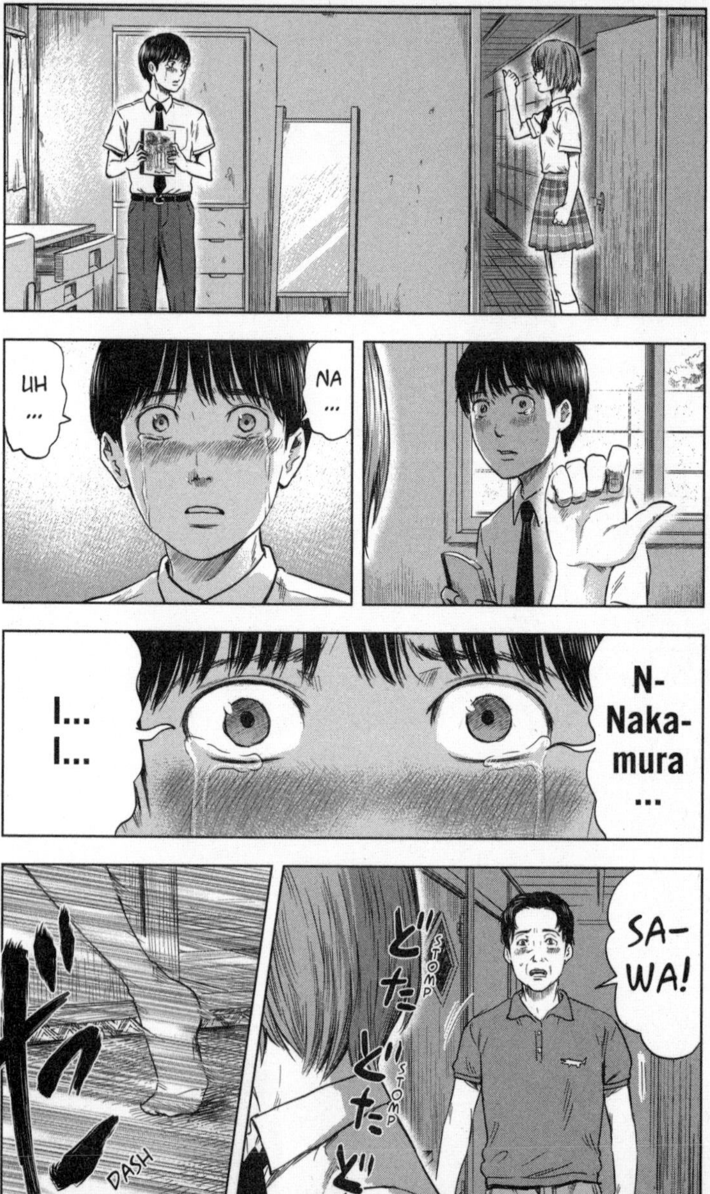
NA ...
UH ...
N-Nakamura ...
I... I...
SA-WA!
どた STOMP
どた STOMP
どた
ダン
DASH

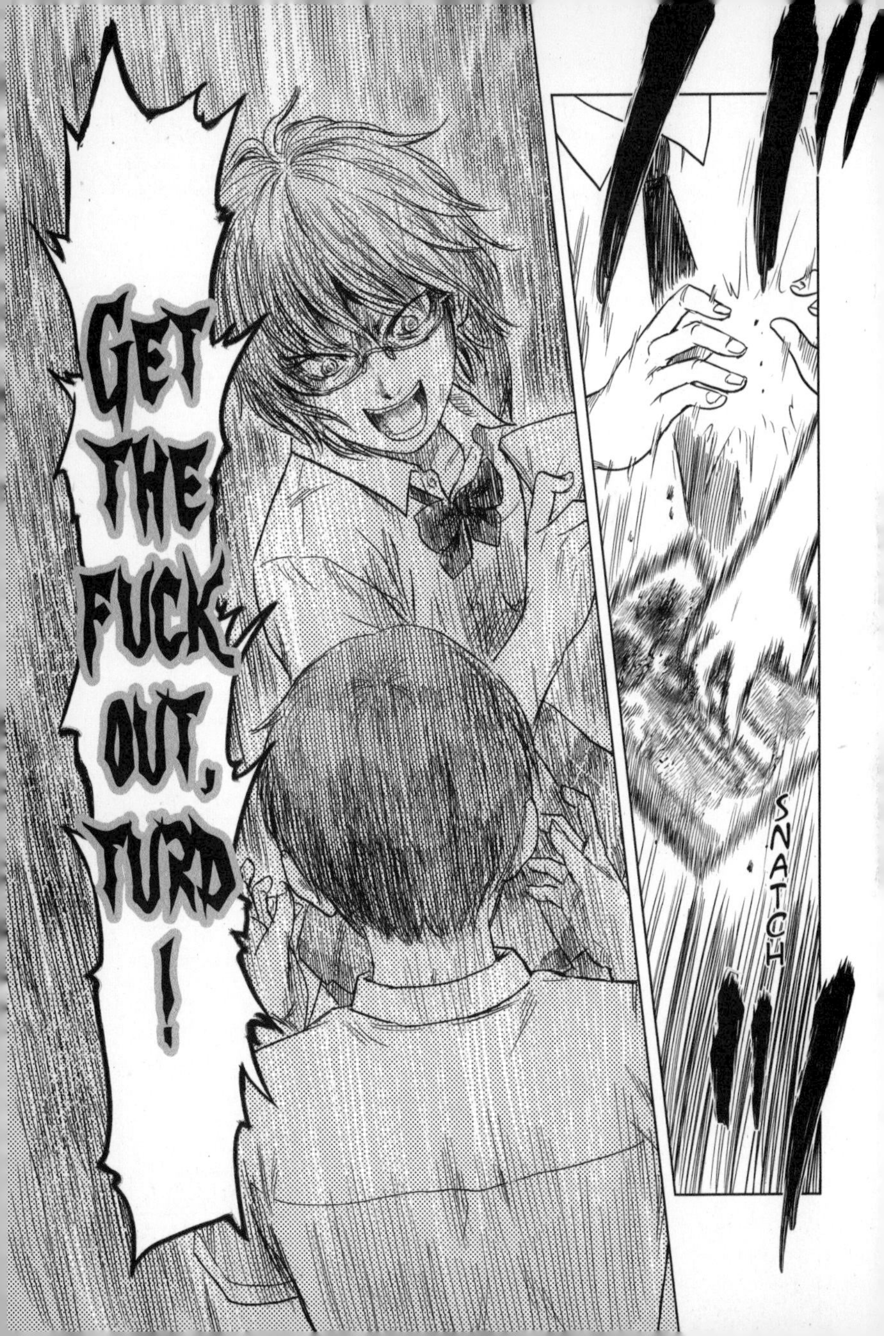
SNATCH
GET THE FUCK OUT, TURD!

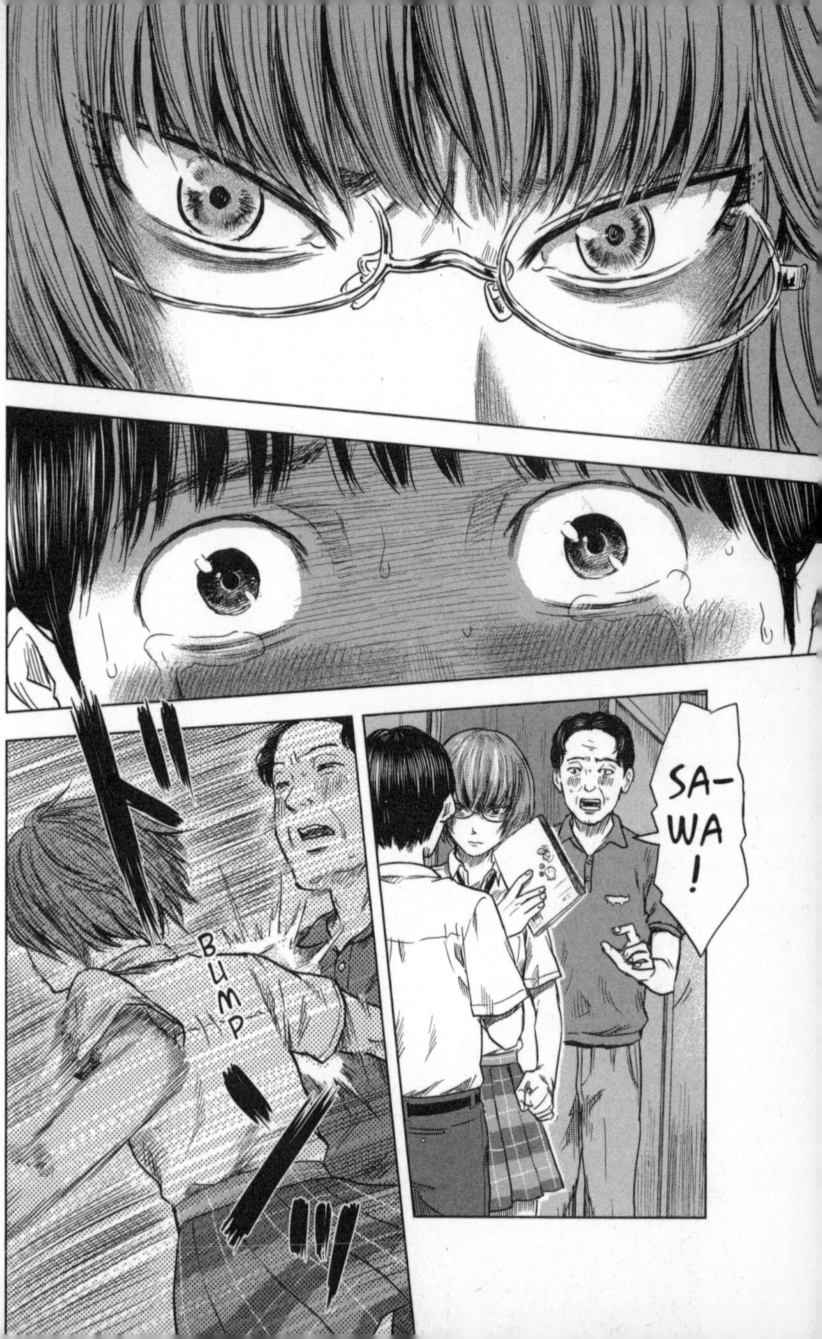
SA-WA!
BUMP

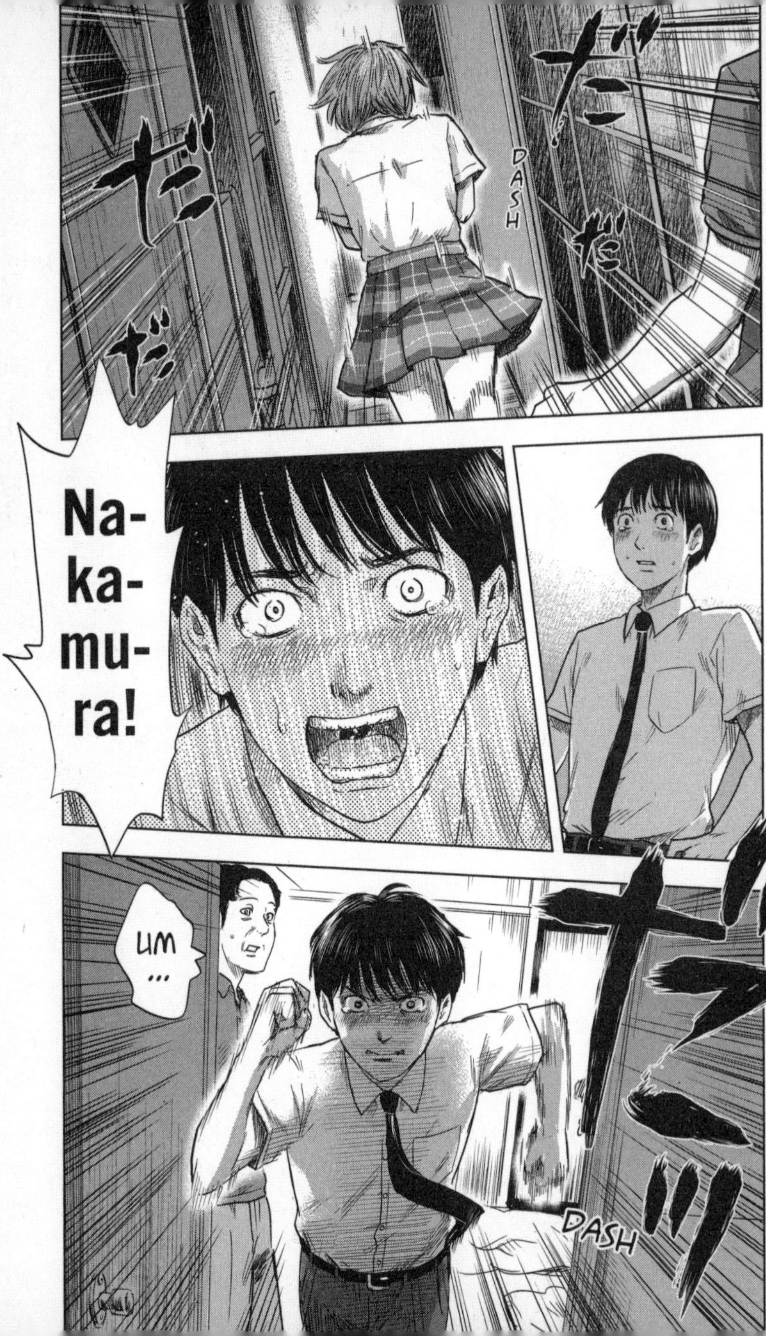
DASH
Na-ka-mu-ra!
um ...
DASH

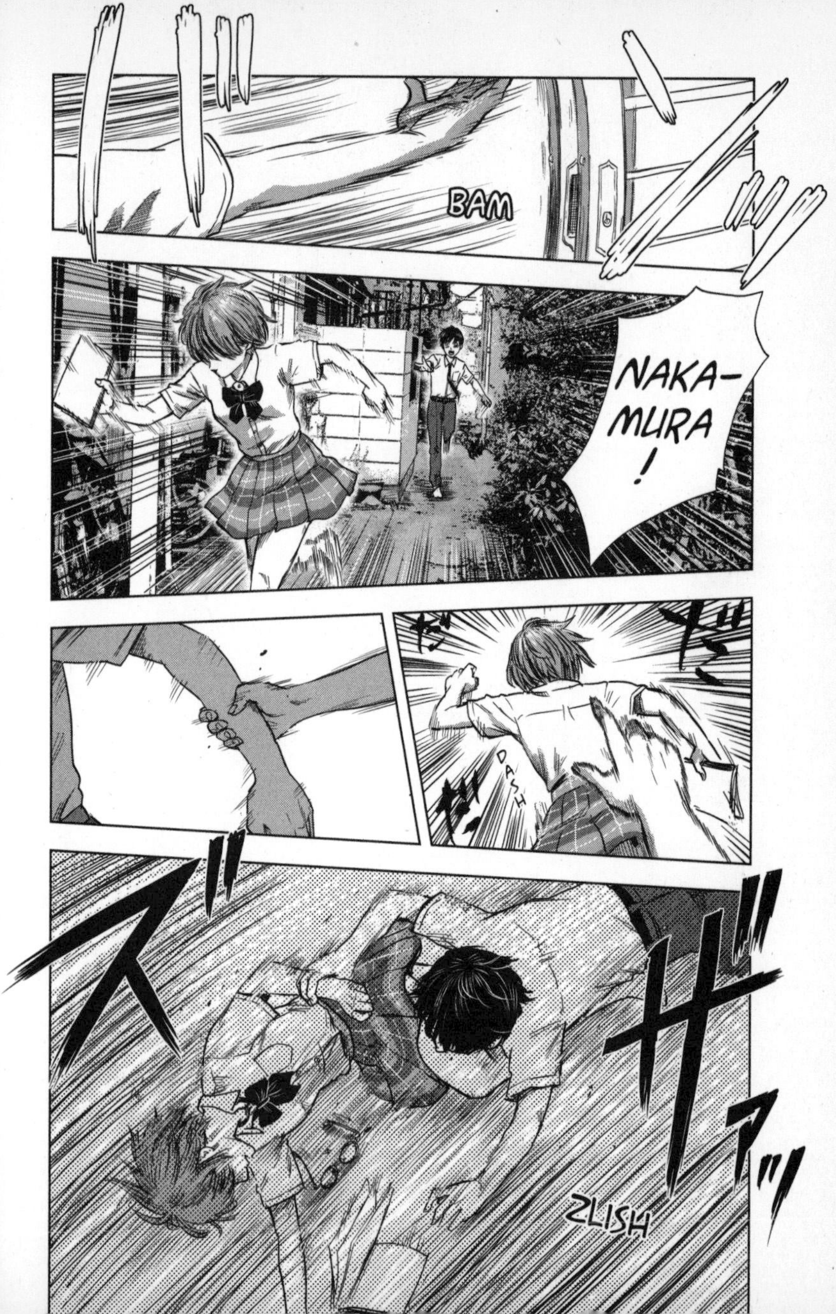
BAM
NAKA-
MURA
!
DASH
ZLISH

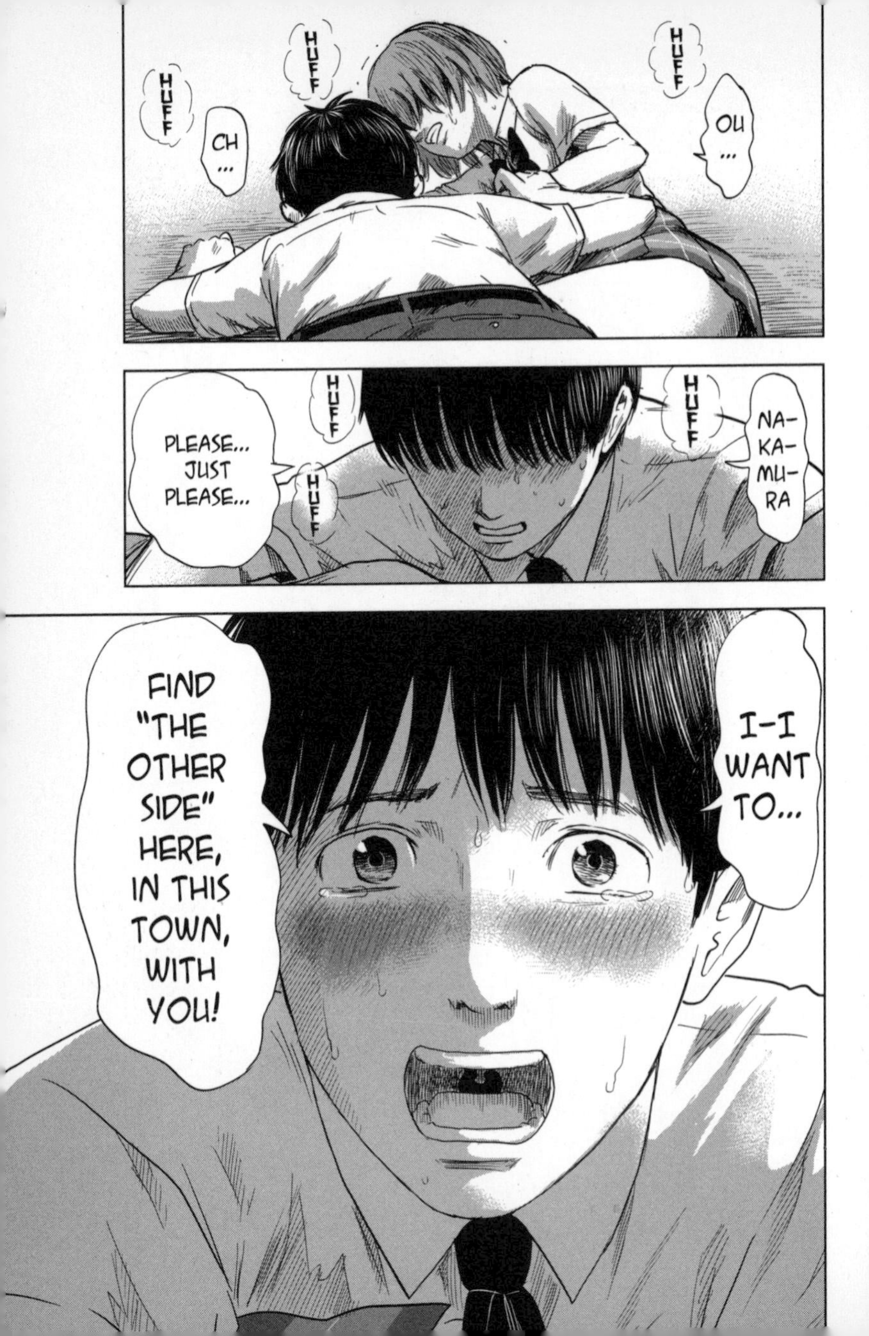
HUFF
OU...
HUFF
HUFF
CH...
NA-KA-MU-RA
HUFF
HUFF
PLEASE... JUST PLEASE...
HUFF
I-I WANT TO...
FIND "THE OTHER SIDE" HERE, IN THIS TOWN, WITH YOU!

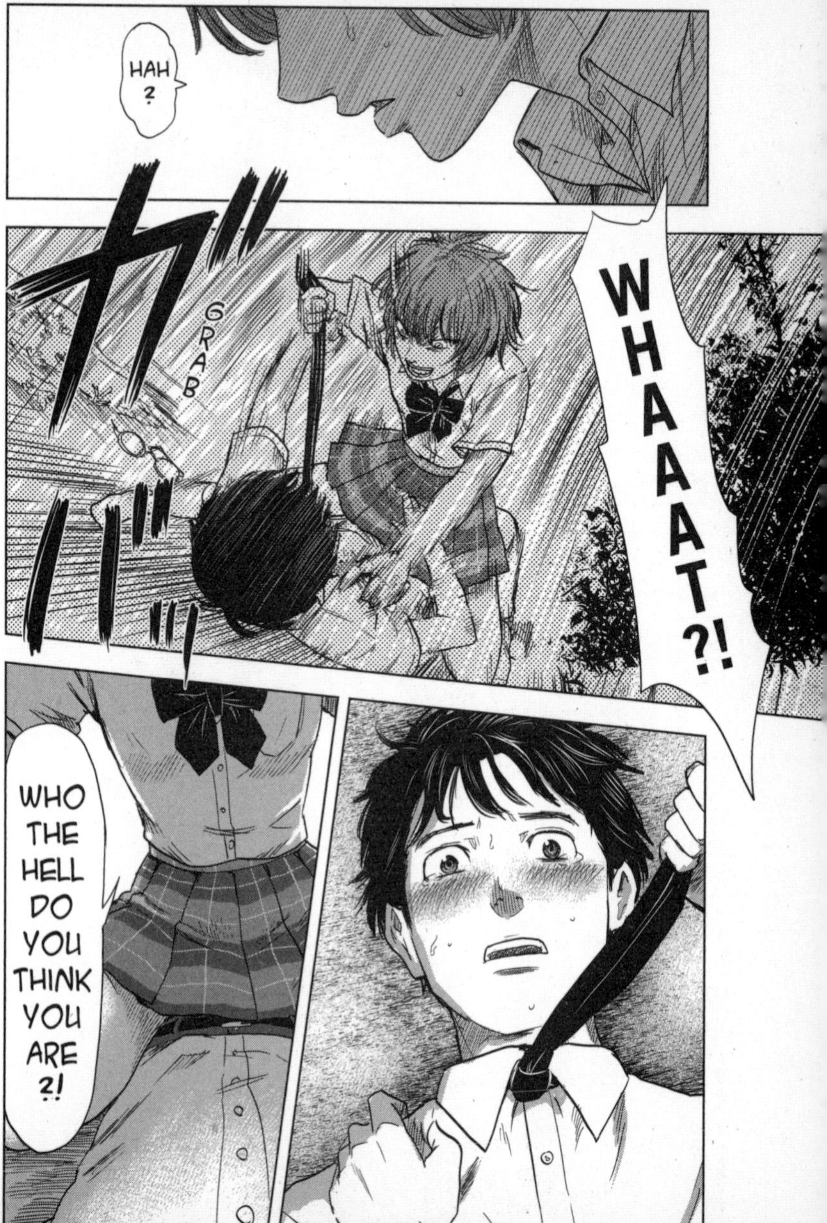

HAH?
WHAAAT?!
GRAB
WHO THE HELL DO YOU THINK YOU ARE?!

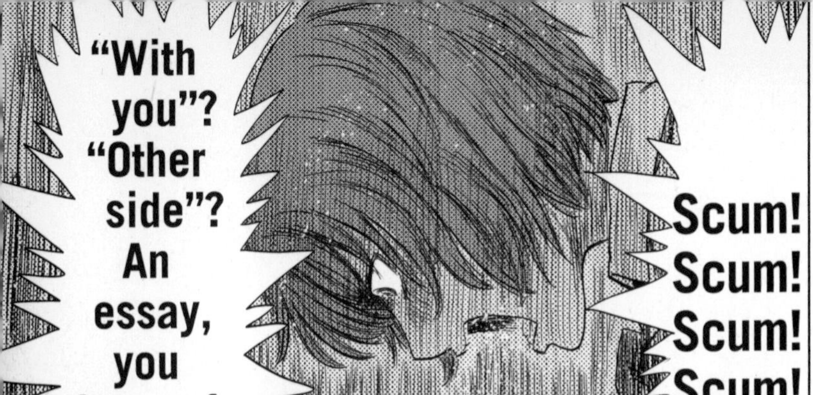
Scum! Scum! Scum! Scum! Scum! Scum! Scum!
"With you"? "Other side"? An essay, you lump of mud?! Scum Scum Scum Scum Scum

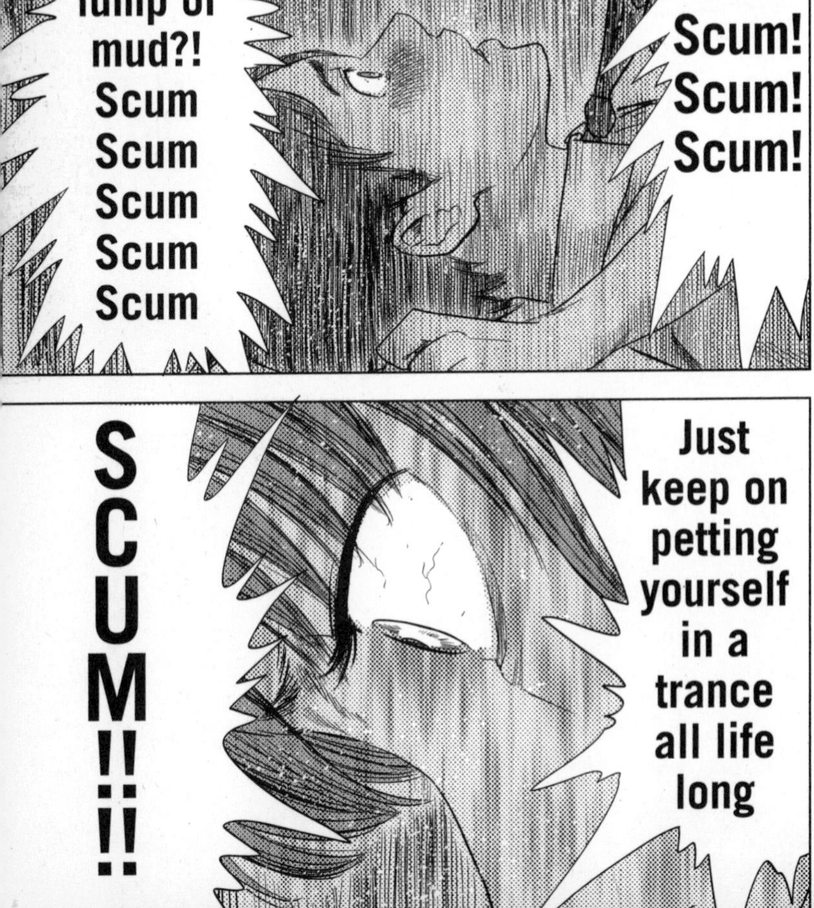
Just keep on petting yourself in a trance all life long
SCUM!!!!

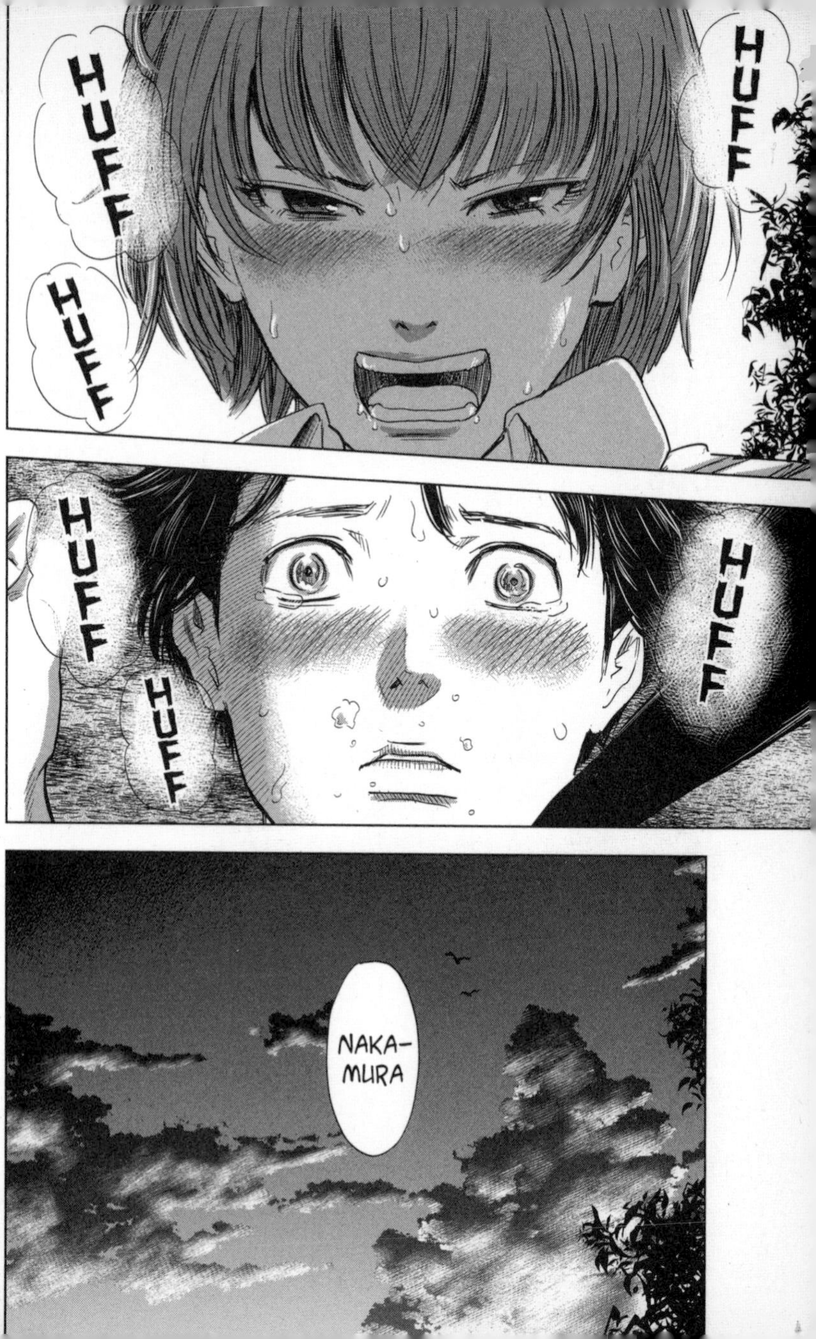
HUFF
HUFF
HUFF
HUFF
HUFF
HUFF
NAKA-MURA

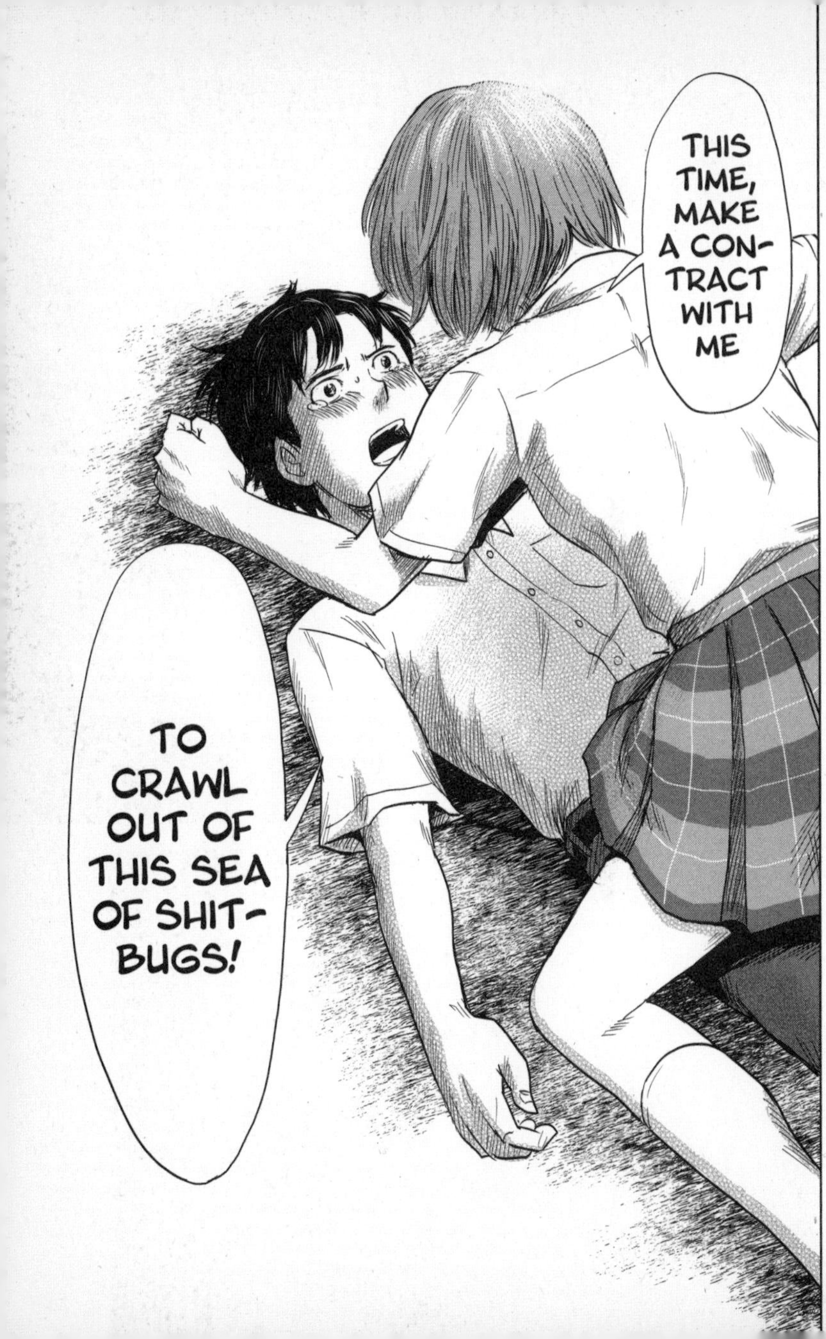
THIS TIME, MAKE A CON-TRACT WITH ME
TO CRAWL OUT OF THIS SEA OF SHIT-BUGS!

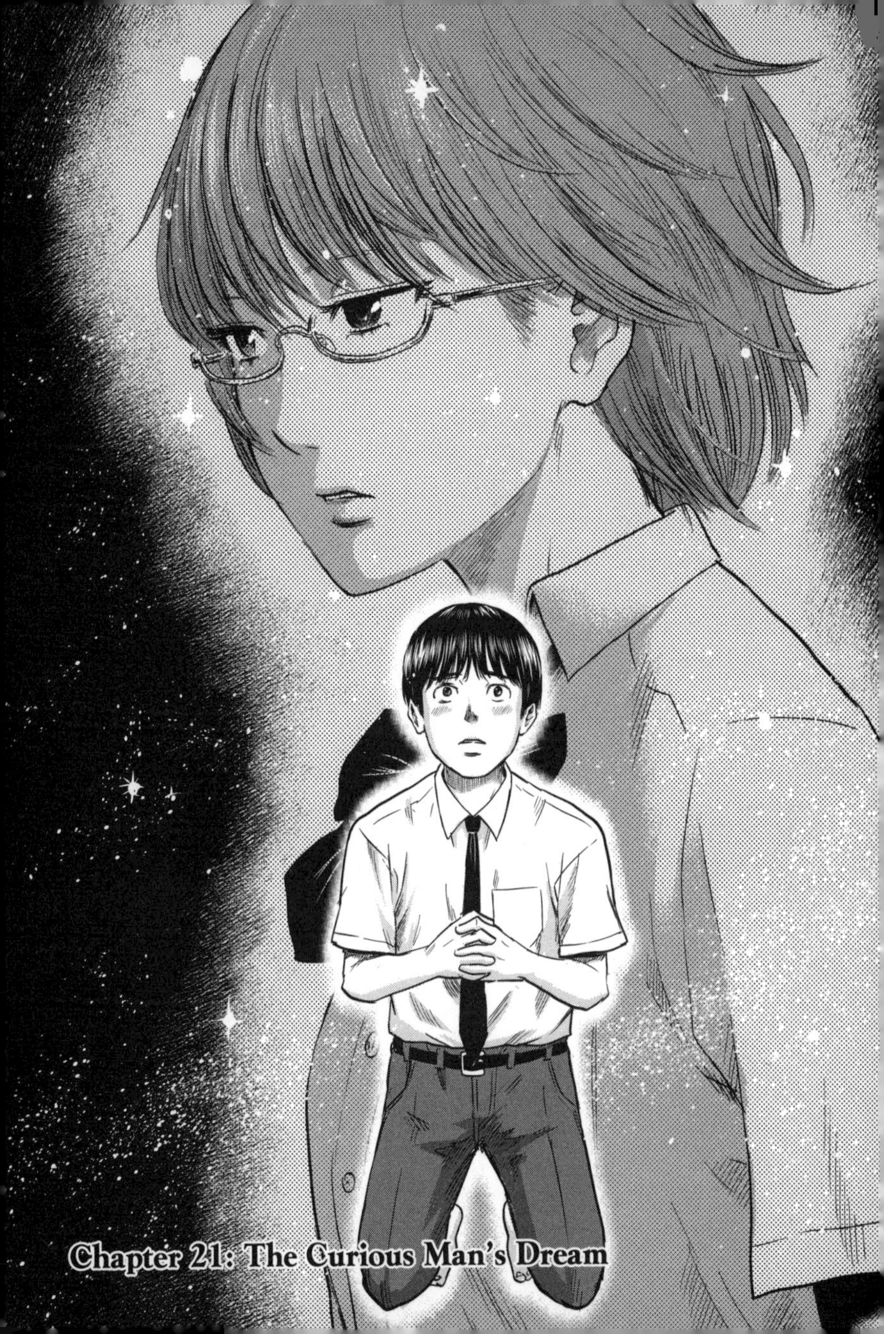

Chapter 21: The Curious Man's Dream

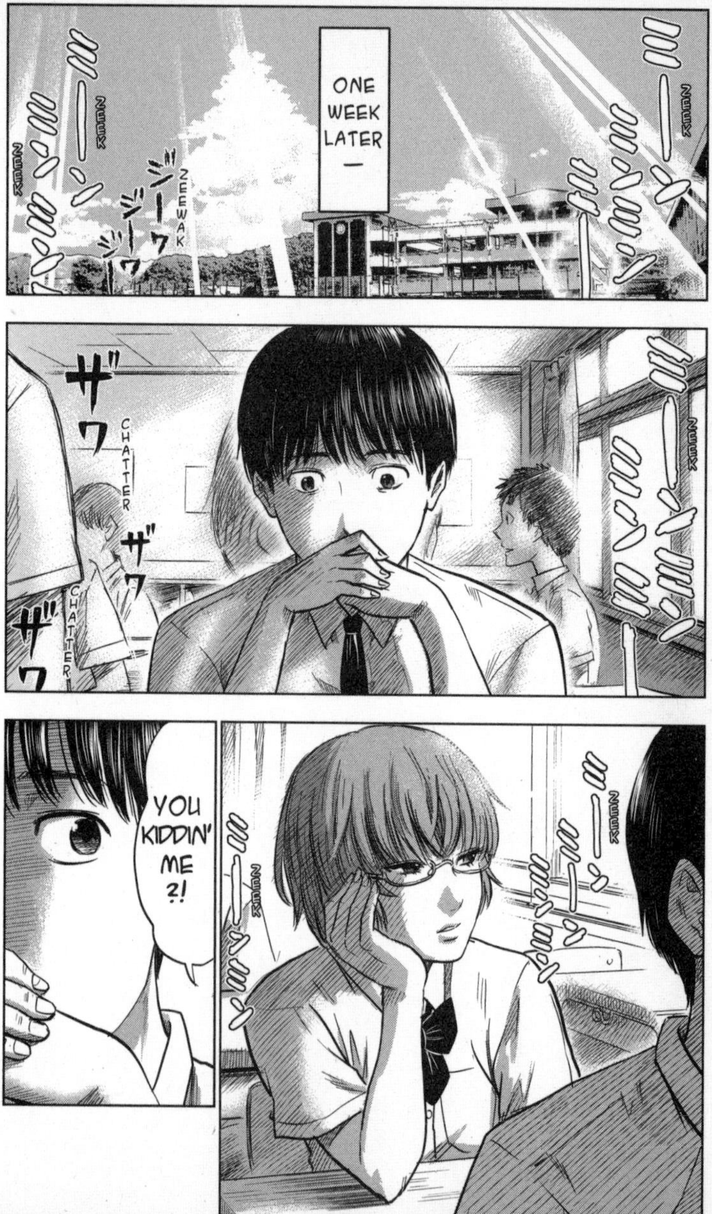
ZEEK
ONE WEEK LATER —
ZEEWAK
ZEEK
ZEEK
ZEEK
CHATTER
CHATTER
ZEEK
ZEEK
YOU KIDDIN' ME ?!

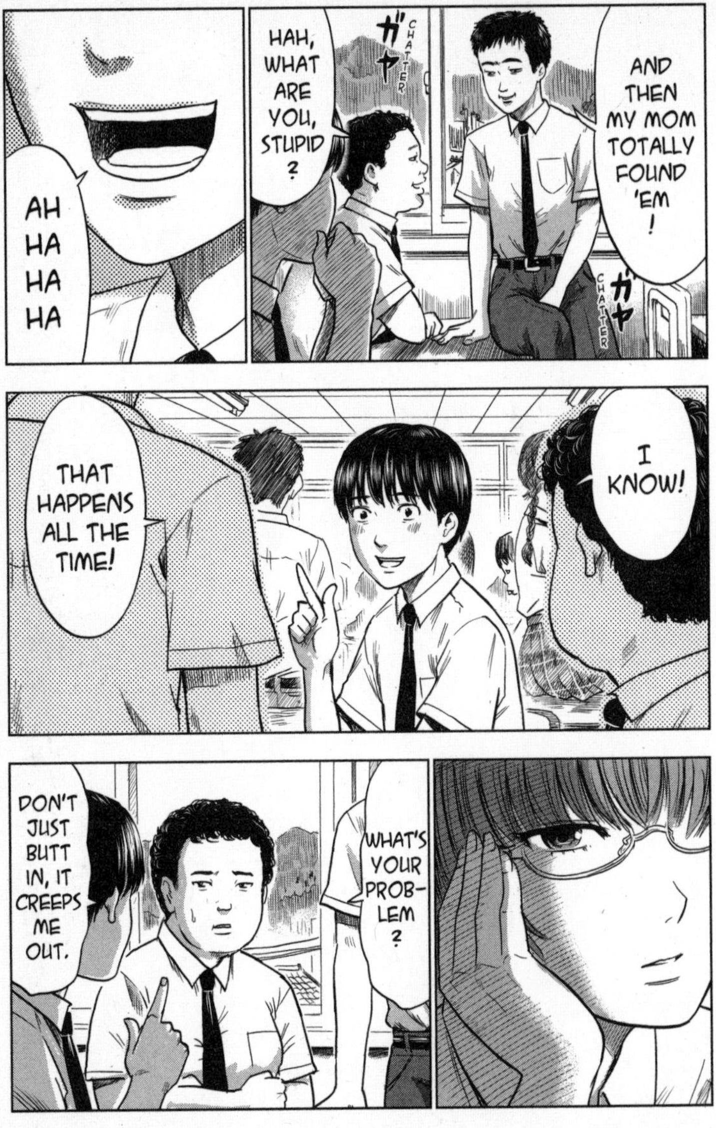
AND THEN MY MOM TOTALLY FOUND 'EM!
ガヤ CHATTER
HAH, WHAT ARE YOU, STUPID?
ガヤ CHATTER
AH HA HA HA
I KNOW!
THAT HAPPENS ALL THE TIME!
WHAT'S YOUR PROB-LEM?
DON'T JUST BUTT IN, IT CREEPS ME OUT.

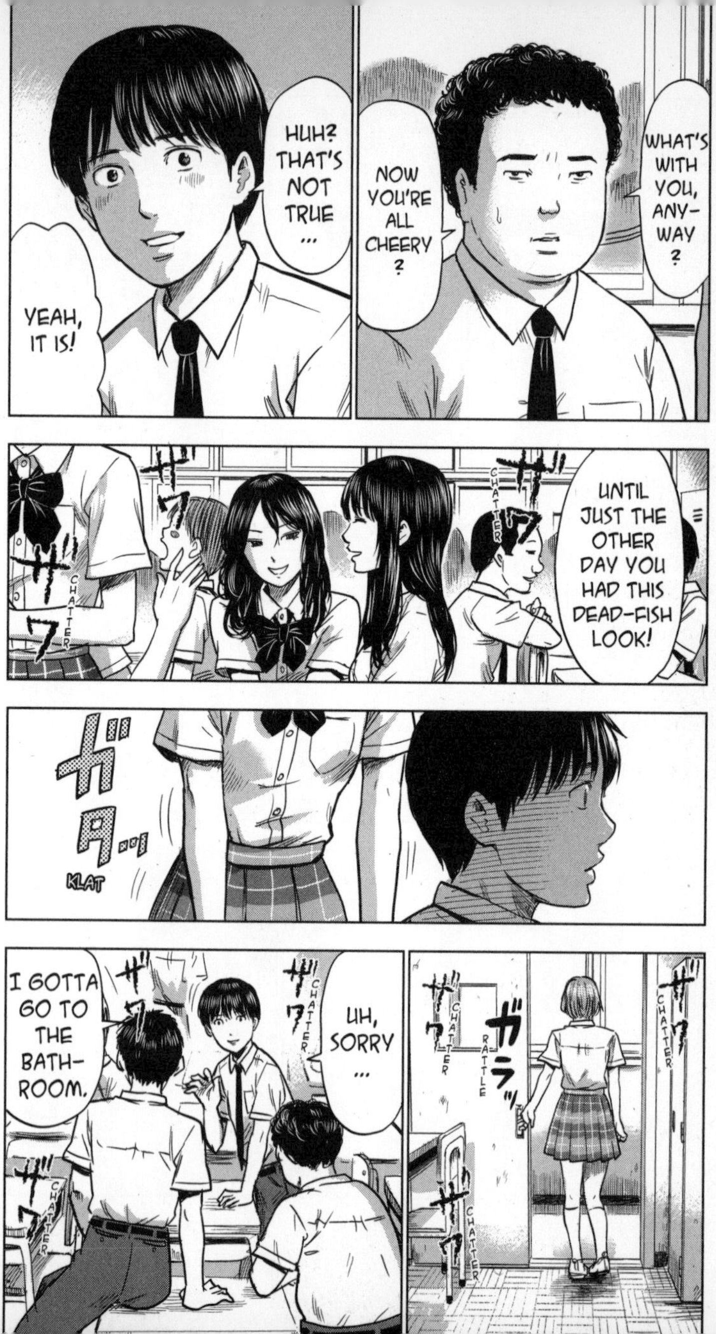
WHAT'S WITH YOU, ANY-WAY?
NOW YOU'RE ALL CHEERY?
HUH? THAT'S NOT TRUE...
YEAH, IT IS!
CHATTER
UNTIL JUST THE OTHER DAY YOU HAD THIS DEAD-FISH LOOK!
CHATTER
KLAT
CHATTER
RATTLE
CHATTER
CHATTER
CHATTER
UH, SORRY...
I GOTTA GO TO THE BATH-ROOM.
CHATTER

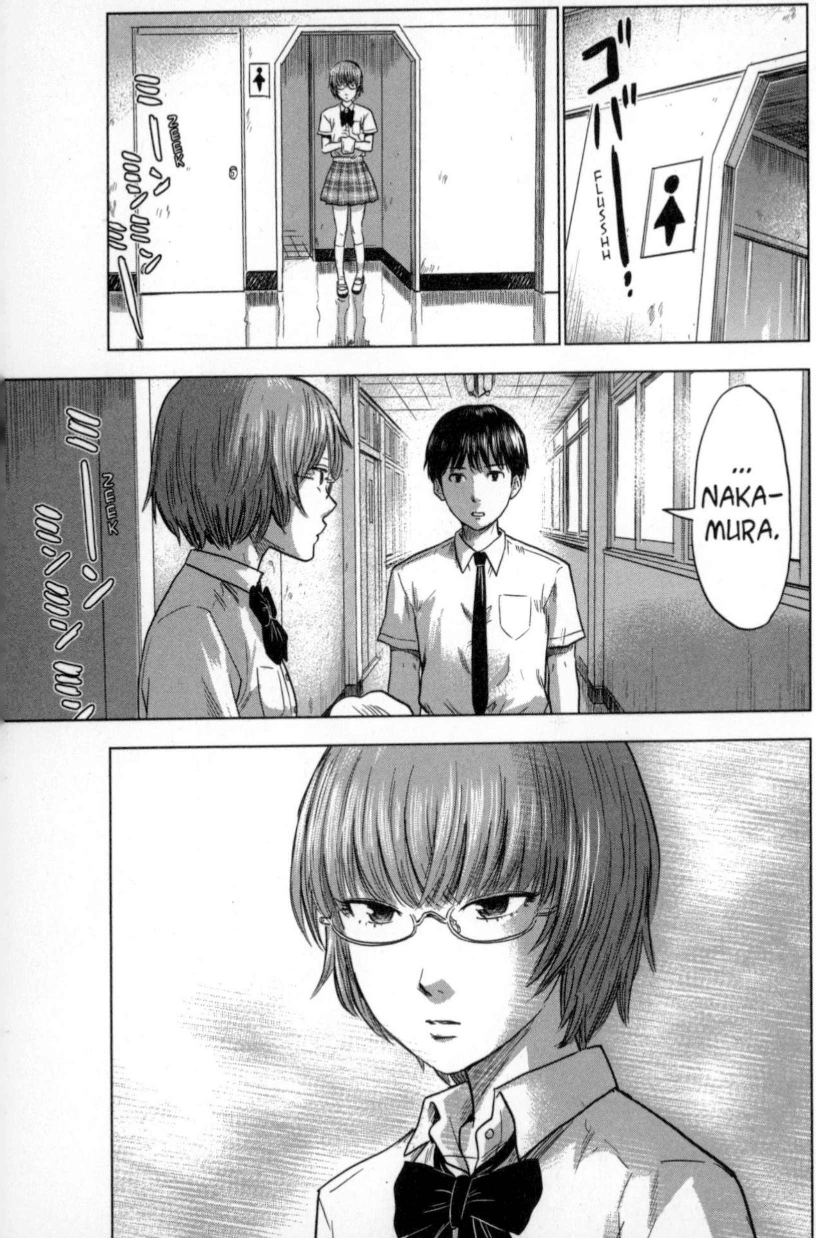
ゴバー!
FLUSSHH
ZEEEK
ZEEEK
... NAKA-MURA.

JUST... WAIT A TINY BIT MORE.

I'M SORRY ...

HERE IN THIS TOWN, I SWEAR ...

I'LL SHOW YOU "THE OTHER SIDE"

...

I'LL SHOW YOU.

HOPE TO DO ?

WHAT COULD A SAD FUCK LIKE YOU

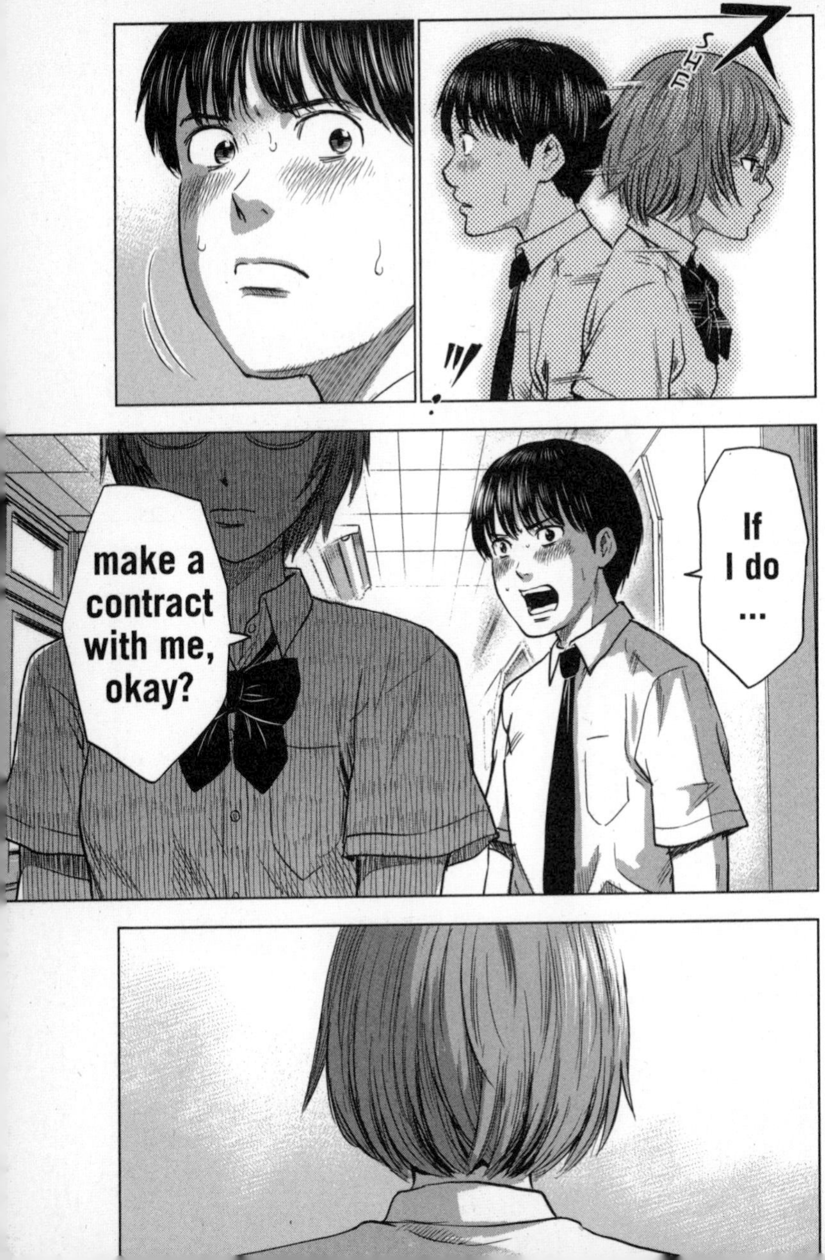
SHU
If I do ...
make a contract with me, okay?

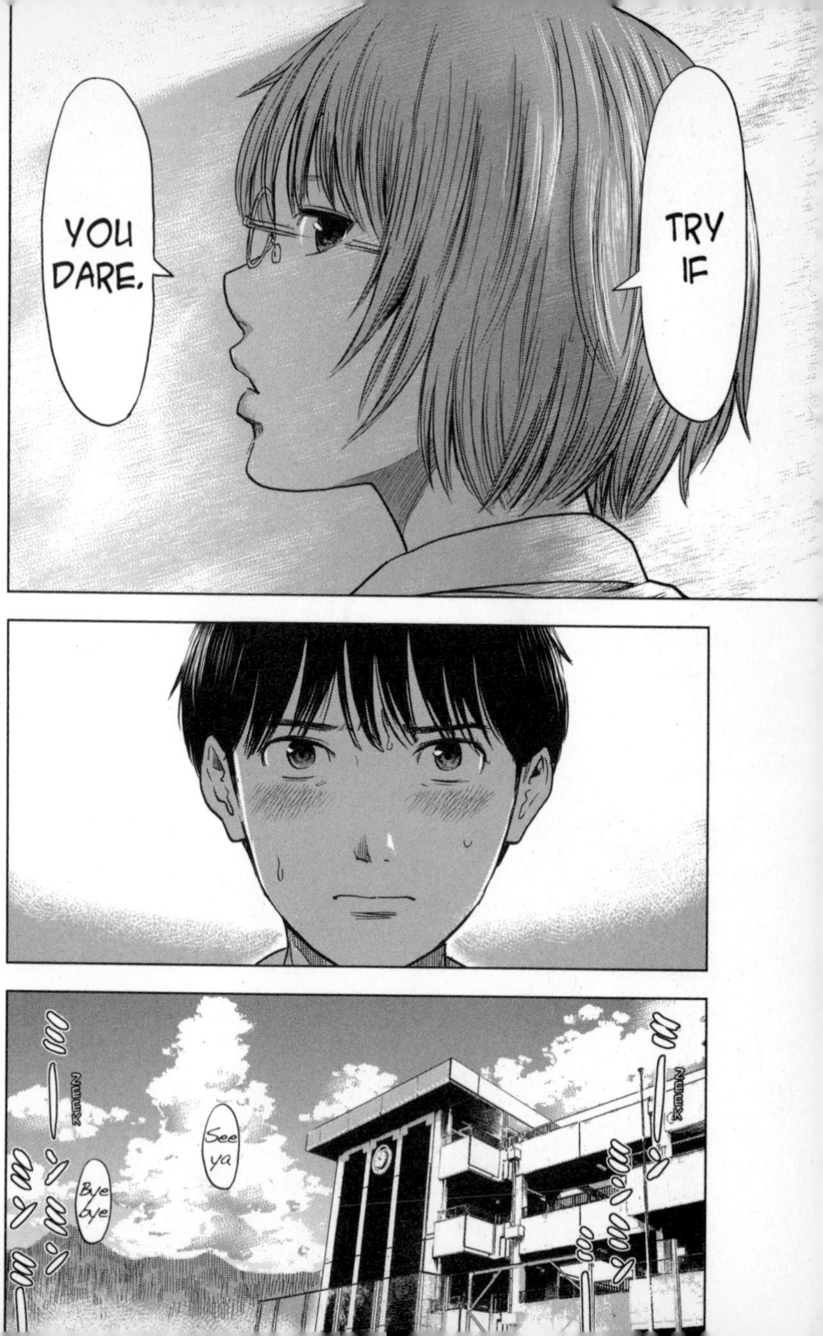
TRY IF
YOU DARE.
KEEEN
See ya
Bye bye
KEEEN

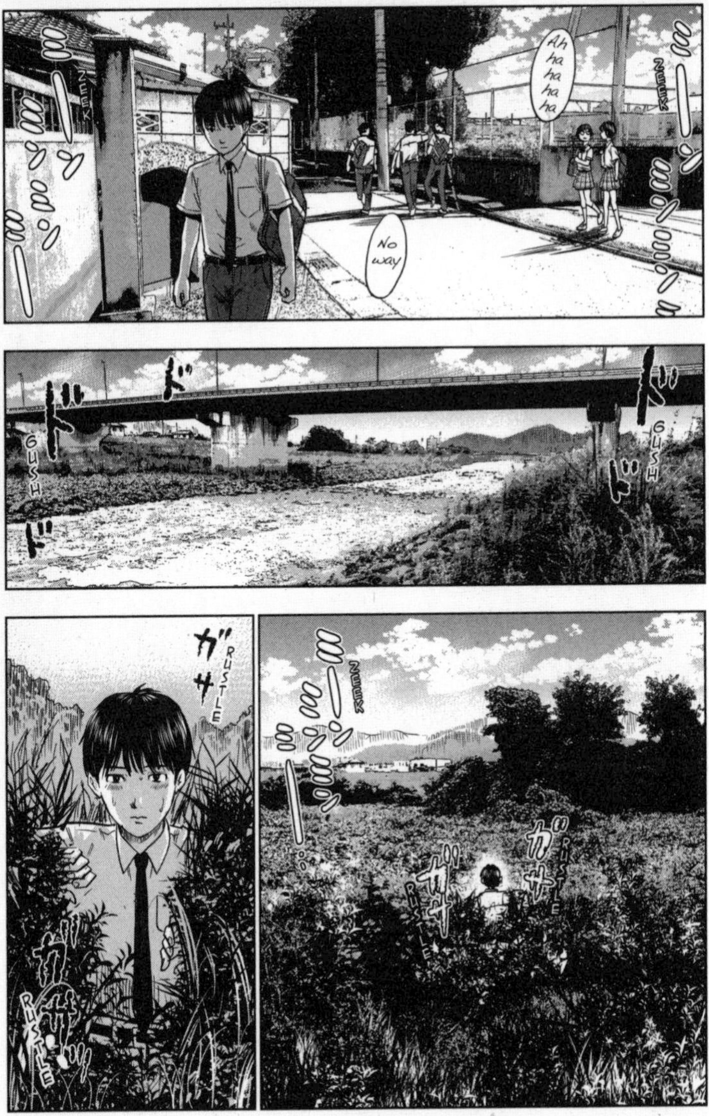
ZEEK
Ah ha ha ha ha ha
No way
ZEEK
GUSH
GUSH
ZEEK
RUSTLE
RUSTLE
RUSTLE
RUSTLE

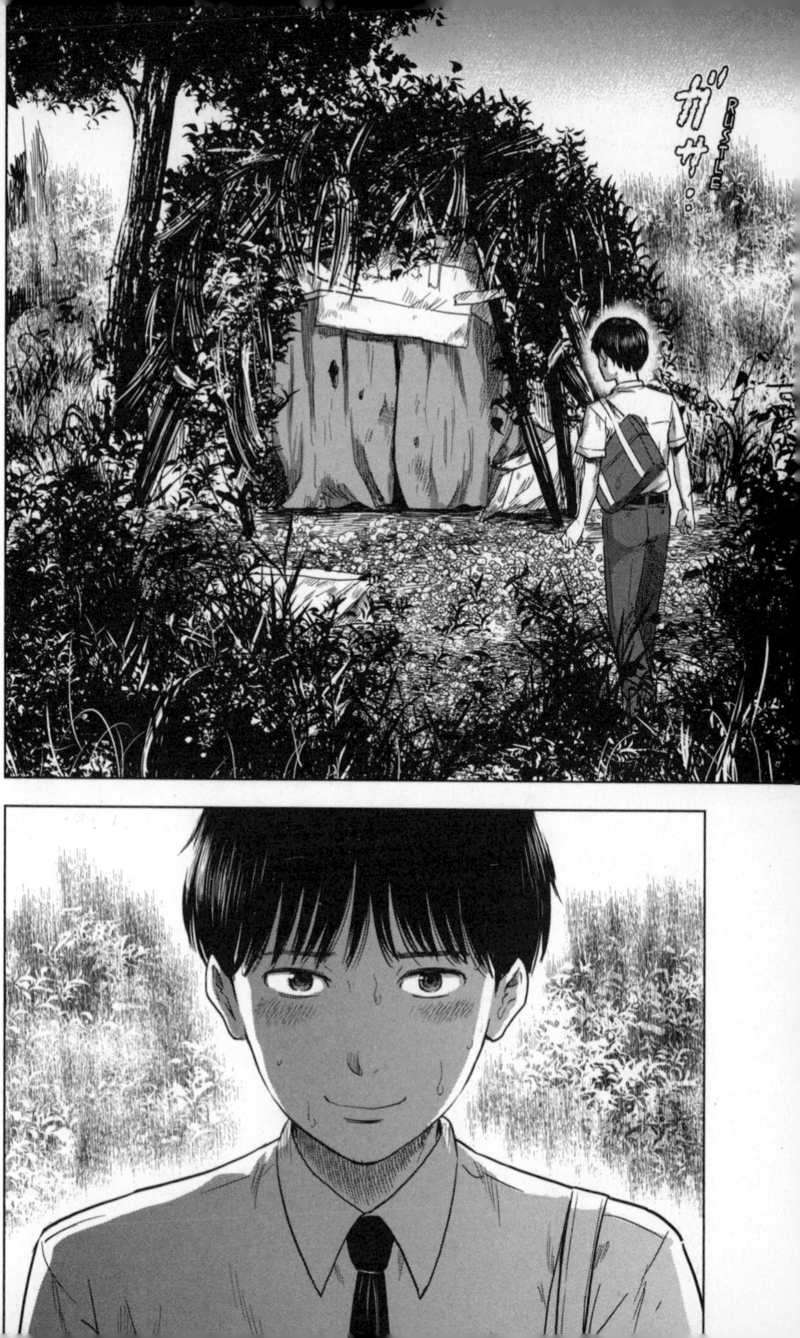
ガサ…
RUSTLE

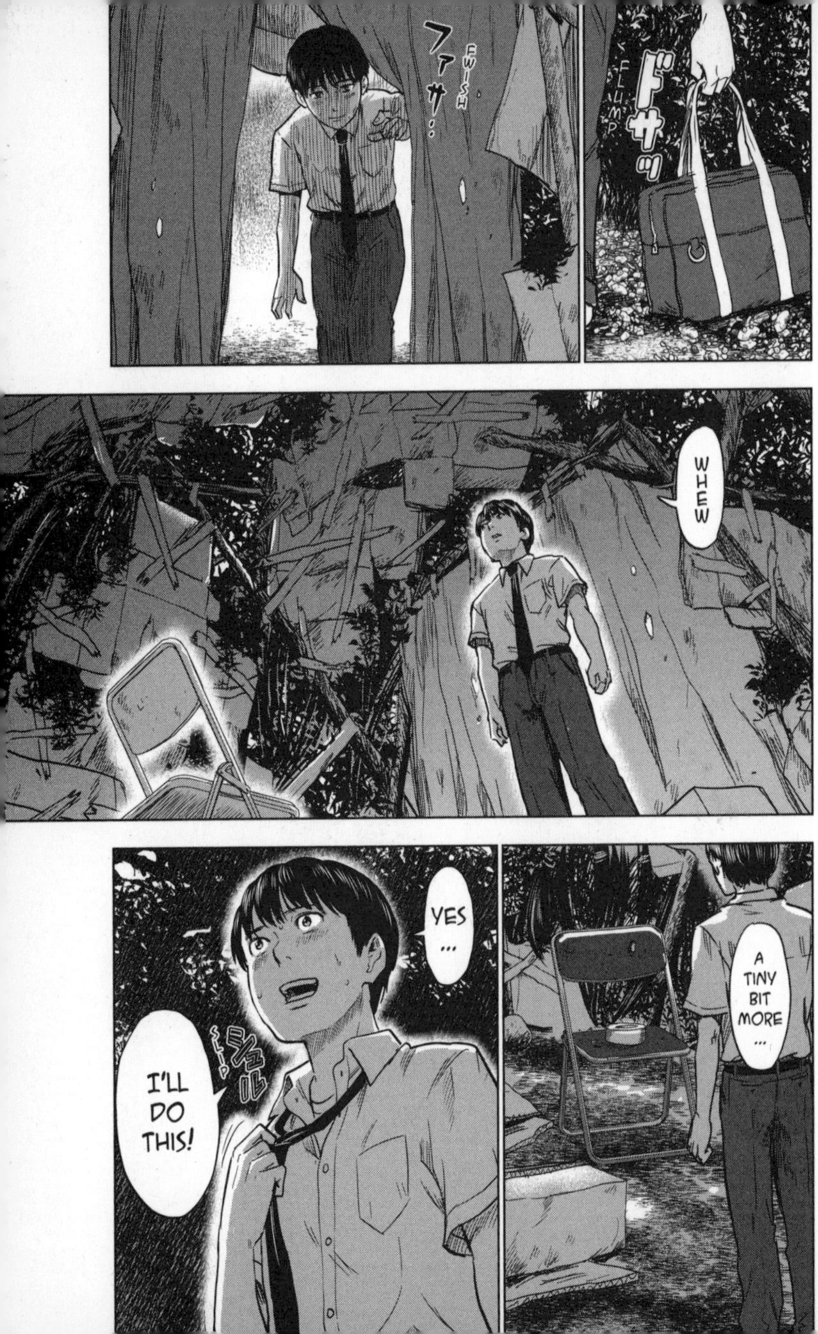
ドサッ
FLUMP
ファサ!!
FWISH
WHEW
A TINY BIT MORE ...
YES ...
シュル
SLIP
I'LL DO THIS!

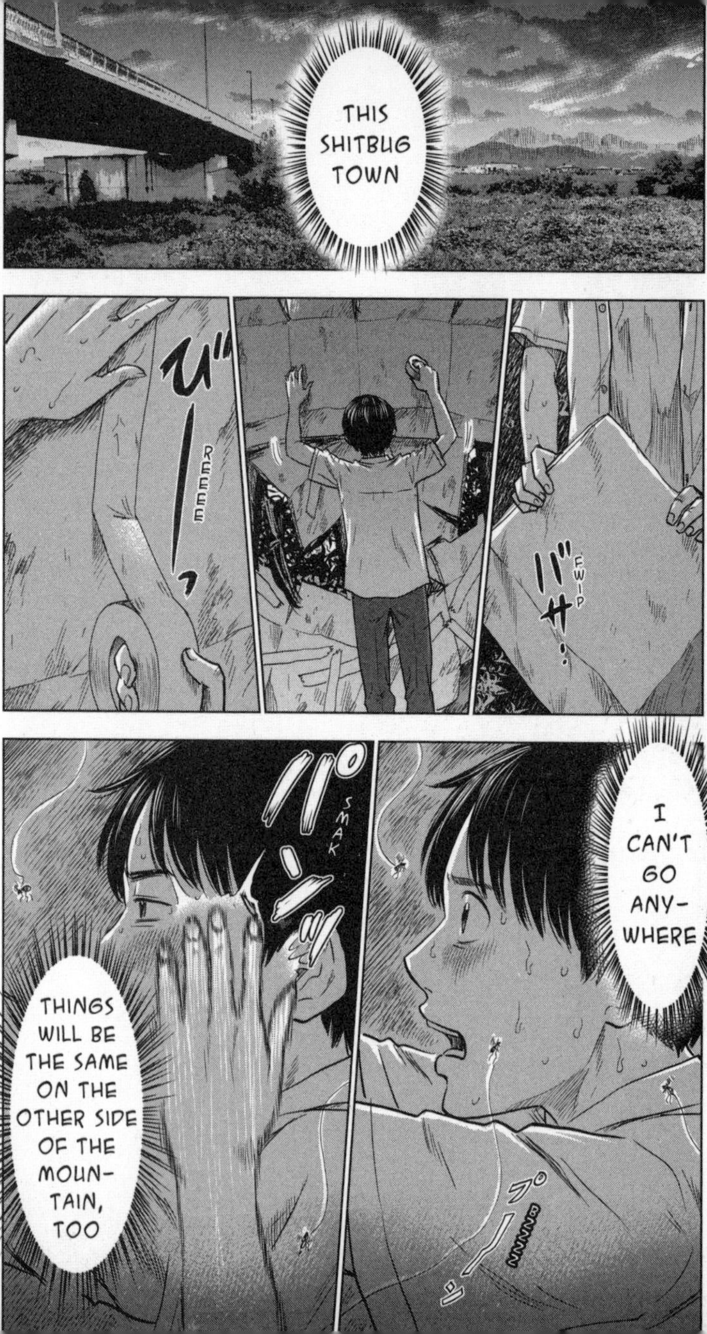
THIS SHITBUG TOWN
FWIP
REEEE
I CAN'T GO ANY-WHERE
BNNNN
SMAK
THINGS WILL BE THE SAME ON THE OTHER SIDE OF THE MOUN-TAIN, TOO

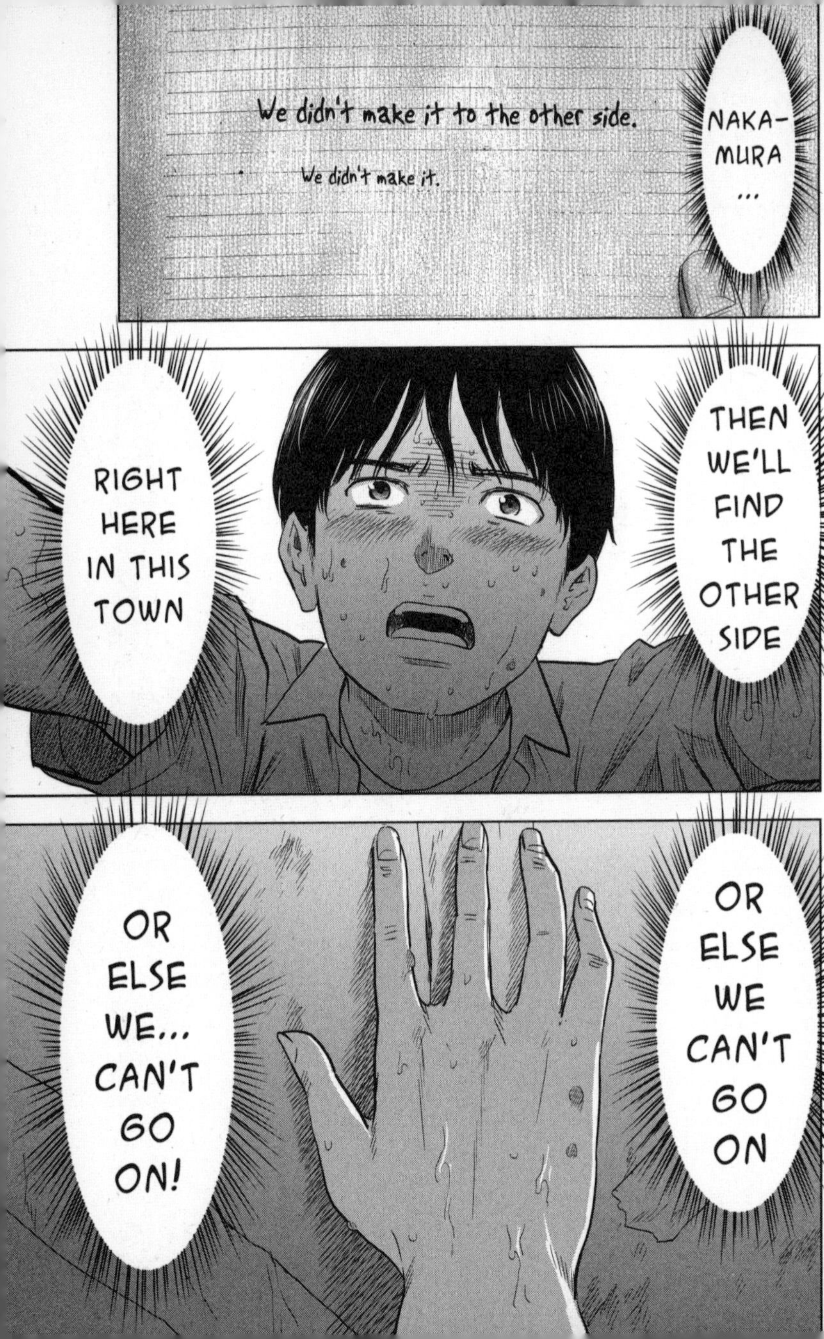
NAKA-MURA...
We didn't make it to the other side.
We didn't make it.
THEN WE'LL FIND THE OTHER SIDE
RIGHT HERE IN THIS TOWN
OR ELSE WE CAN'T GO ON
OR ELSE WE... CAN'T GO ON!

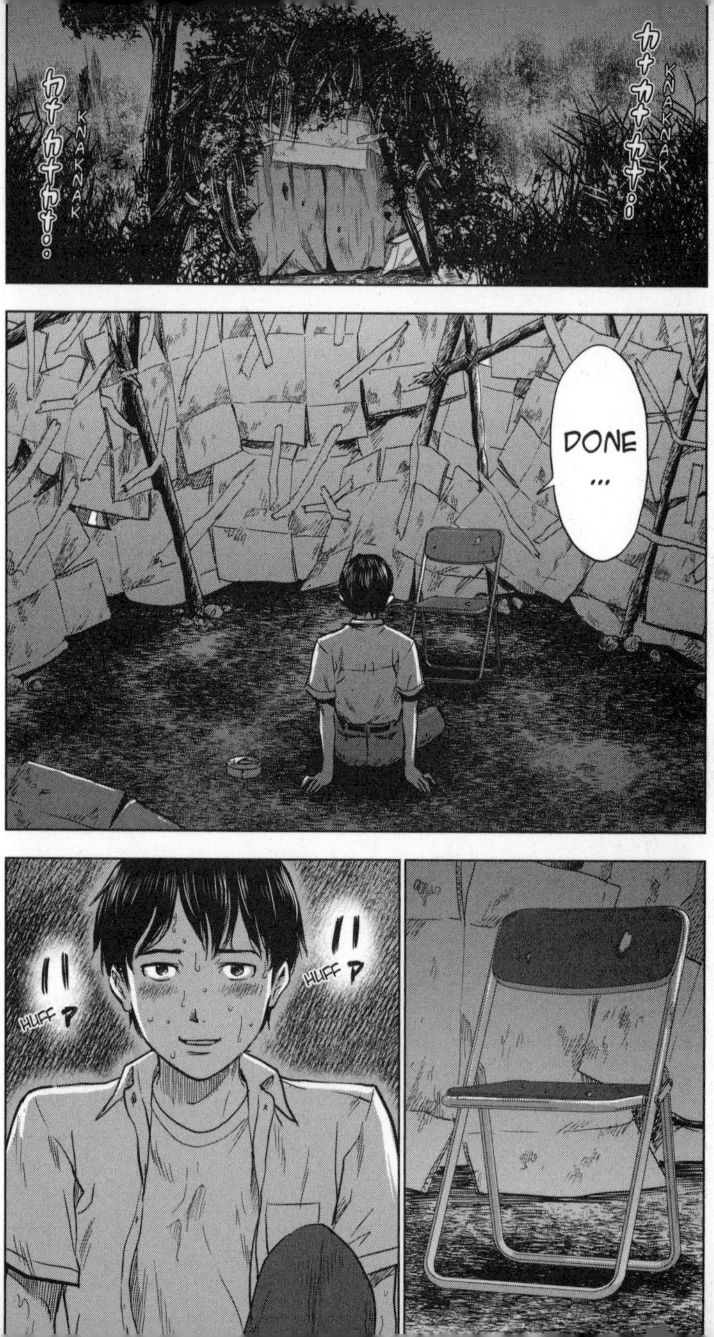

カナカナカナ。。
KNAKNAK
カナカナカナ。。
KNAKNAK
DONE ...
HUFF
HUFF

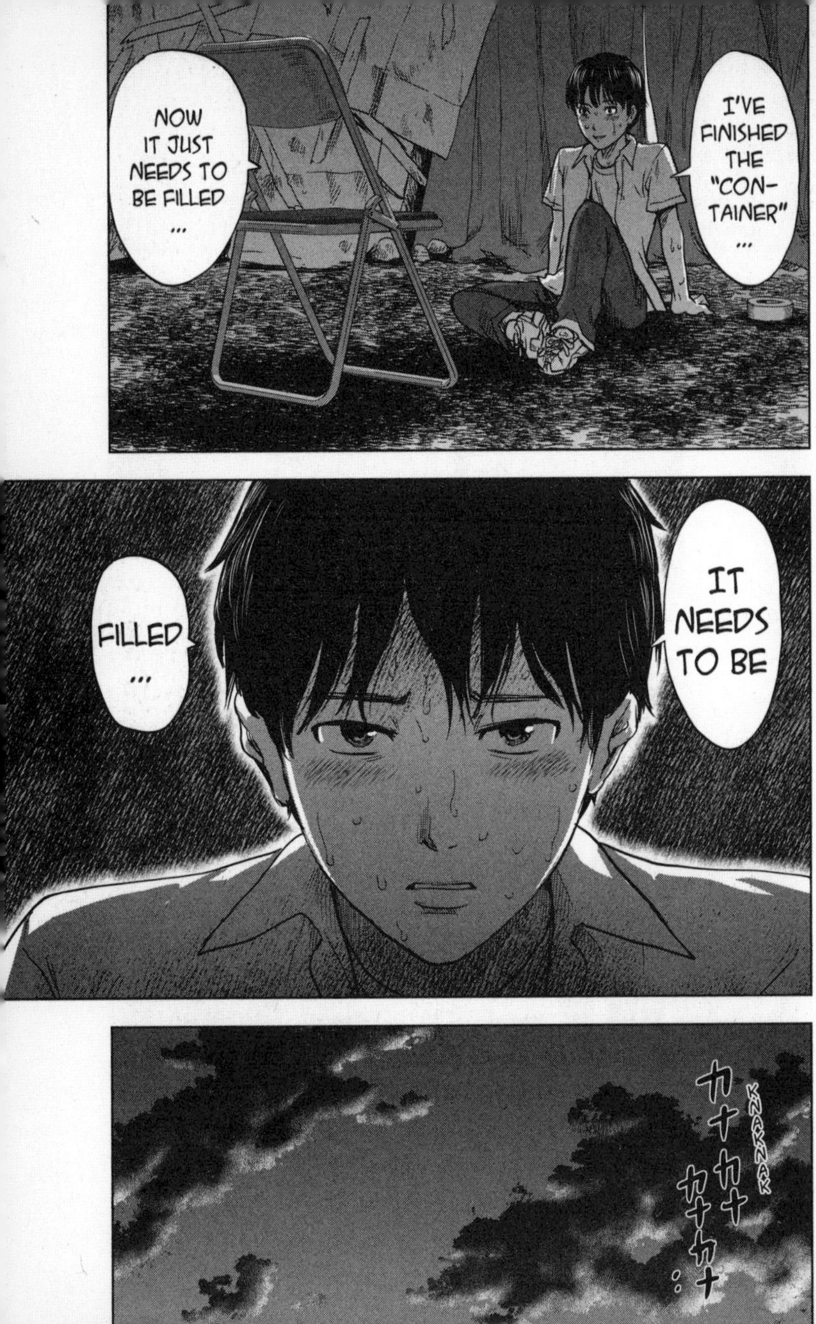
I'VE FINISHED THE "CON-TAINER" ...
NOW IT JUST NEEDS TO BE FILLED ...
IT NEEDS TO BE
FILLED ...
KNAKNAK
カナカナカナカナ…

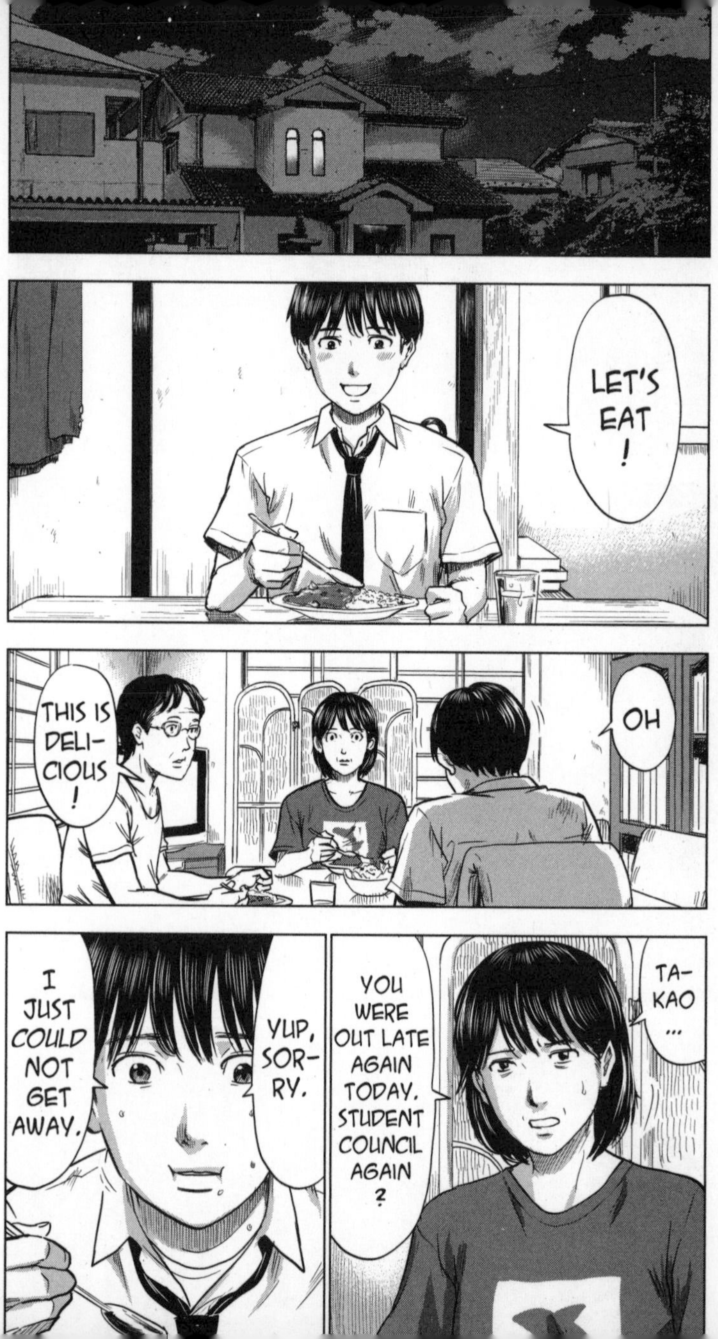
LET'S EAT!
OH
THIS IS DELI-CIOUS!
TA-KAO ...
YOU WERE OUT LATE AGAIN TODAY. STUDENT COUNCIL AGAIN?
YUP, SOR-RY.
I JUST COULD NOT GET AWAY.

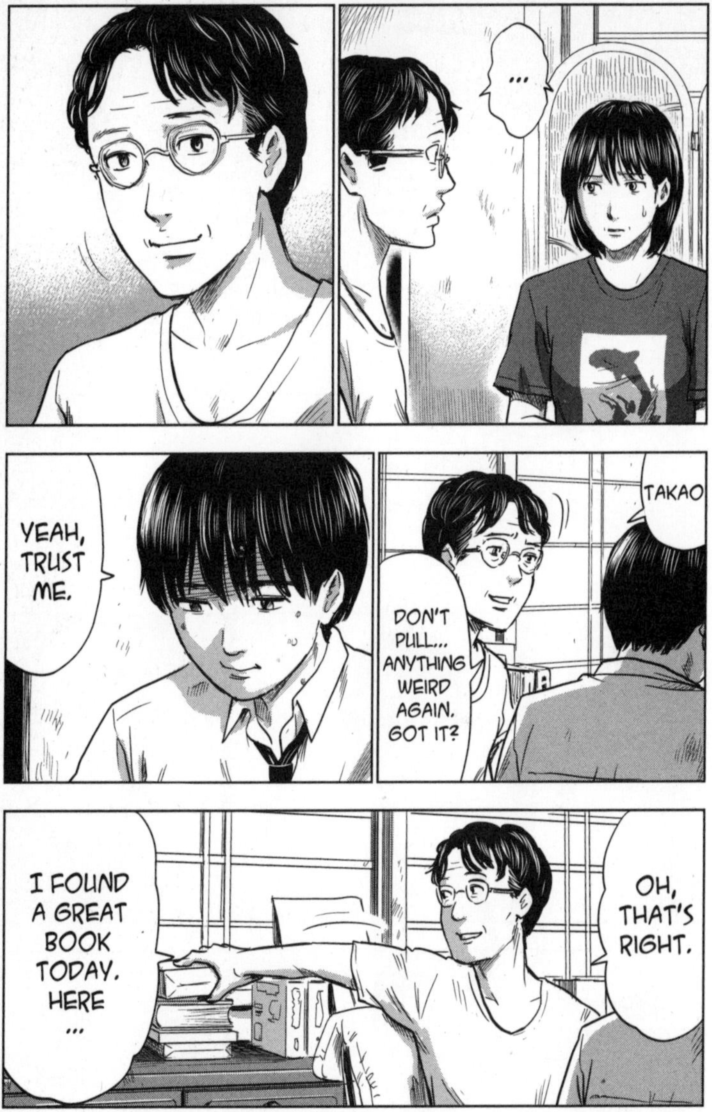
...
TAKAO
DON'T PULL... ANYTHING WEIRD AGAIN. GOT IT?
YEAH, TRUST ME.
OH, THAT'S RIGHT.
I FOUND A GREAT BOOK TODAY. HERE ...

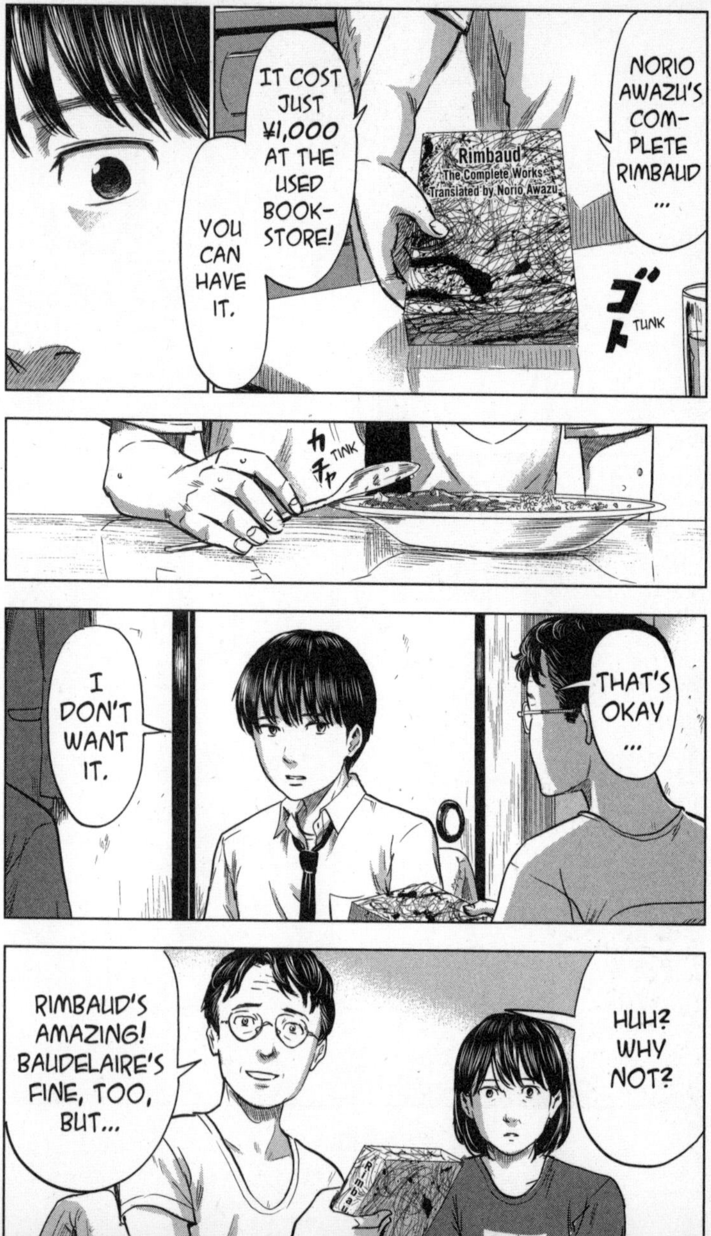
NORIO AWAZU'S COM-PLETE RIMBAUD ...
Rimbaud
The Complete Works
Translated by Norio Awazu
IT COST JUST ¥1,000 AT THE USED BOOK-STORE!
YOU CAN HAVE IT.
ゴト TUNK
カチャ TINK
THAT'S OKAY ...
I DON'T WANT IT.
HUH? WHY NOT?
RIMBAUD'S AMAZING! BAUDELAIRE'S FINE, TOO, BUT...

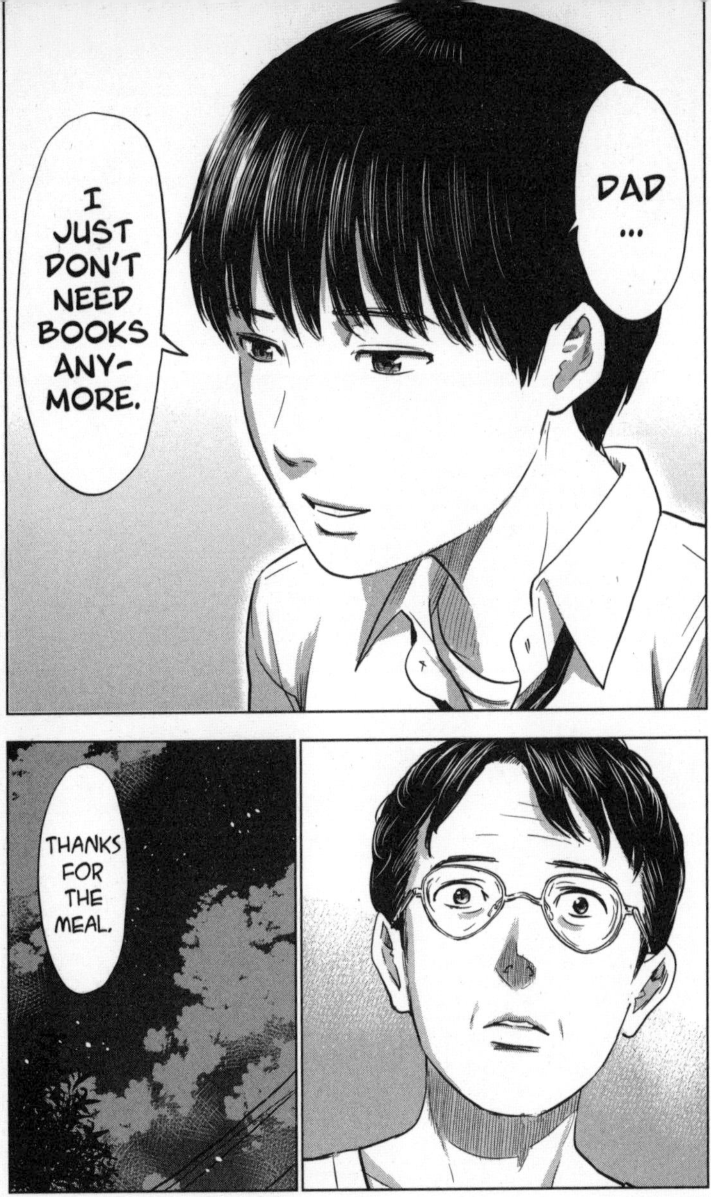
DAD ...
I JUST DON'T NEED BOOKS ANYMORE.
THANKS FOR THE MEAL.

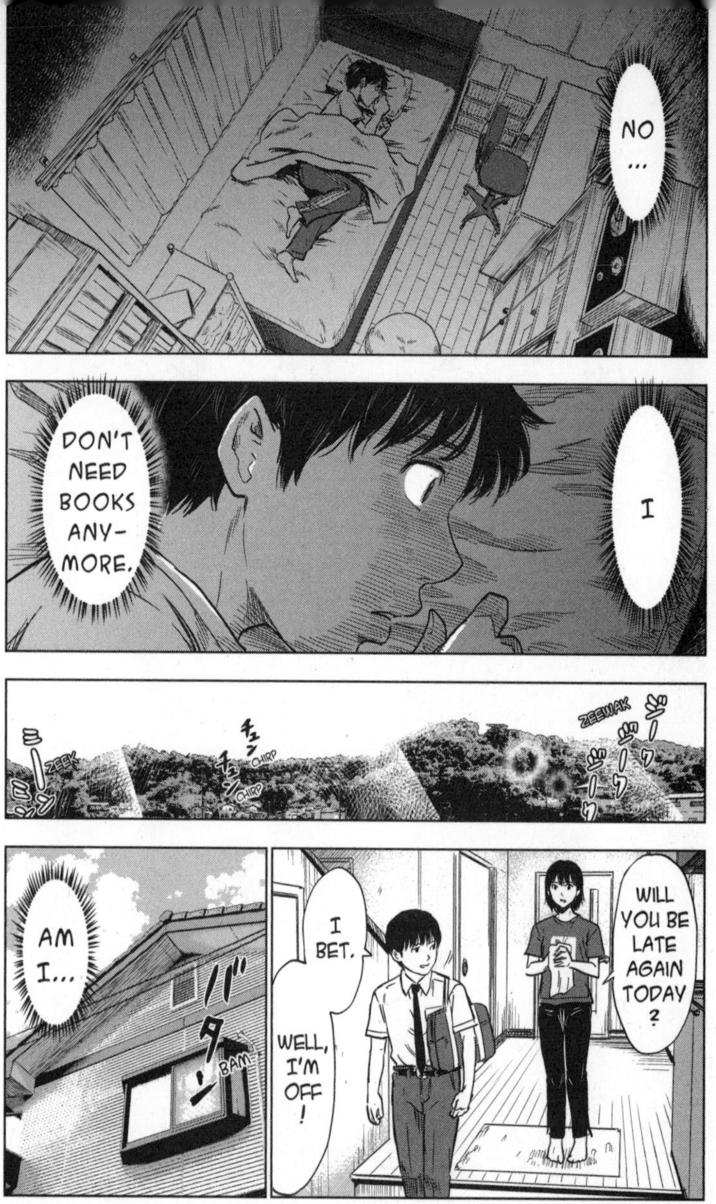
NO ...
I
DON'T NEED BOOKS ANYMORE.
ZEEWAK
CHIRP CHIRP
ZEEK
WILL YOU BE LATE AGAIN TODAY?
I BET.
WELL, I'M OFF!
AM I...
BAM

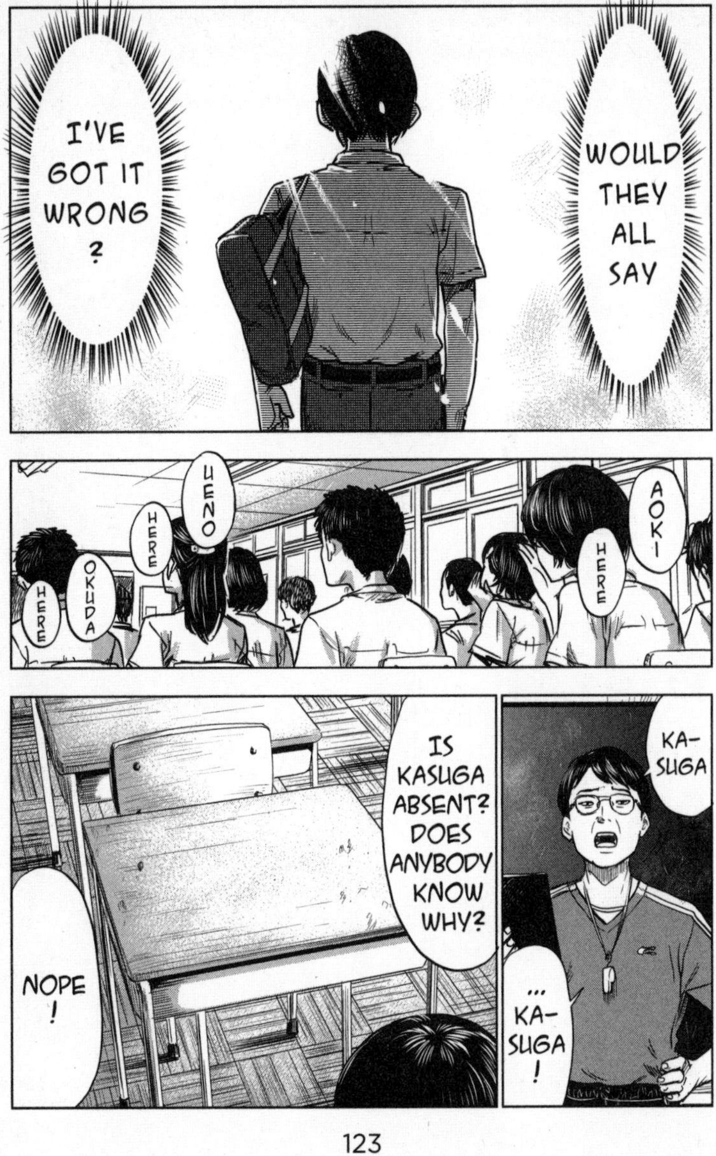
WOULD THEY ALL SAY
I'VE GOT IT WRONG?
AOKI
HERE
UENO
HERE
OKUDA
HERE
KA-SUGA
... KA-SUGA!
IS KASUGA ABSENT? DOES ANYBODY KNOW WHY?
NOPE!

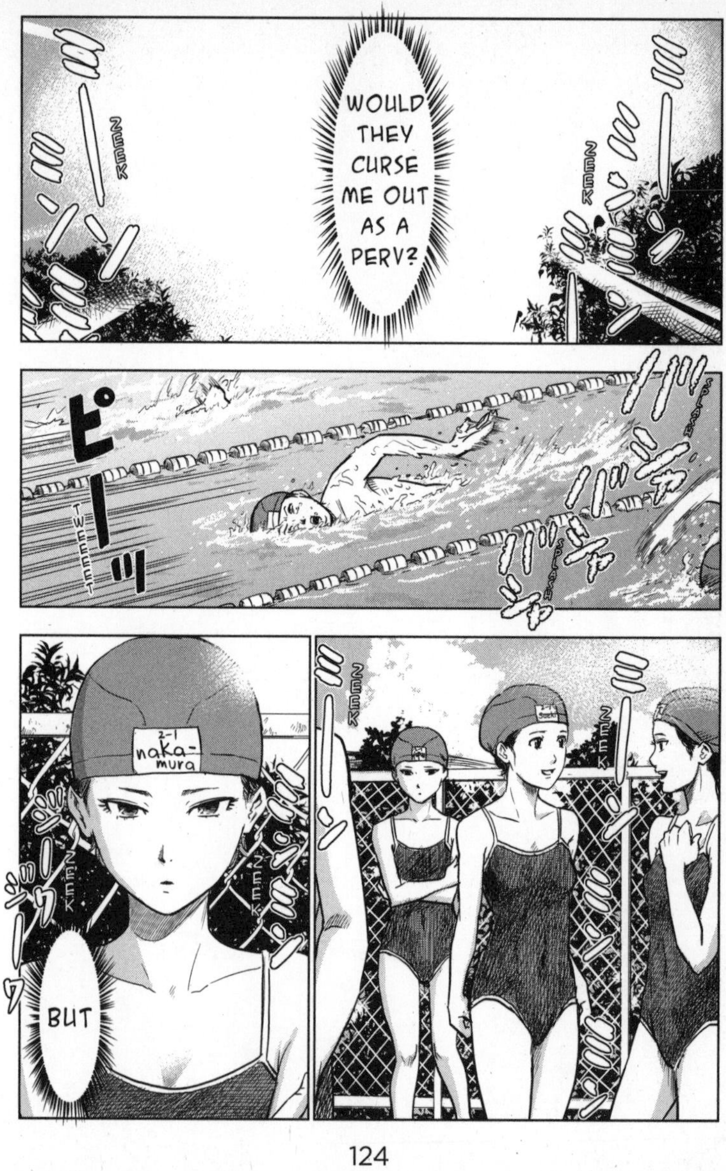
ZEEK
WOULD THEY CURSE ME OUT AS A PERV?
ZEEK
SPLASH
SPLASH
TWEEEET
ZEEK
ZEEK
2-1 naka-mura
ZEEK
ZEEK
BUT

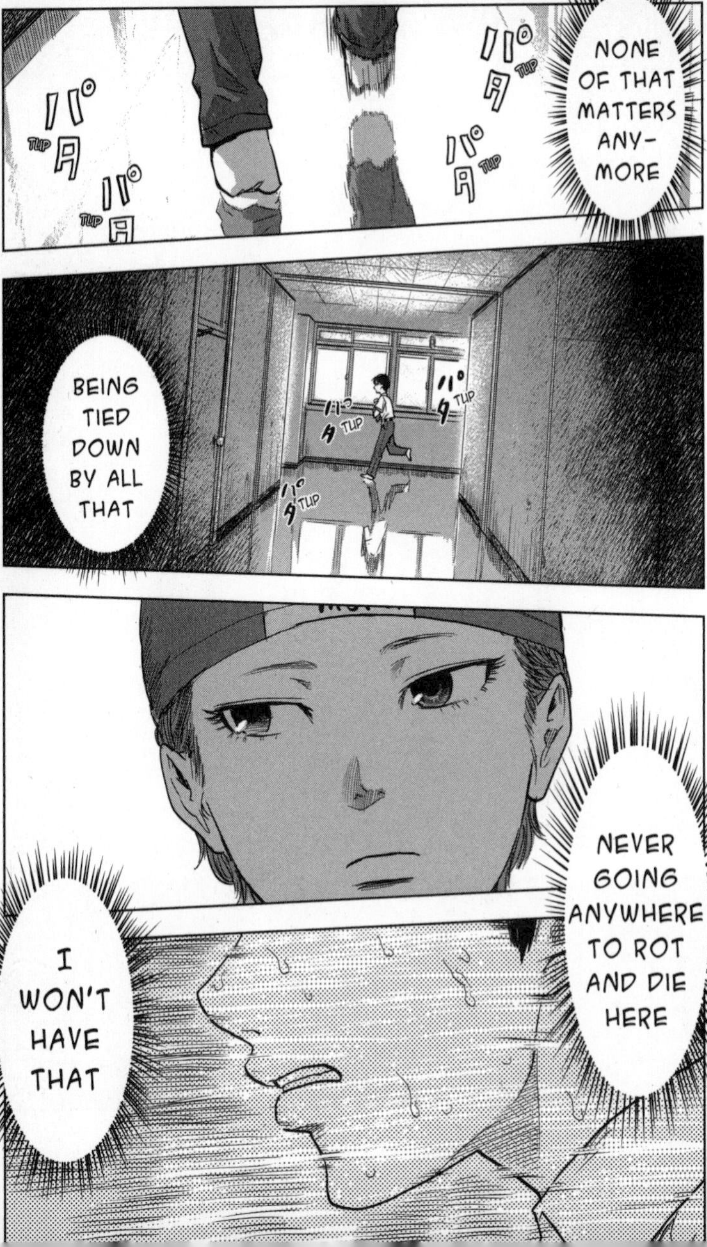
NONE OF THAT MATTERS ANY-MORE
TUP
TUP
TUP
TUP
BEING TIED DOWN BY ALL THAT
TUP
TUP
TUP
NEVER GOING ANYWHERE TO ROT AND DIE HERE
I WON'T HAVE THAT

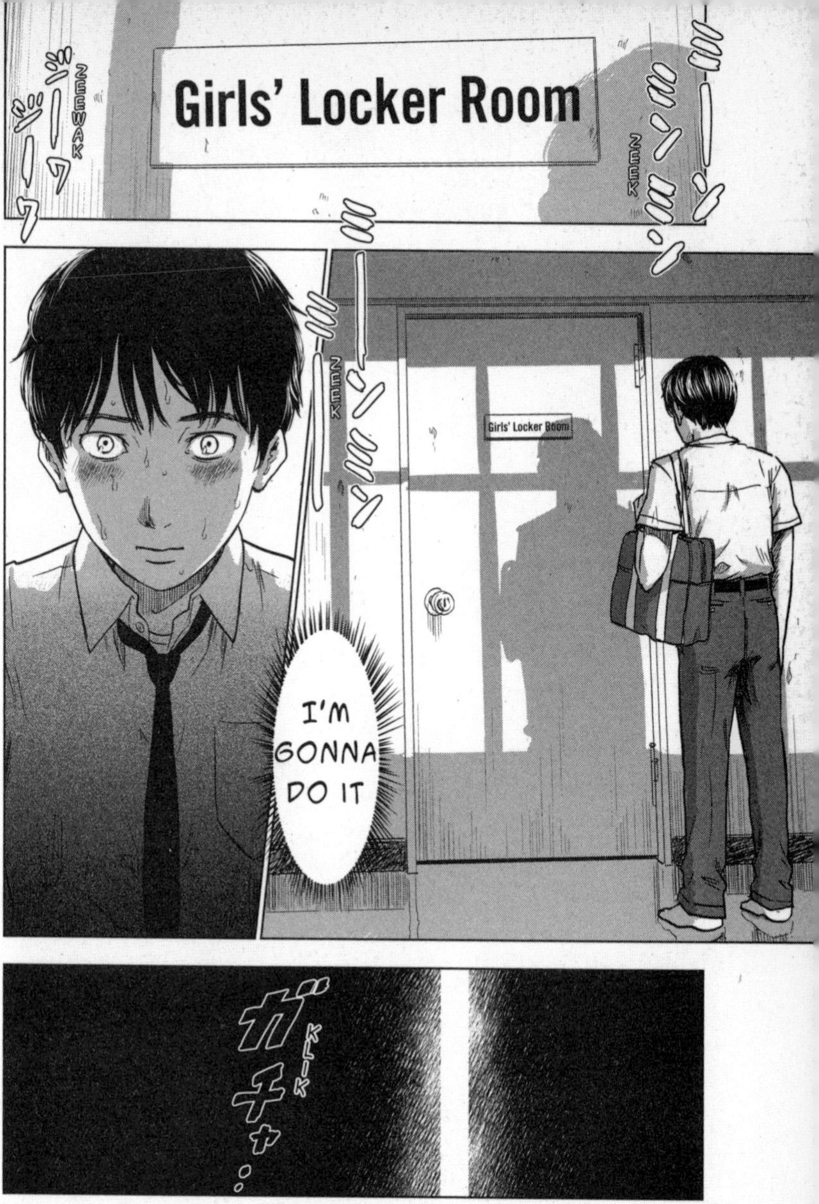
ZEEK
Girls' Locker Room
ZEEWAK
Girls' Locker Room
ZEEK
I'M GONNA DO IT
KLIK

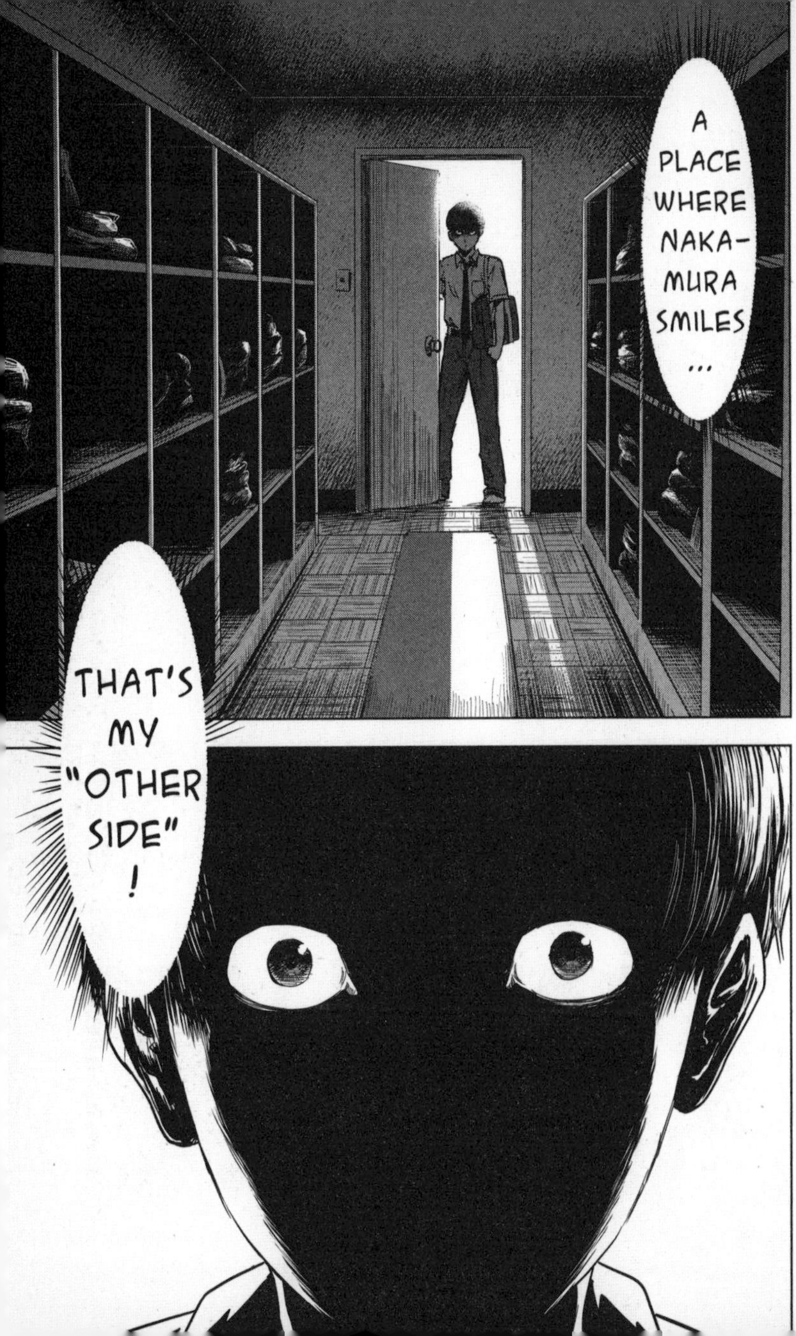
A PLACE WHERE NAKA-MURA SMILES ...
THAT'S MY "OTHER SIDE" !

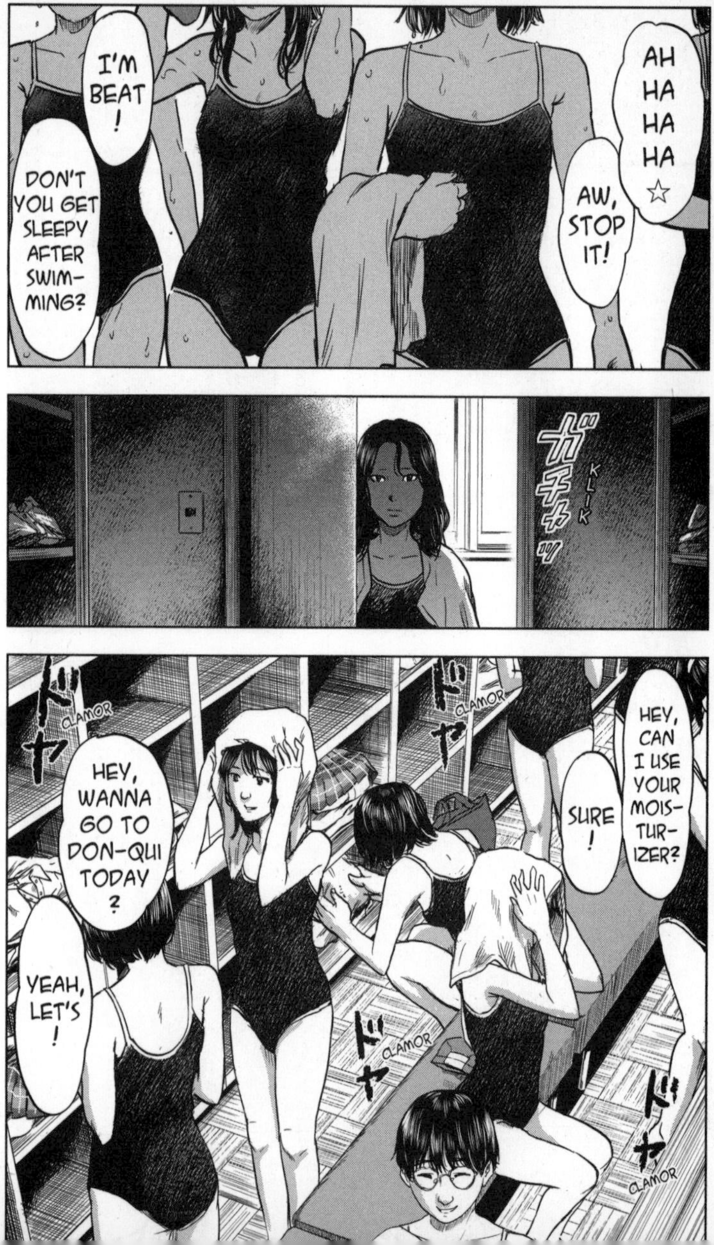
AH HA HA HA ☆
AW, STOP IT!
I'M BEAT!
DON'T YOU GET SLEEPY AFTER SWIM-MING?
KLIK
HEY, CAN I USE YOUR MOIS-TUR-IZER?
SURE!
CLAMOR
CLAMOR
HEY, WANNA GO TO DON-QUI TODAY?
YEAH, LET'S!
CLAMOR
CLAMOR

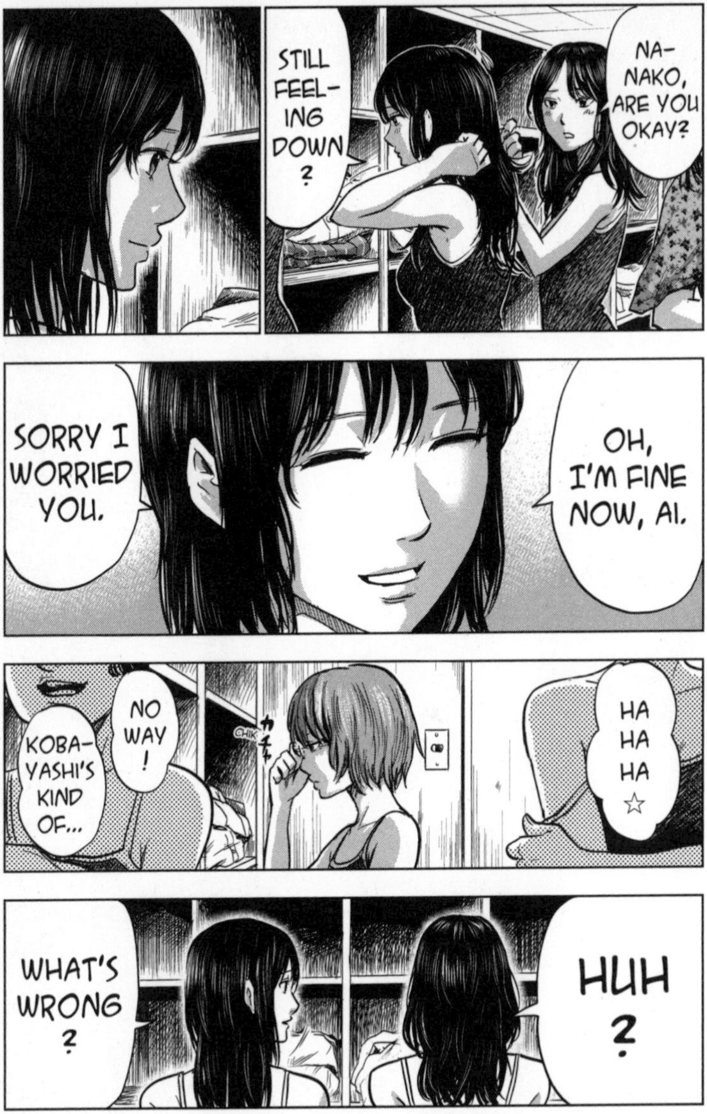
NA-NAKO, ARE YOU OKAY?
STILL FEEL-ING DOWN?
OH, I'M FINE NOW, AI.
SORRY I WORRIED YOU.
HA HA HA ☆
CHIK
NO WAY!
KOBA-YASHI'S KIND OF...
HUH?
WHAT'S WRONG?

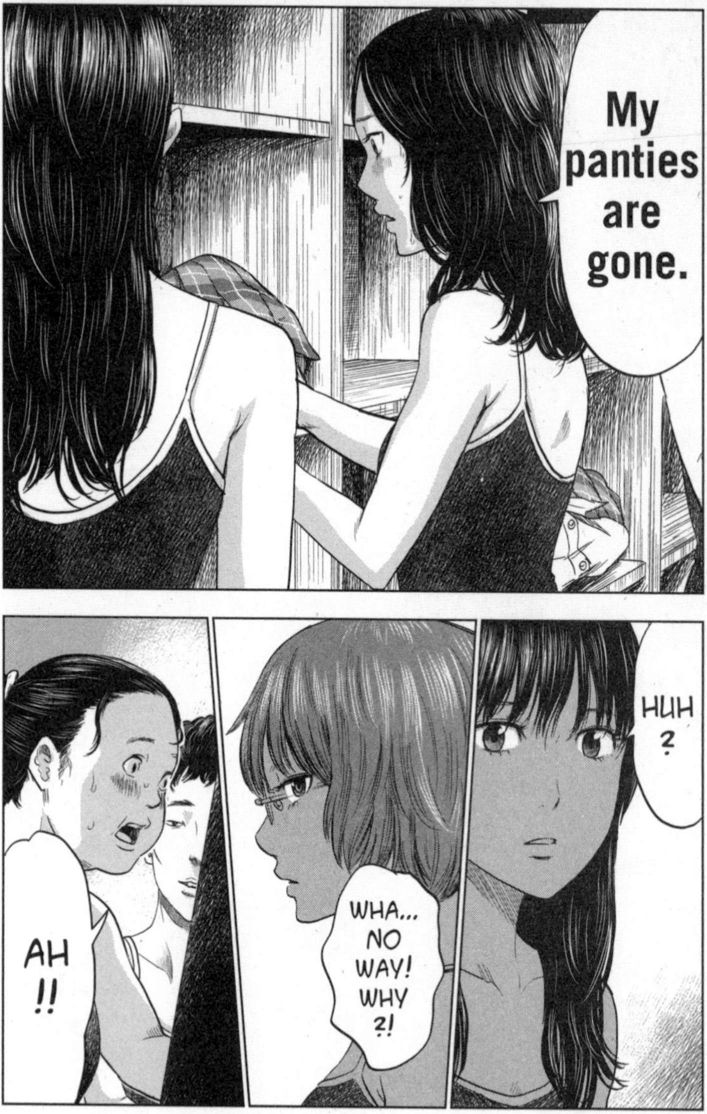
My panties are gone.
HUH?
WHA... NO WAY! WHY?!
AH!!

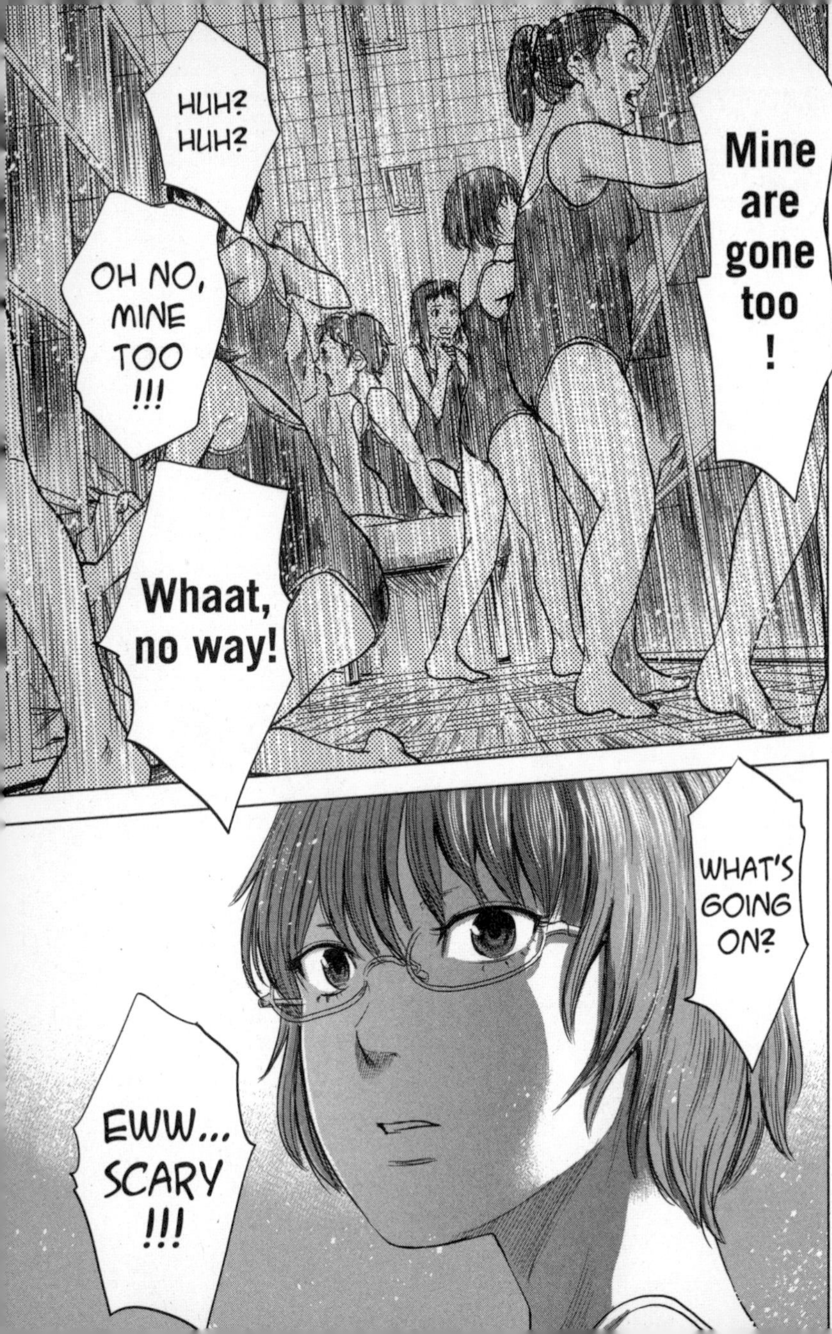
Mine are gone too!
HUH? HUH?
OH NO, MINE TOO!!!
Whaat, no way!
WHAT'S GOING ON?
EWW... SCARY!!!

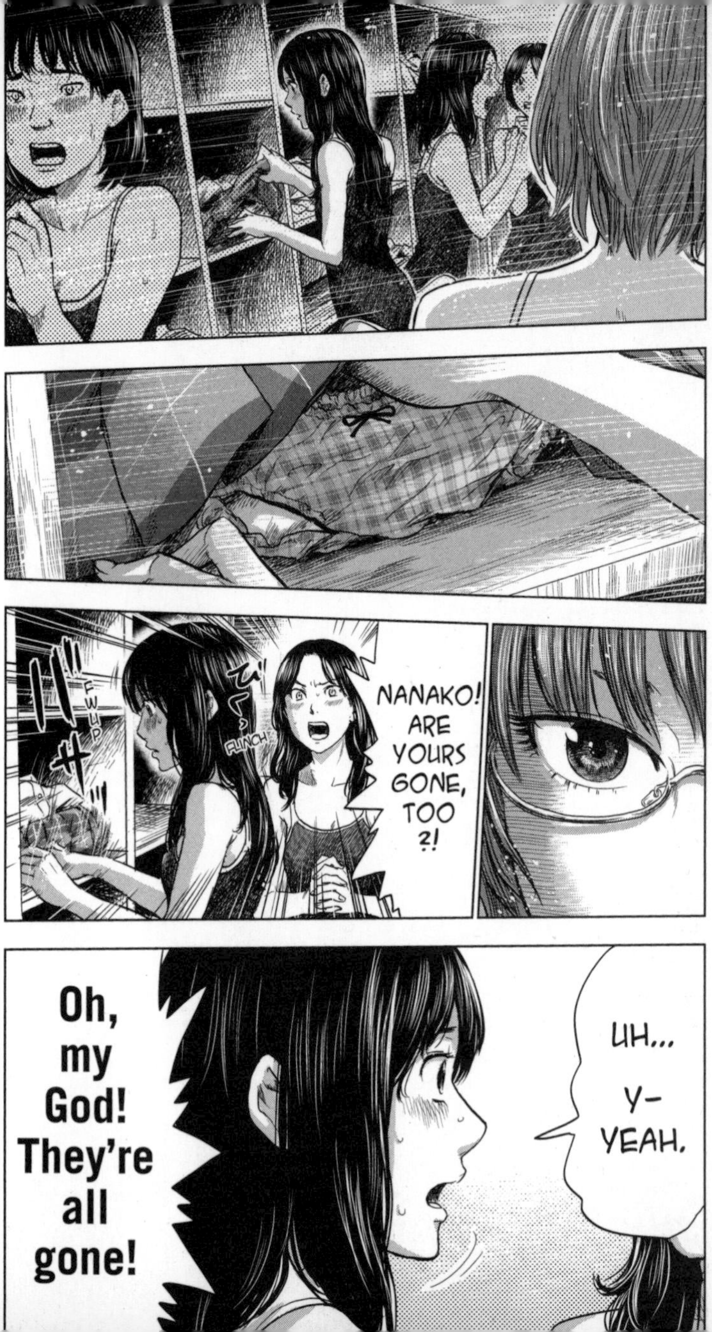
NANAKO! ARE YOURS GONE, TOO?!
FLINCH
FWUP
UH...
Y-YEAH.
Oh, my God! They're all gone!

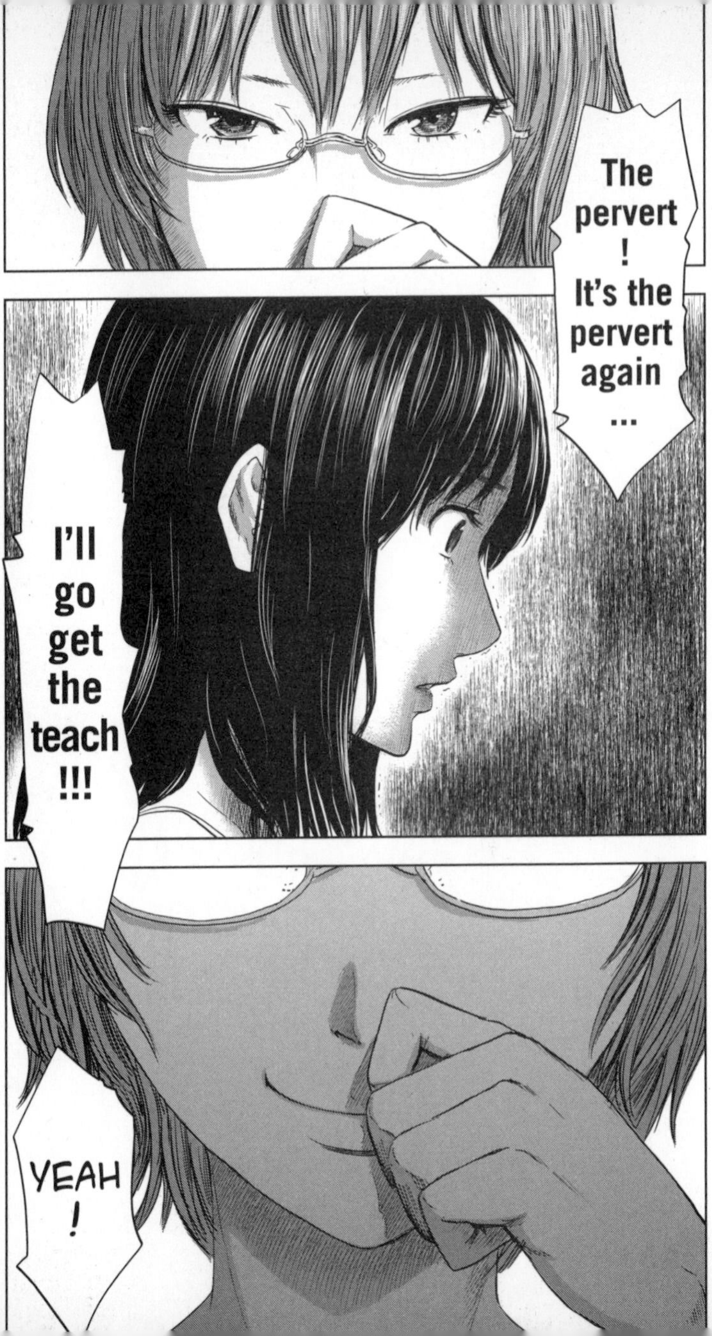
The pervert! It's the pervert again...
I'll go get the teach!!!
YEAH!

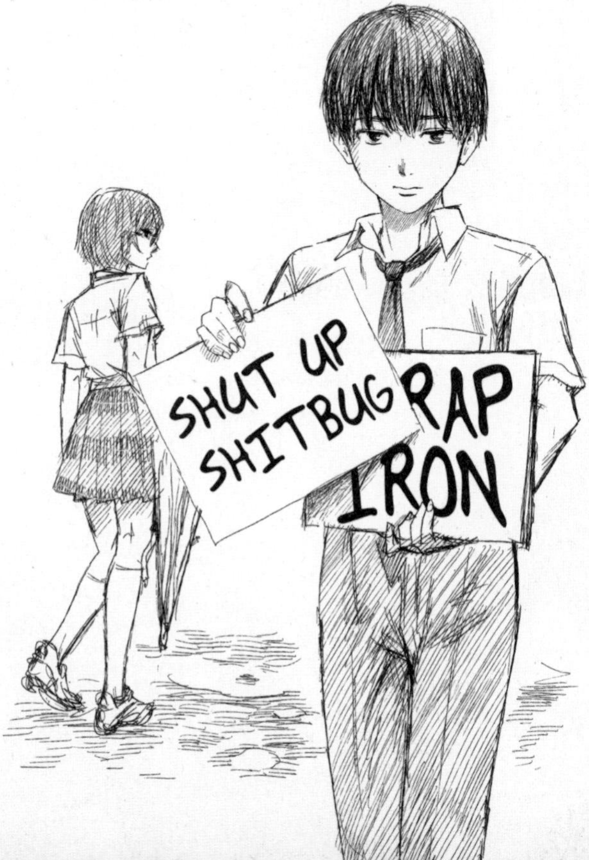
SHUT UP
SHITBUG
RAP
IRON

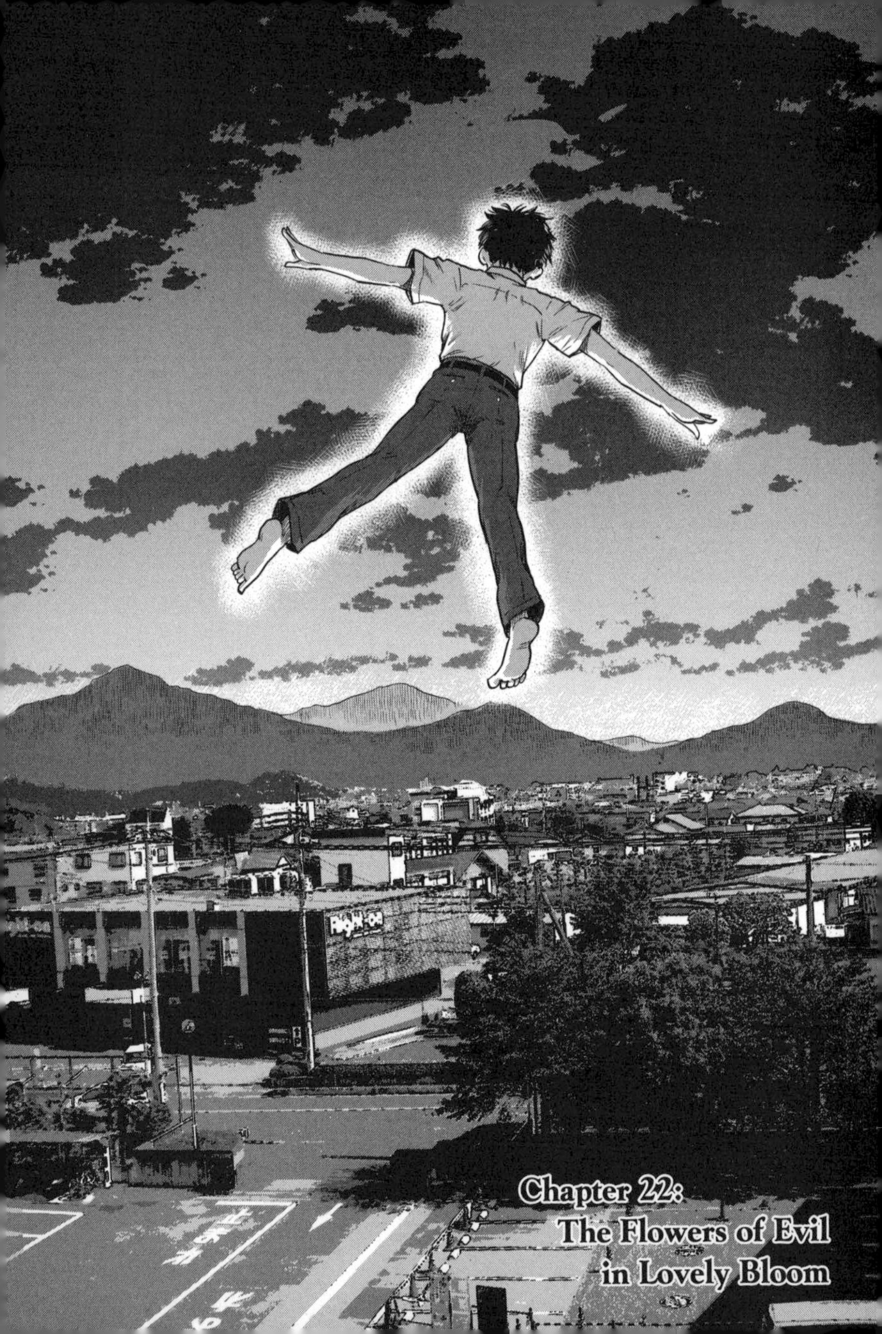

Chapter 22: The Flowers of Evil in Lovely Bloom

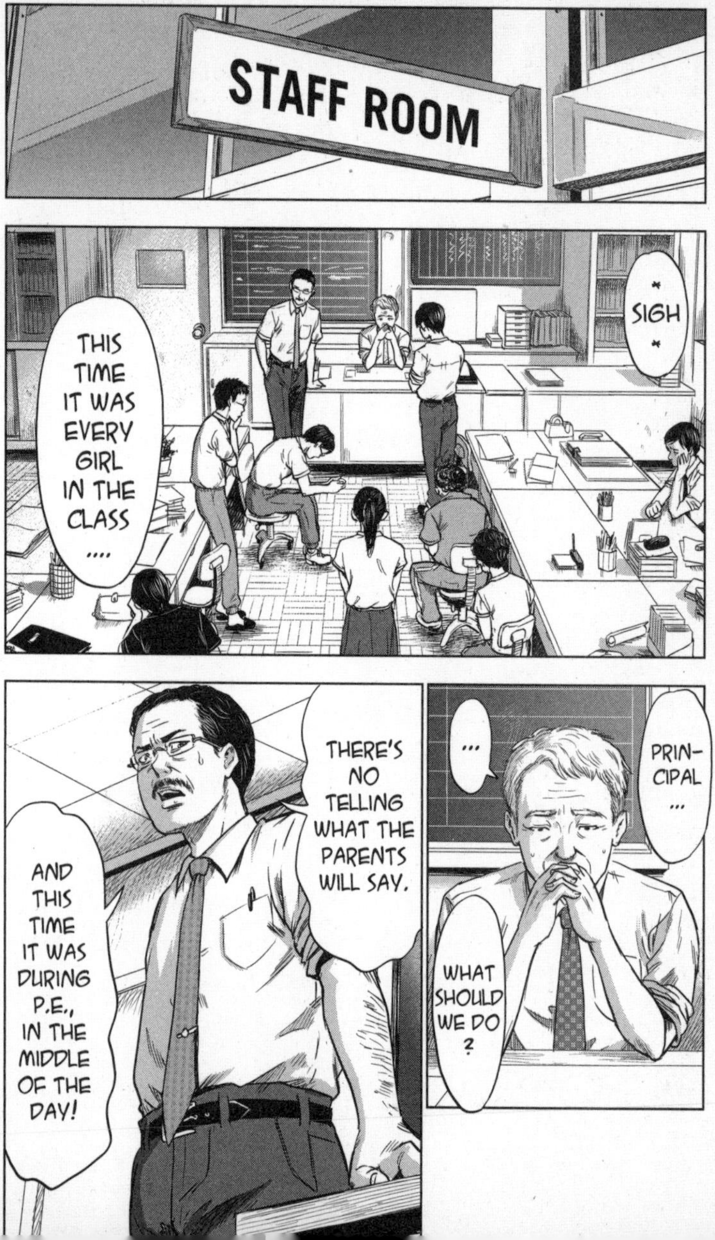
STAFF ROOM
* SIGH *
THIS TIME IT WAS EVERY GIRL IN THE CLASS ....
PRIN-CIPAL ...
...
WHAT SHOULD WE DO?
THERE'S NO TELLING WHAT THE PARENTS WILL SAY.
AND THIS TIME IT WAS DURING P.E., IN THE MIDDLE OF THE DAY!

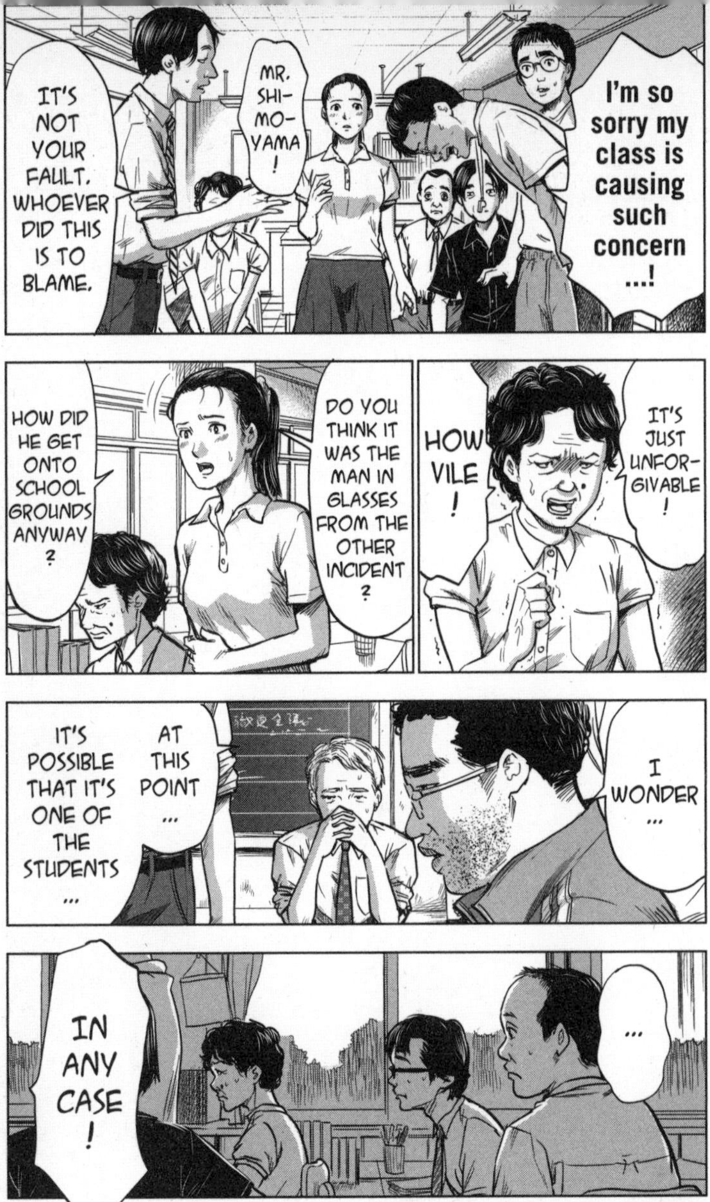

I'm so sorry my class is causing such concern...!
MR. SHI-MO-YAMA!
IT'S NOT YOUR FAULT. WHOEVER DID THIS IS TO BLAME.
IT'S JUST UNFORGIVABLE!
HOW VILE!
DO YOU THINK IT WAS THE MAN IN GLASSES FROM THE OTHER INCIDENT?
HOW DID HE GET ONTO SCHOOL GROUNDS ANYWAY?
I WONDER...
AT THIS POINT...
IT'S POSSIBLE THAT IT'S ONE OF THE STUDENTS...
...
IN ANY CASE!

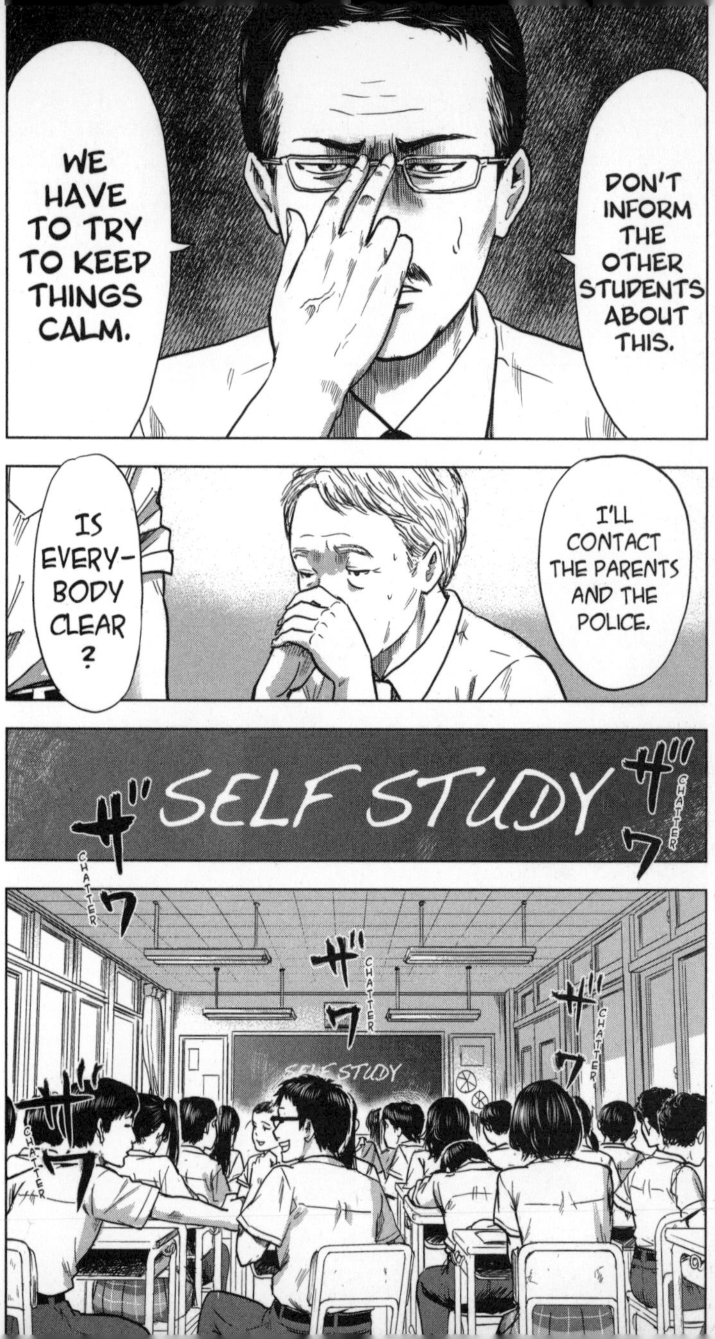
DON'T INFORM THE OTHER STUDENTS ABOUT THIS.
WE HAVE TO TRY TO KEEP THINGS CALM.
I'LL CONTACT THE PARENTS AND THE POLICE.
IS EVERYBODY CLEAR?
ザワ
CHATTER
SELF STUDY
ザワ
CHATTER
ザワ
CHATTER
ザワ
CHATTER
ザワ
CHATTER
SELF STUDY
ザワ
CHATTER

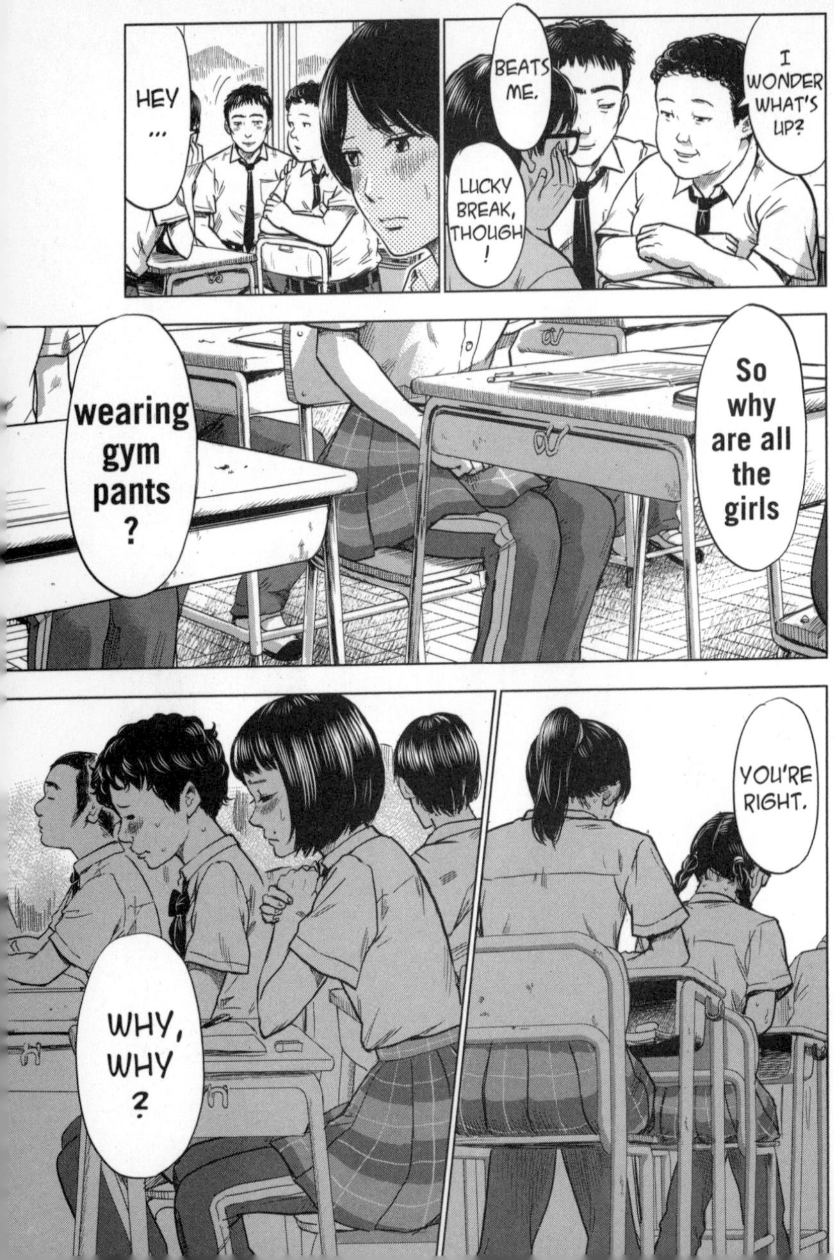
I WONDER WHAT'S UP?
BEATS ME.
LUCKY BREAK, THOUGH!
HEY ...
So why are all the girls
wearing gym pants?
YOU'RE RIGHT.
WHY, WHY?

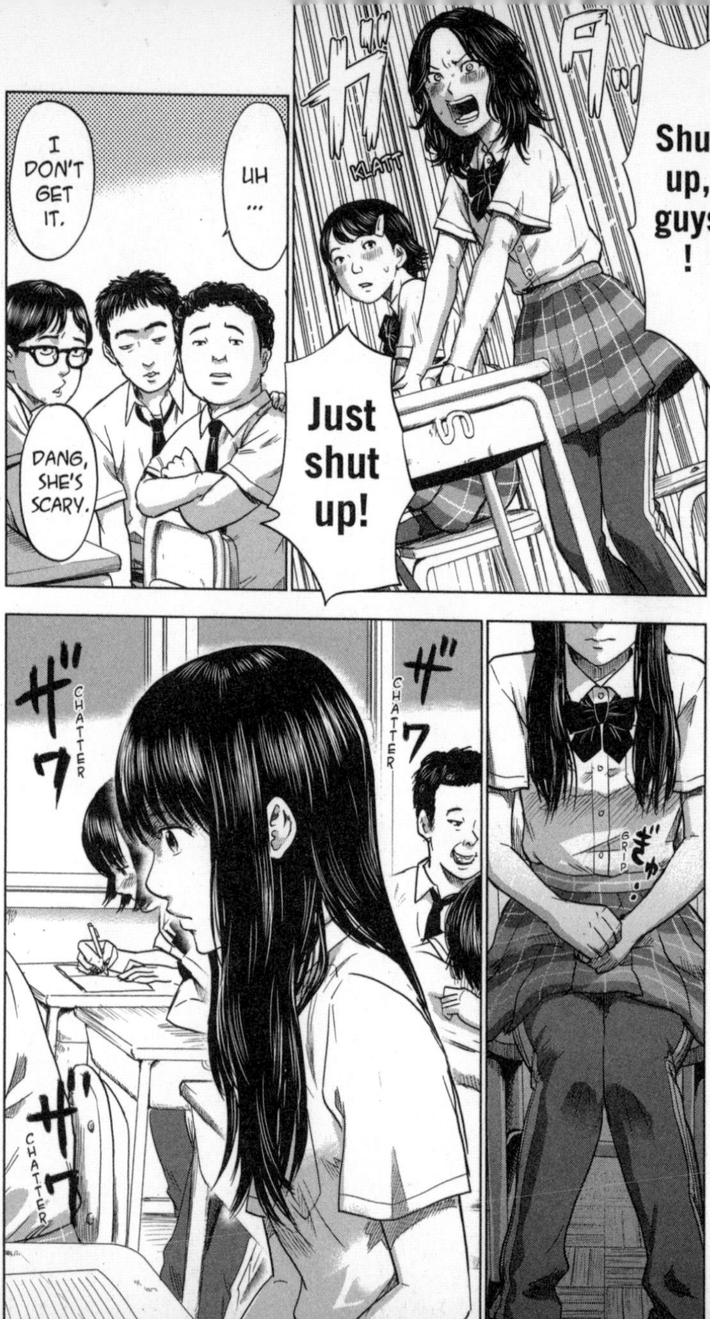

Shut up, guys!
ダッ
ガタ
KLATT
Just shut up!
UH ...
I DON'T GET IT.
DANG, SHE'S SCARY.
ぎゅ
GRIP
ザワ
CHATTER
ザワ
CHATTER
ザワ
CHATTER

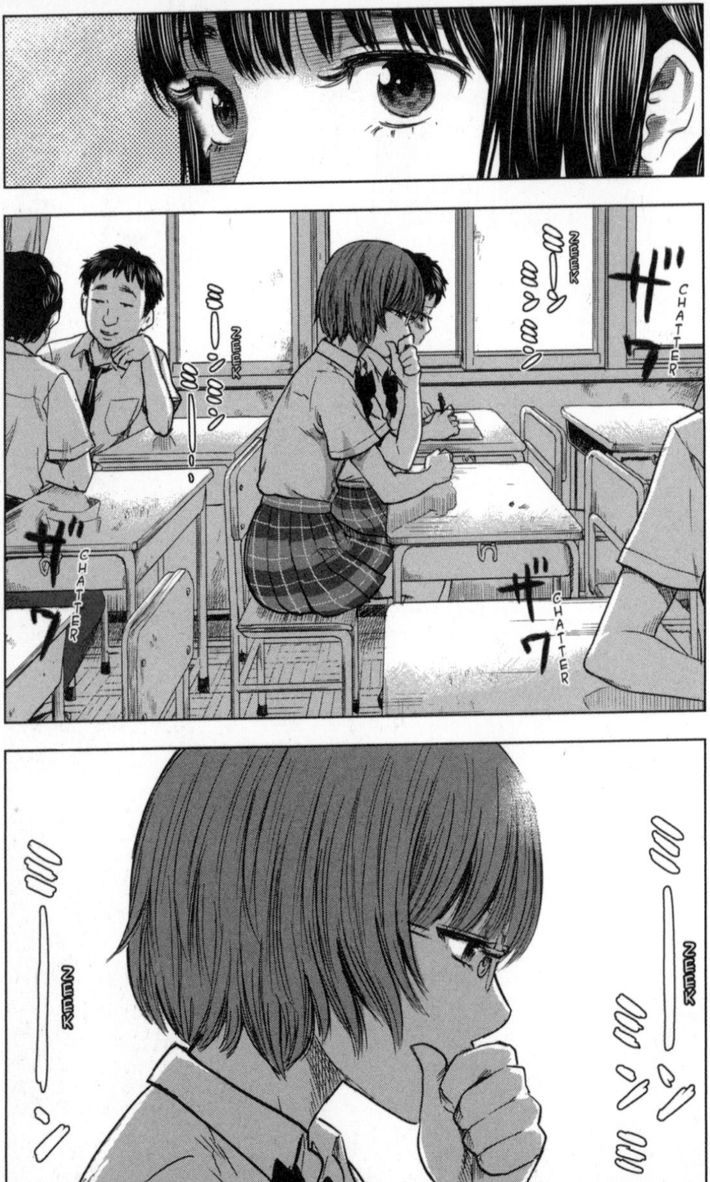
ザワ
CHATTER
ミーンミンミン
ZEEK
ミーンミンミー
ZEEK
ザワ
CHATTER
ザワ
CHATTER
ミーンミンミン
ZEEK
ミーン
ZEEK

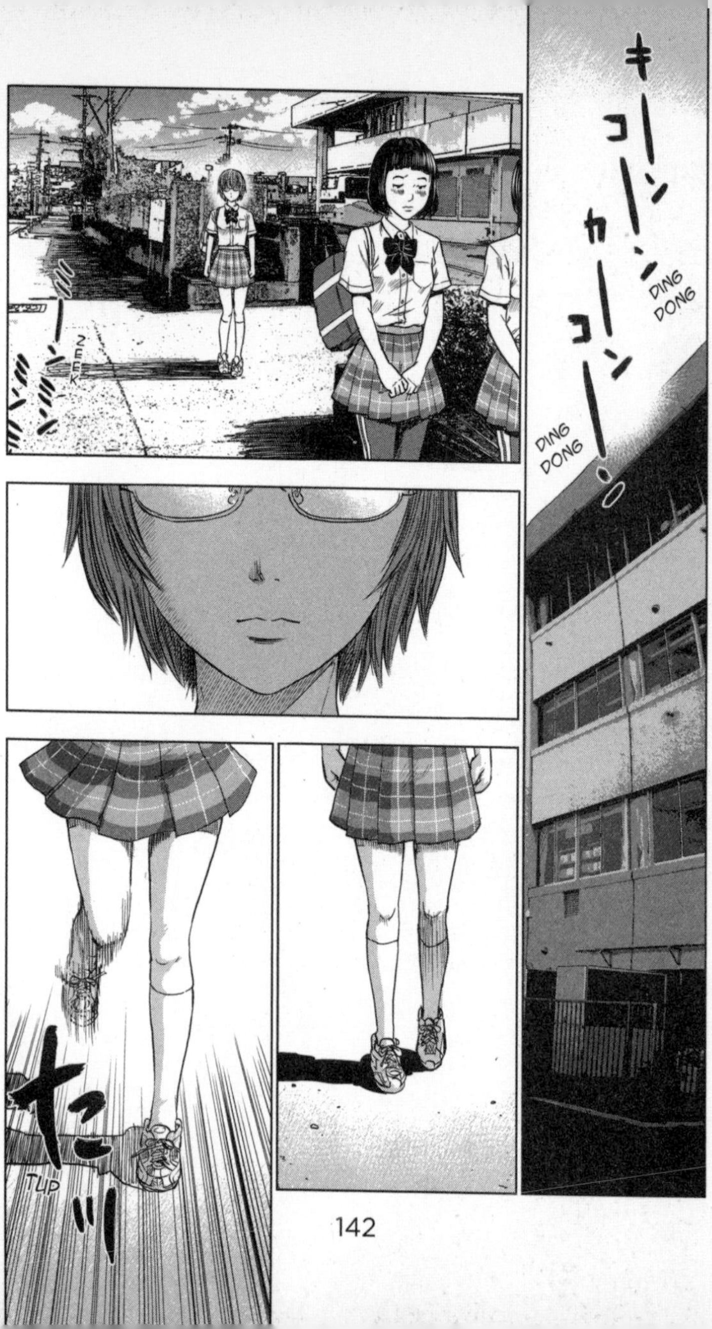
キーンコーンカーンコーン
DING DONG
DING DONG
ZEEK
タッ
TUP

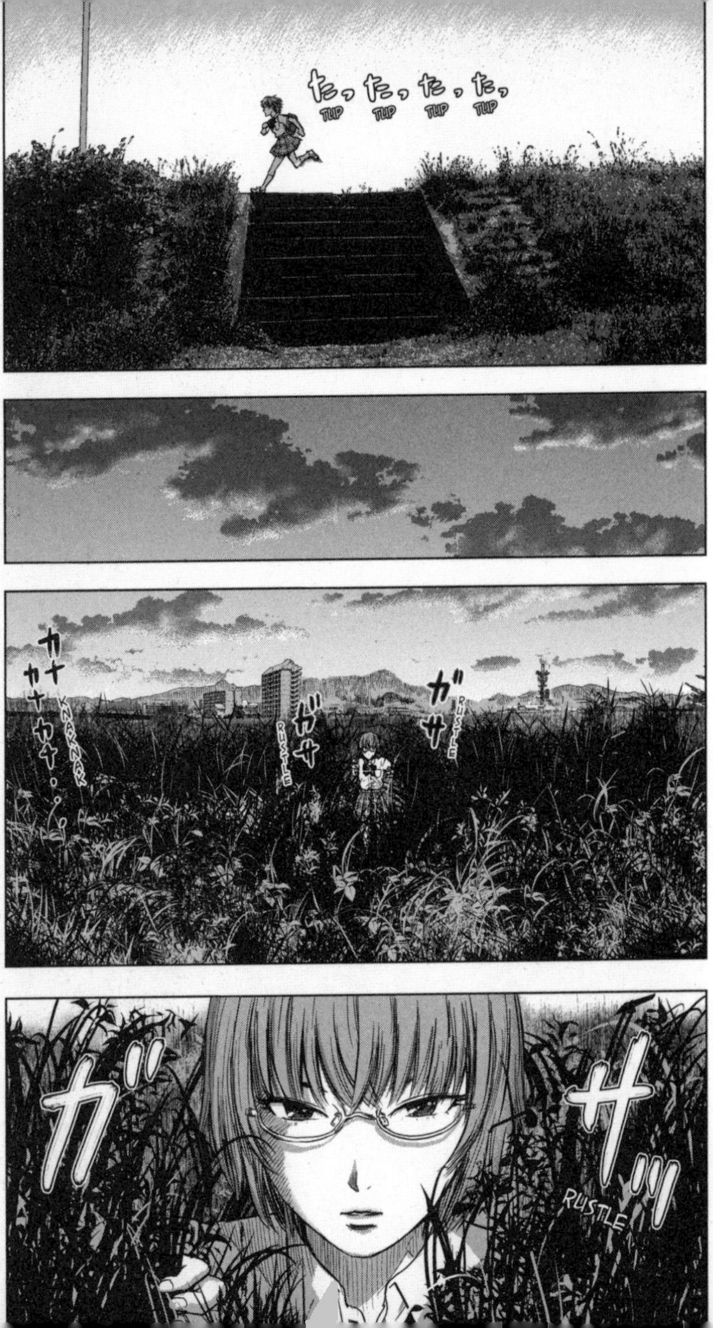
たっ たっ たっ たっ
TUP TUP TUP TUP
ガサ
RUSTLE
ガサ
RUSTLE
カサカサカサ・・・
KNAKNAK
ガサッ
RUSTLE

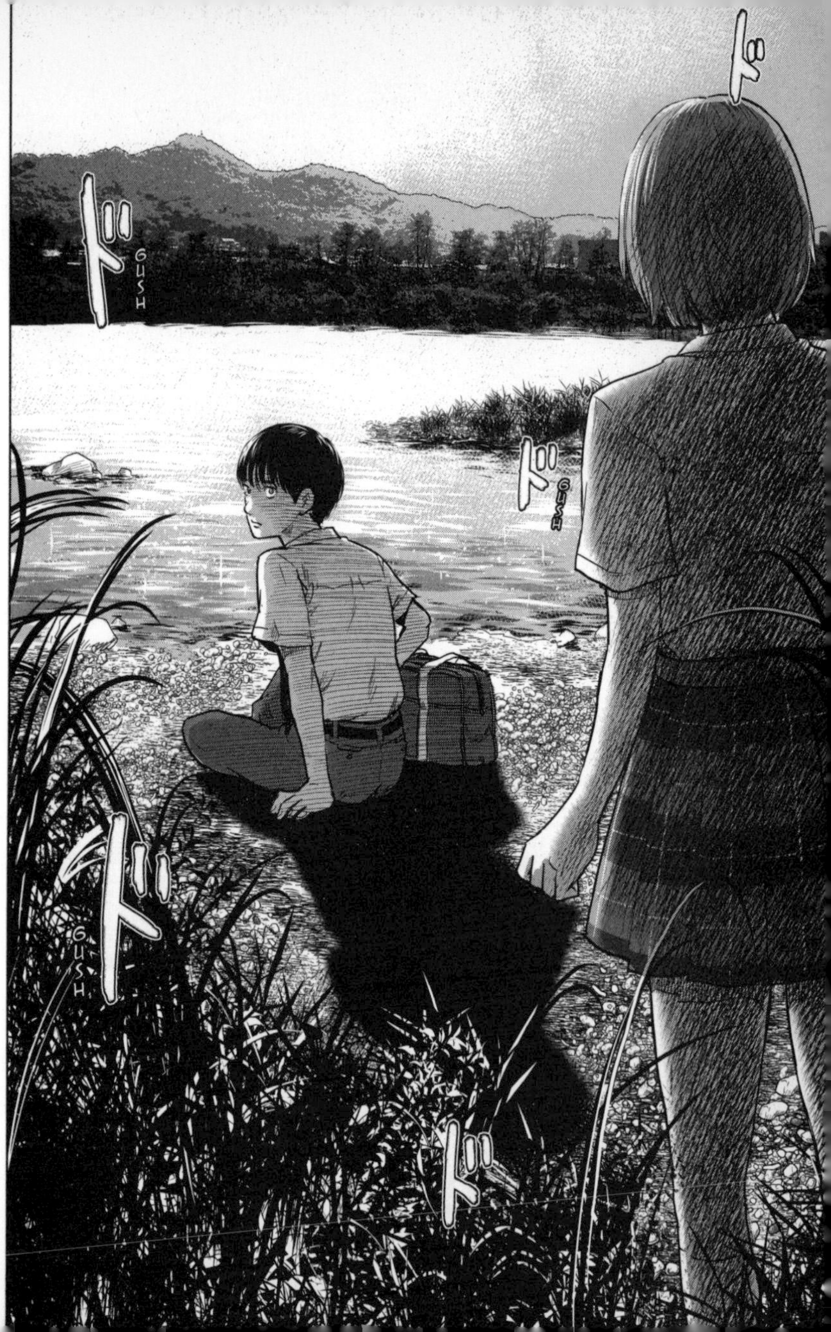
ド
ド
GUSH
ド
GUSH
ド
GUSH
ド

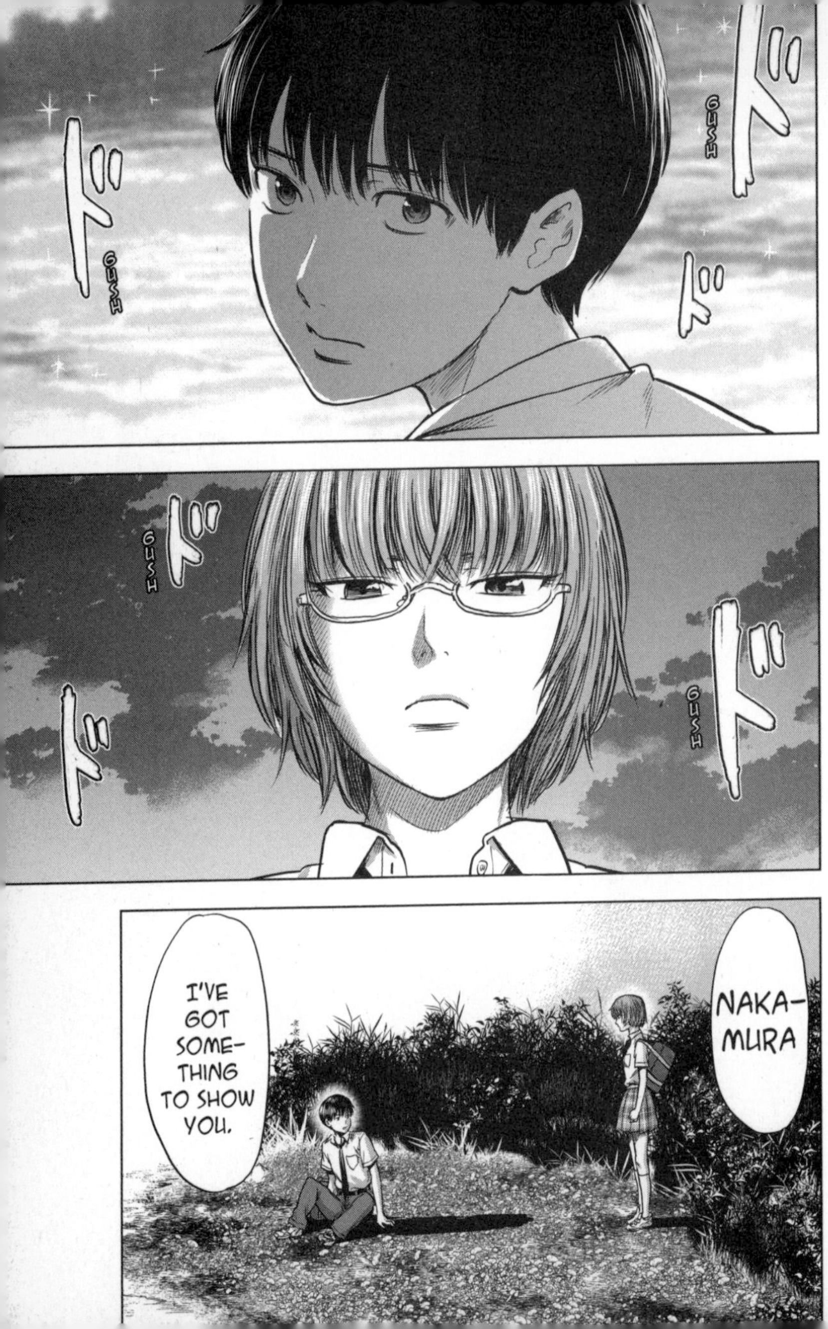
GUSH
GUSH
GUSH
GUSH
NAKA-
MURA
I'VE GOT SOME-THING TO SHOW YOU.

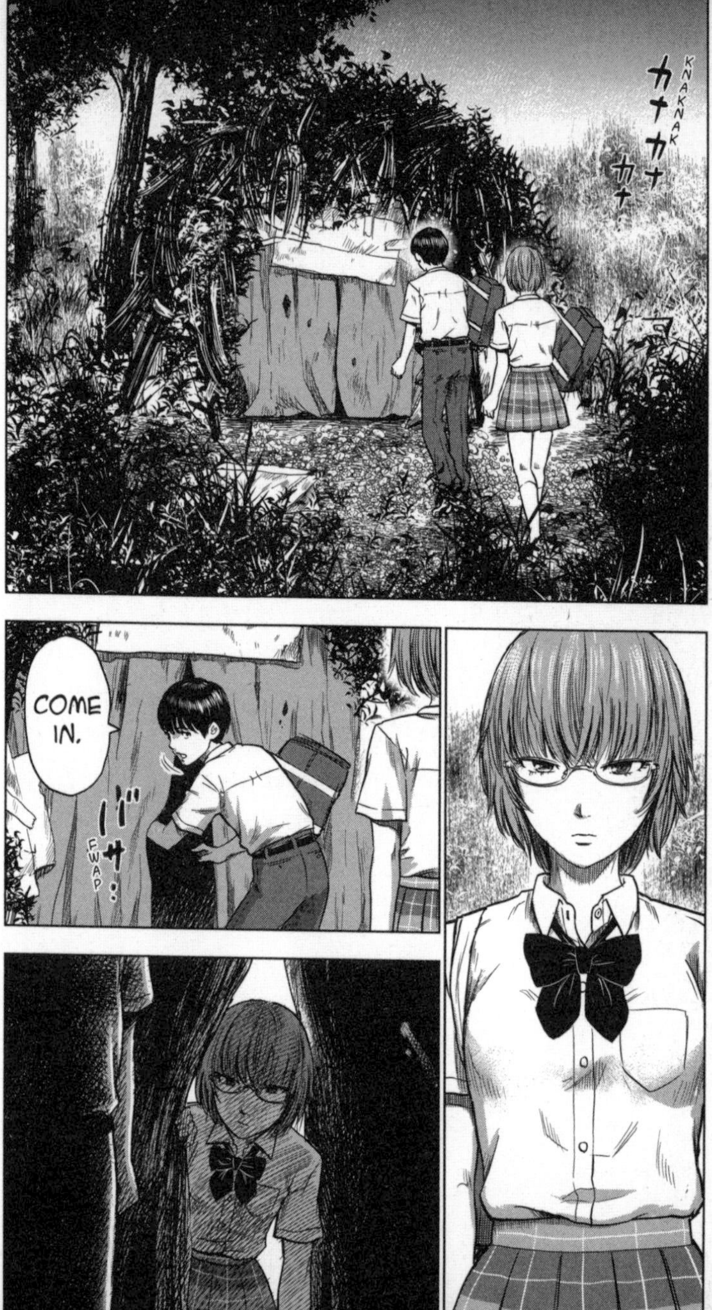
KNAKNAK
カナカナカナ
COME IN.
バサッ
FWAP

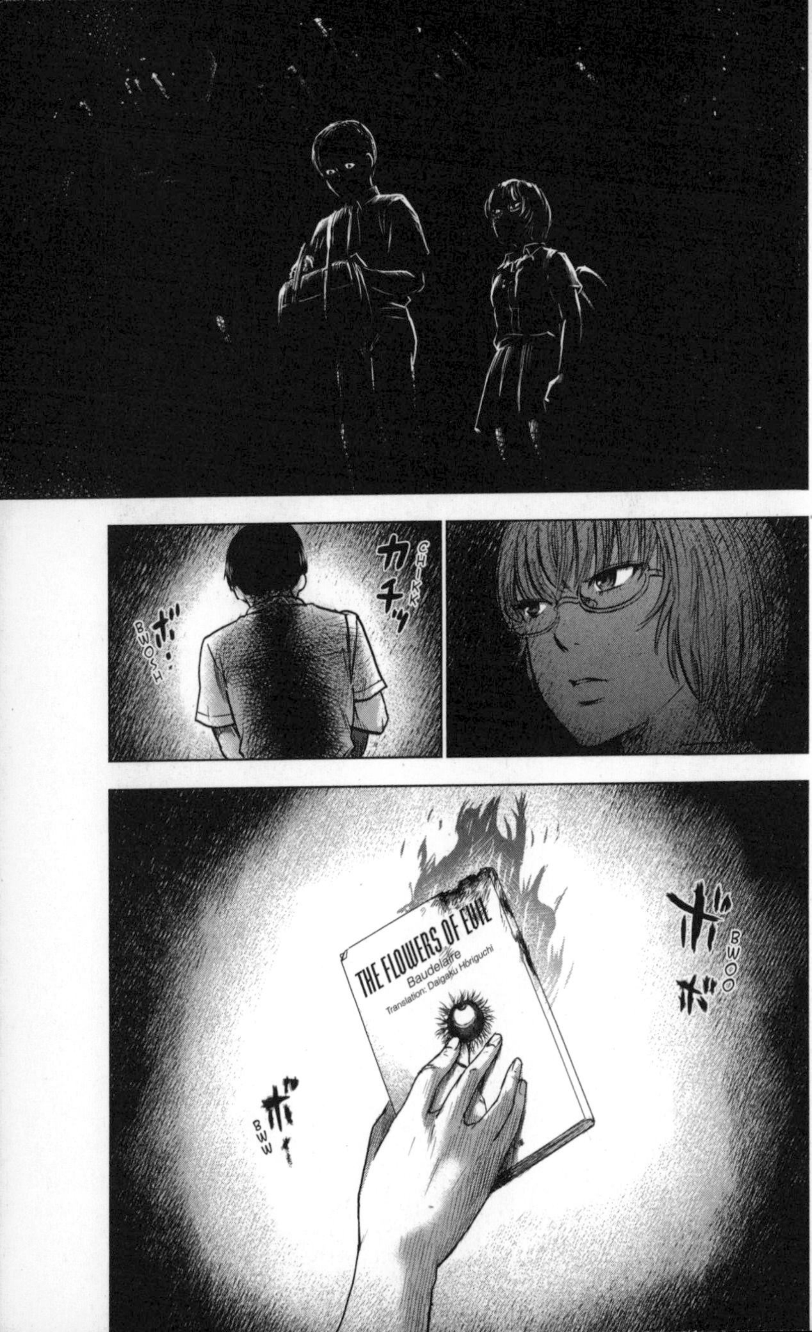

カチッ
CHIKK
ボ…
BWOSH
ボボ
BWOO
THE FLOWERS OF EVIL
Baudelaire
Translation: Daigaku Horiguchi
ボォ
BWW

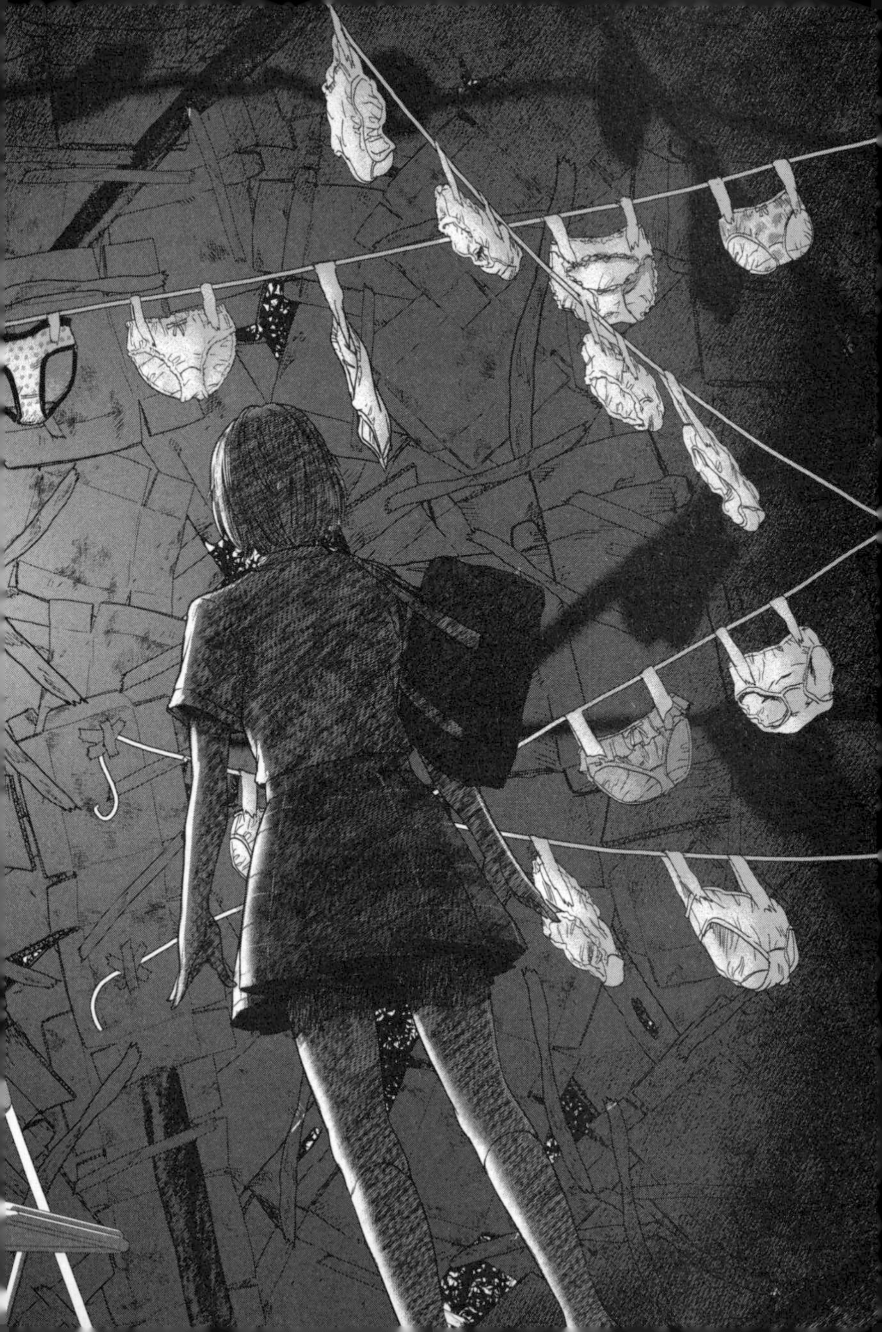

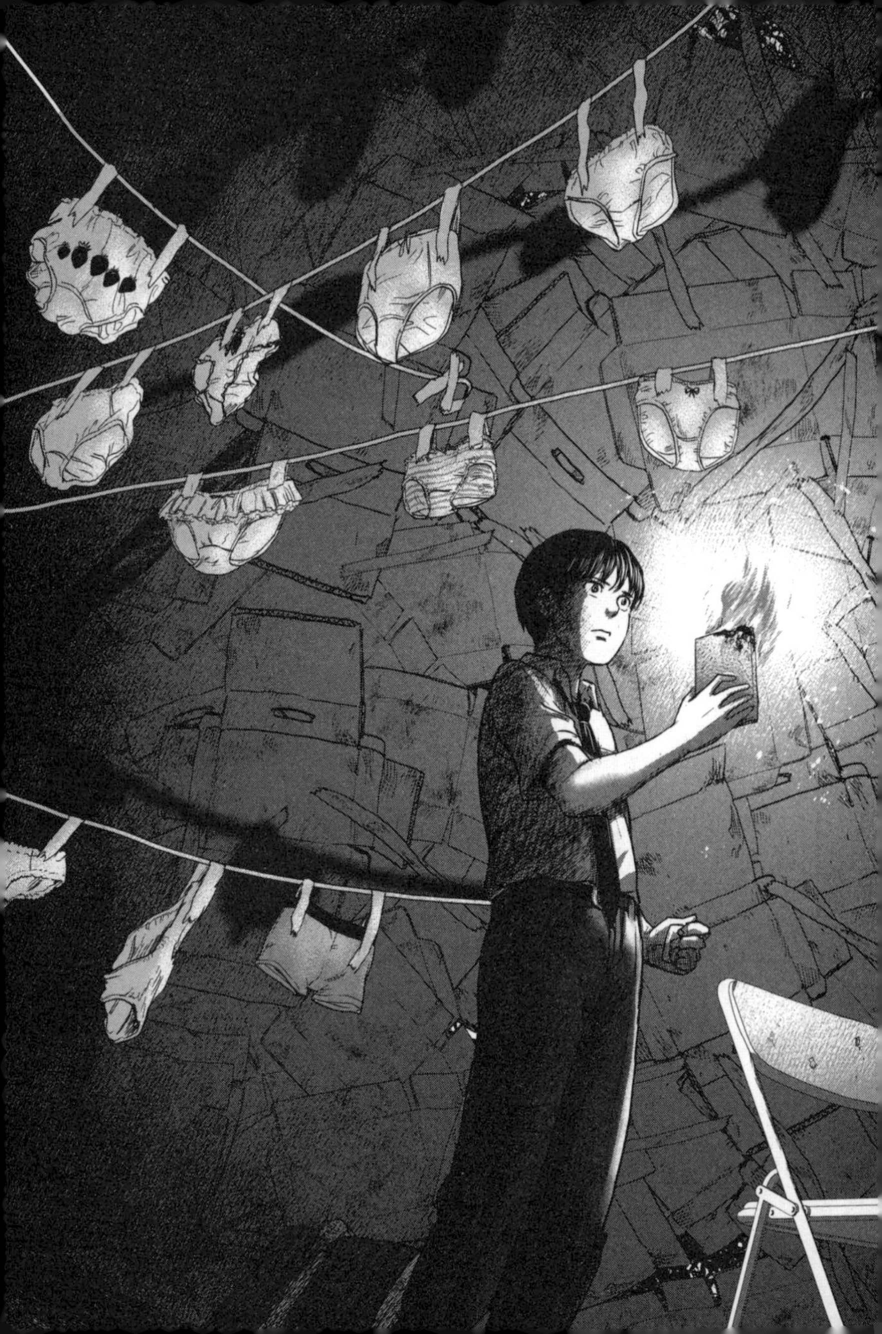

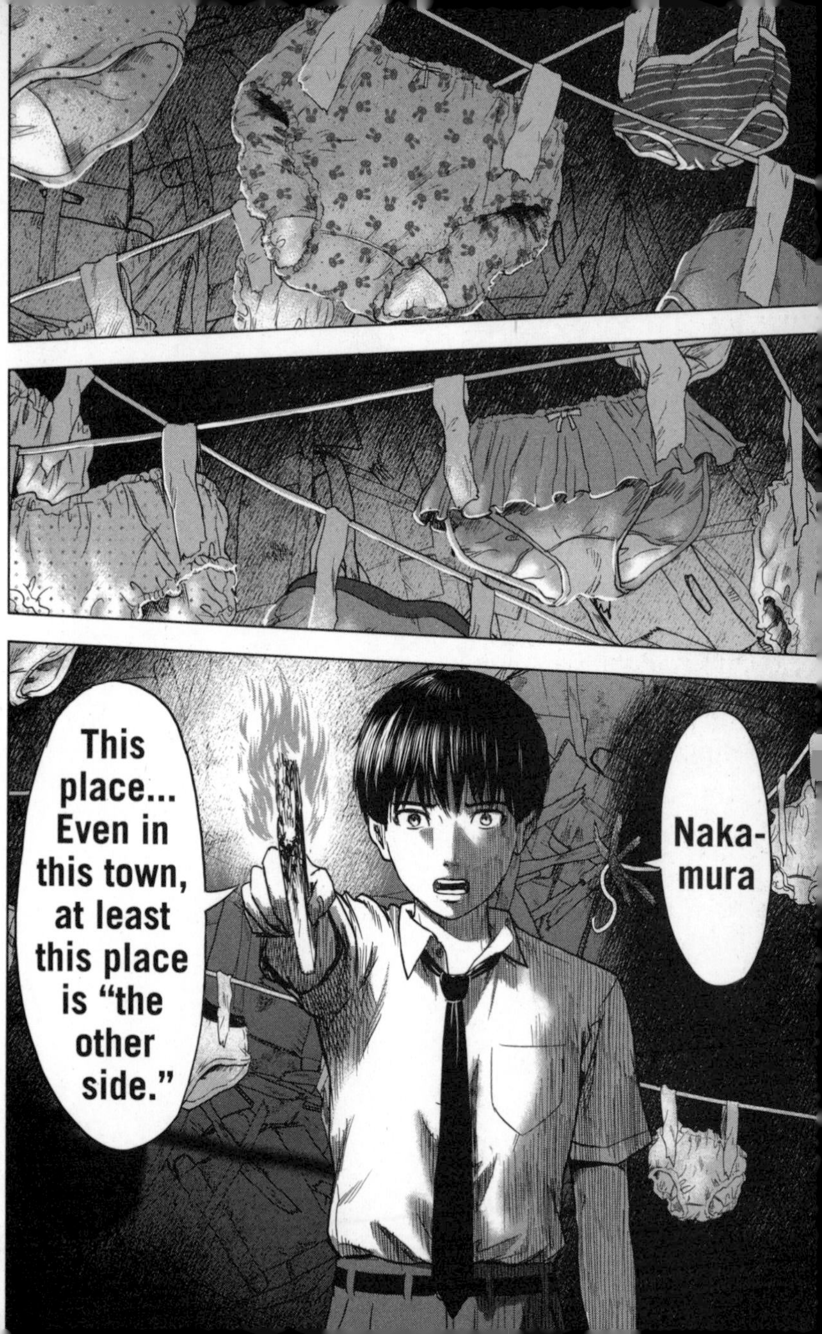
Naka-mura
This place... Even in this town, at least this place is "the other side."

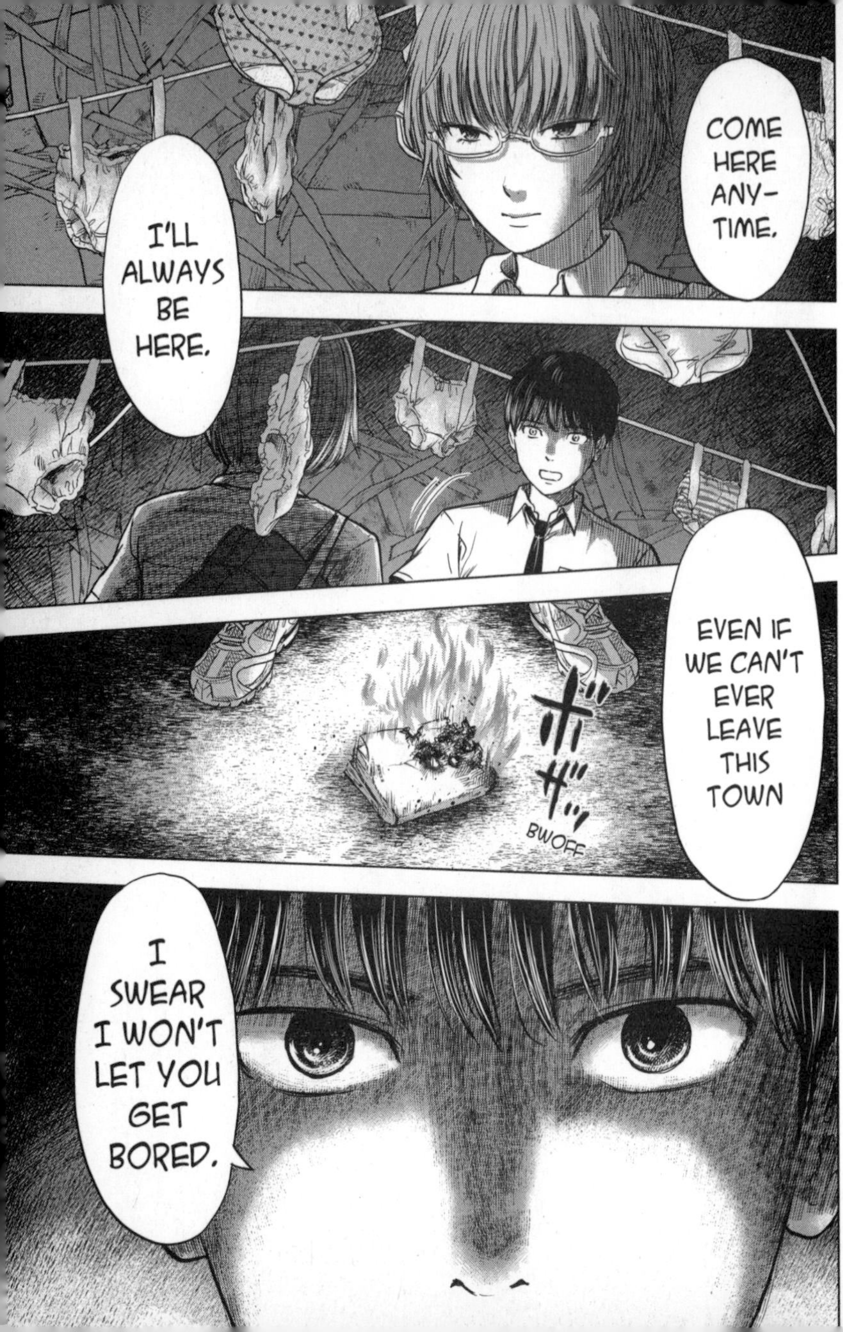
COME HERE ANY-TIME.
I'LL ALWAYS BE HERE.
EVEN IF WE CAN'T EVER LEAVE THIS TOWN
ボザッ
BWOFF
I SWEAR I WON'T LET YOU GET BORED.

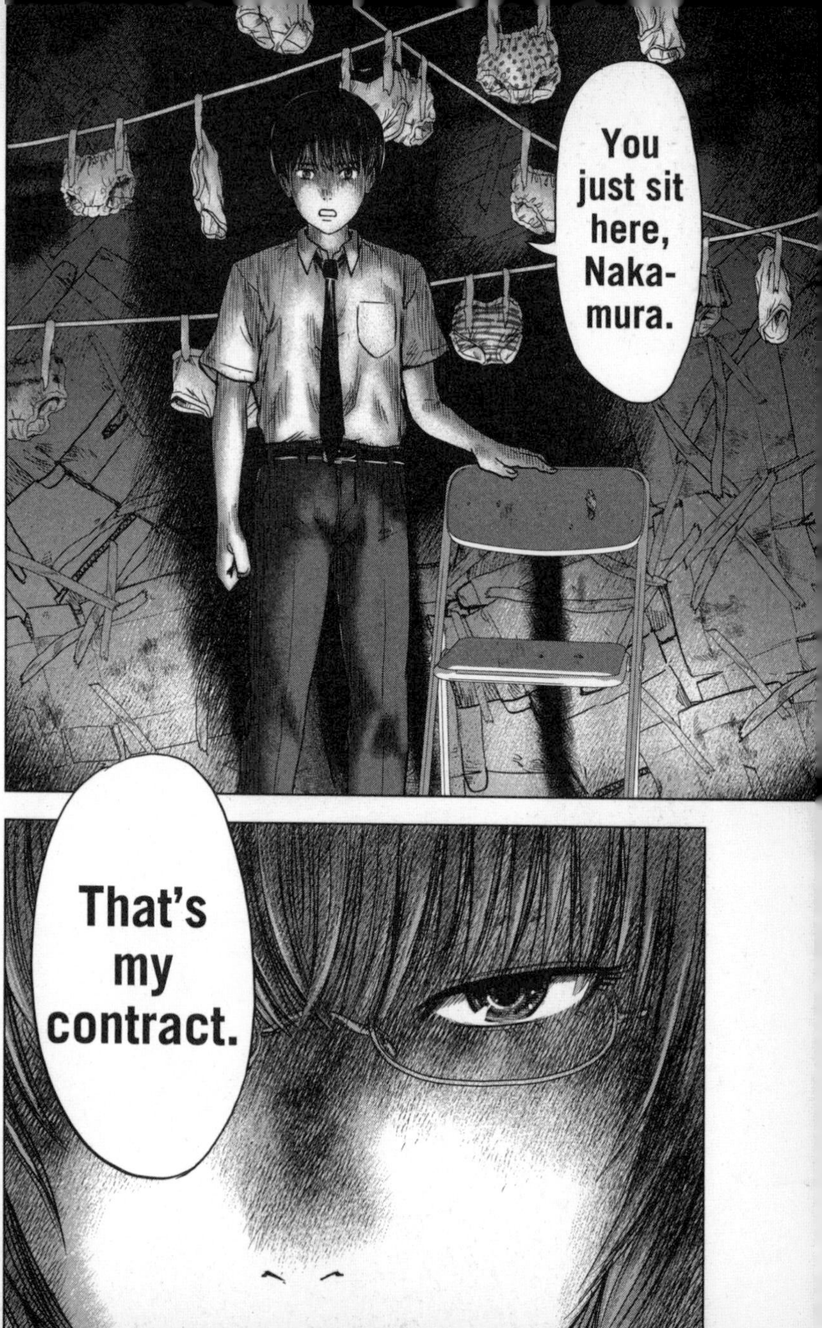
You just sit here, Naka-mura.
That's my contract.

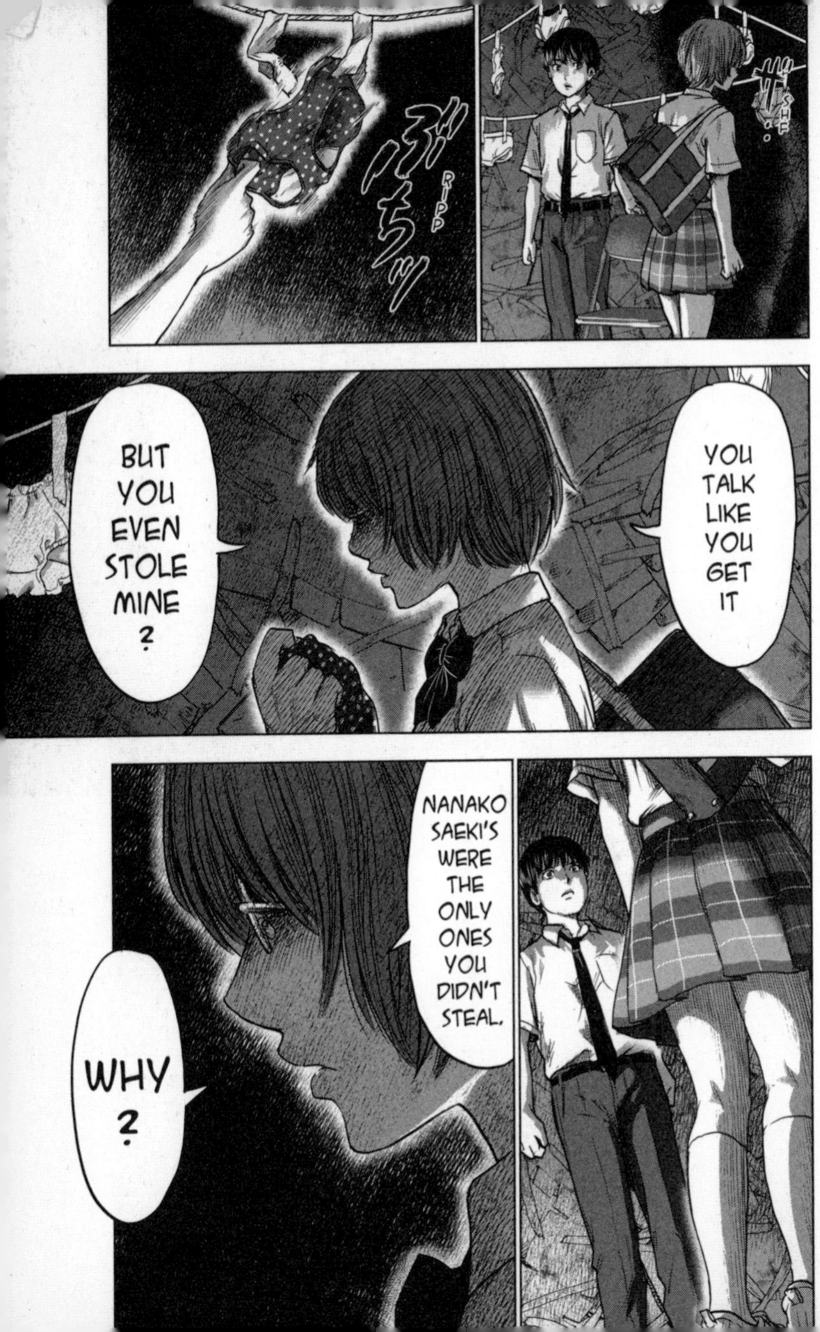
SHF
RIPP
YOU TALK LIKE YOU GET IT
BUT YOU EVEN STOLE MINE?
NANAKO SAEKI'S WERE THE ONLY ONES YOU DIDN'T STEAL.
WHY?

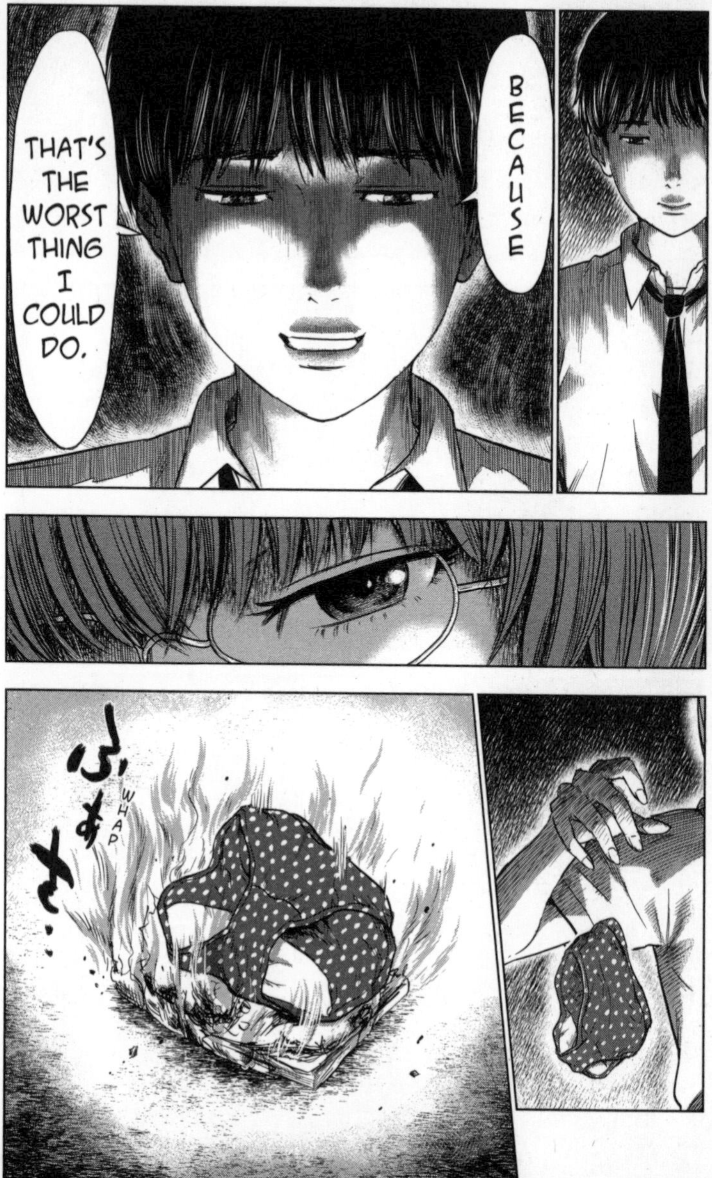
BECAUSE
THAT'S THE WORST THING I COULD DO.
ふぁさ…
WHAP

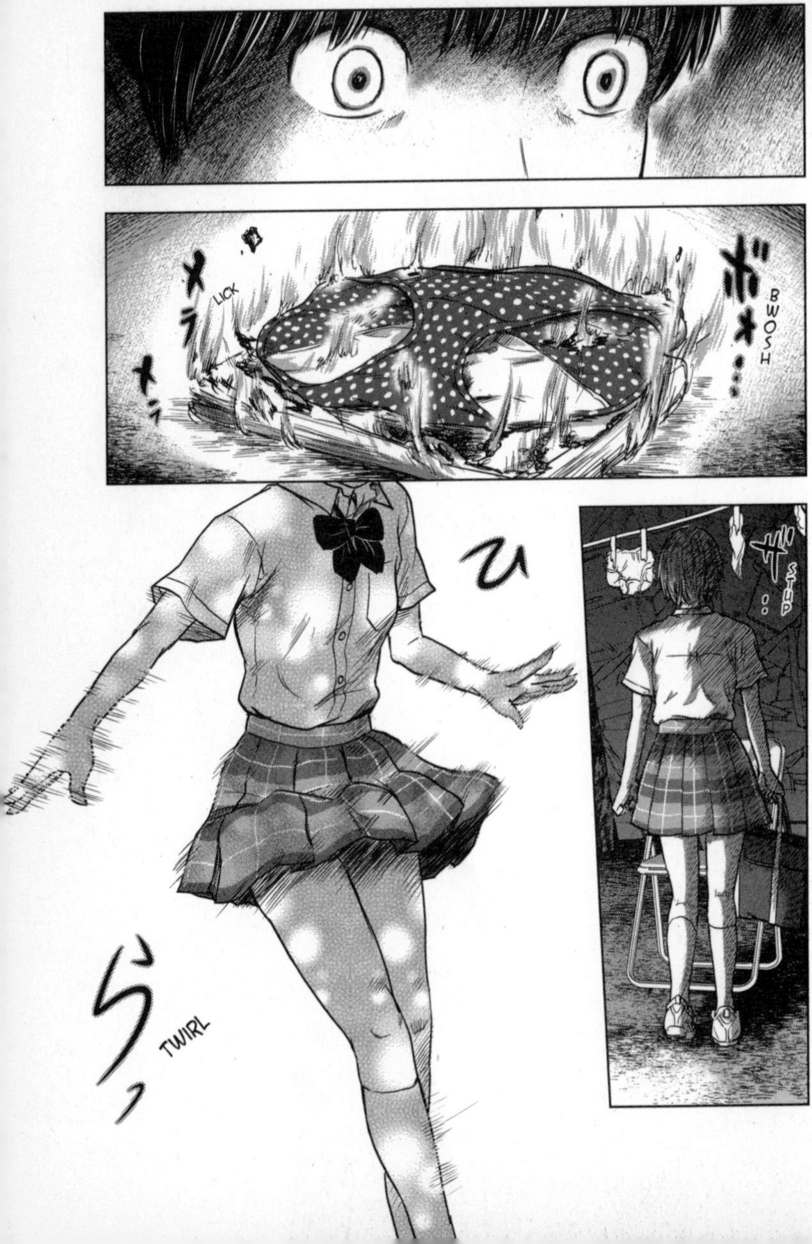
ボォ…
BWOSH
メラ メラ
LICK
ザッ‥
STUP
ひらっ
TWIRL

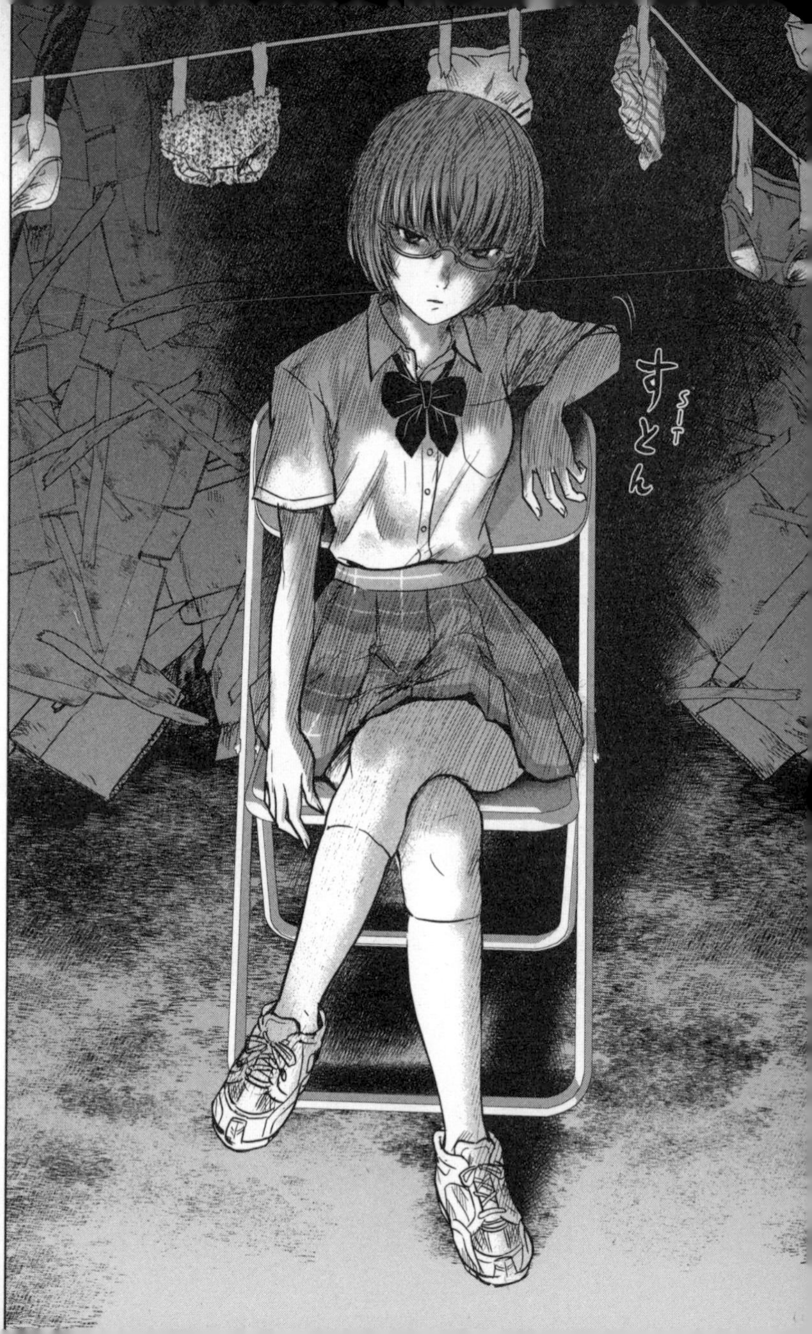
すとん
SIT

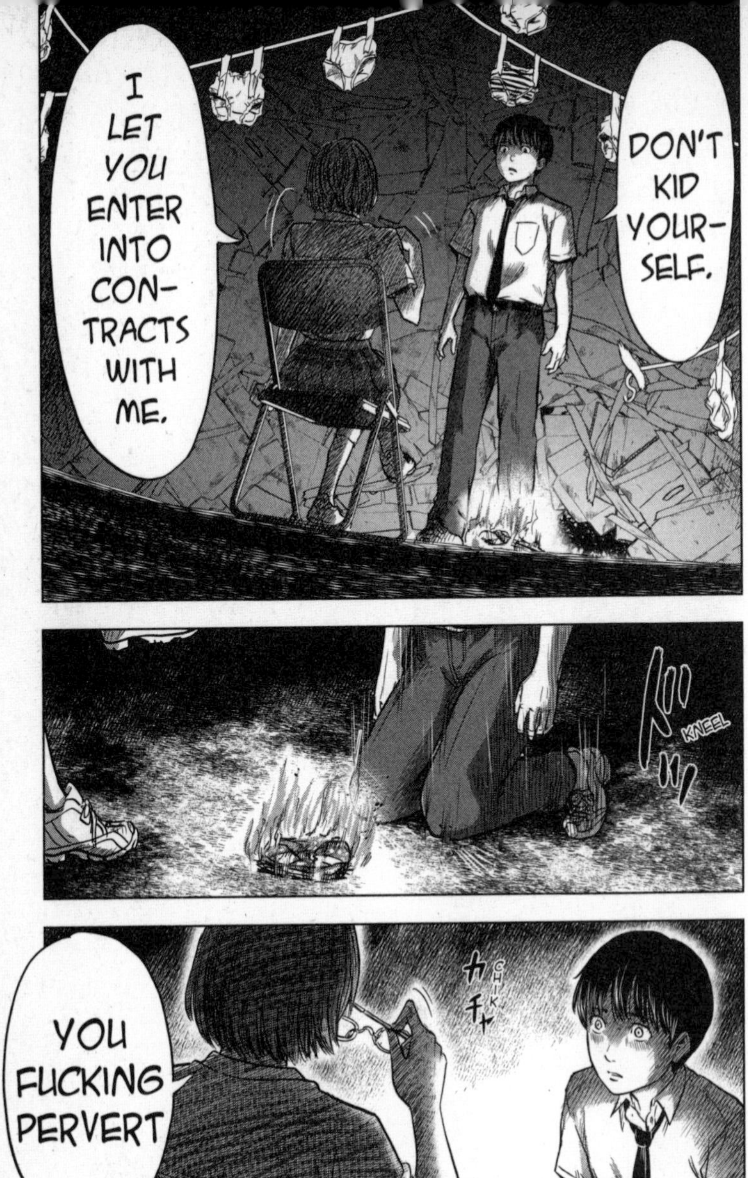
DON'T KID YOURSELF.
I LET YOU ENTER INTO CONTRACTS WITH ME.
KNEEL
CHIK
YOU FUCKING PERVERT

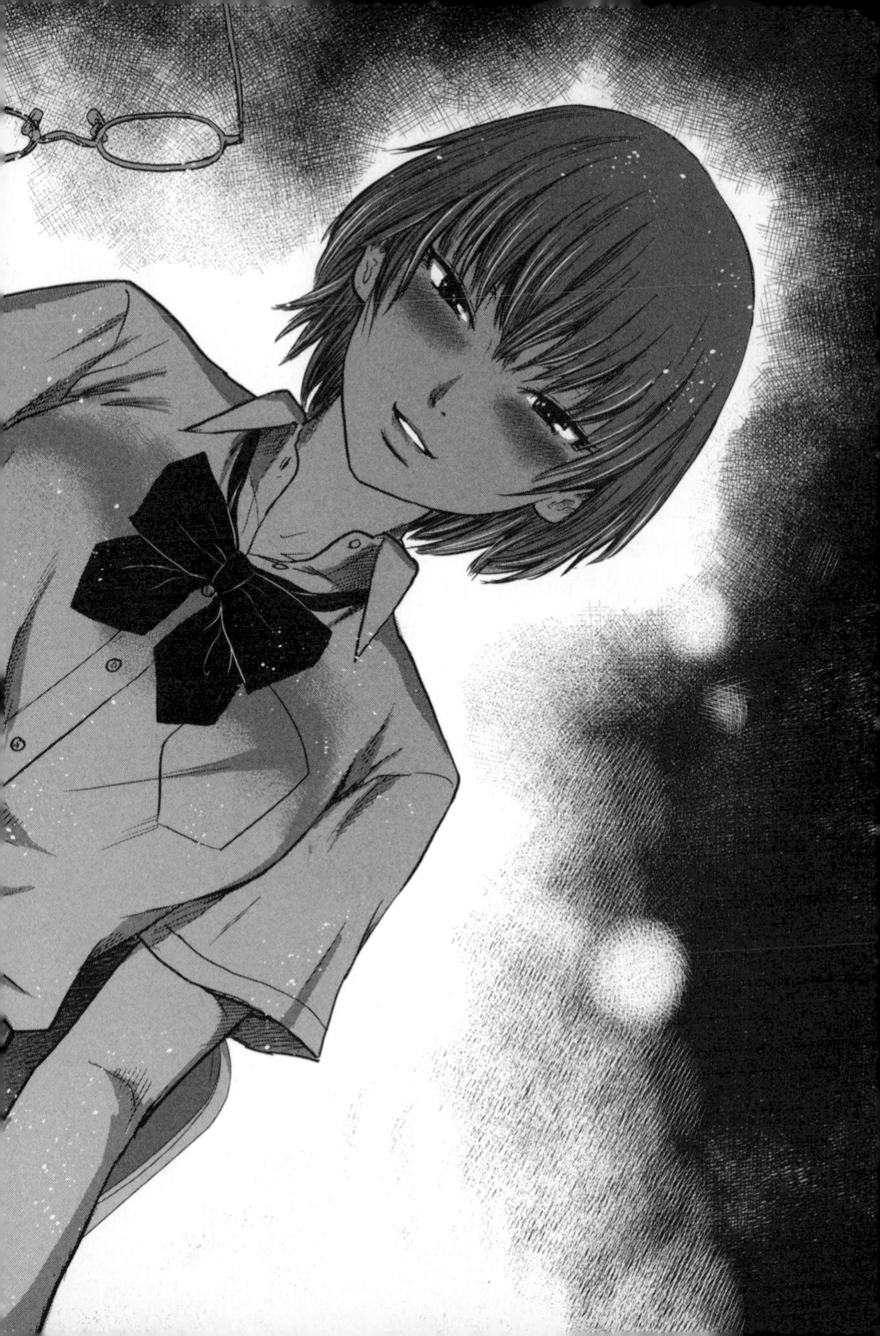

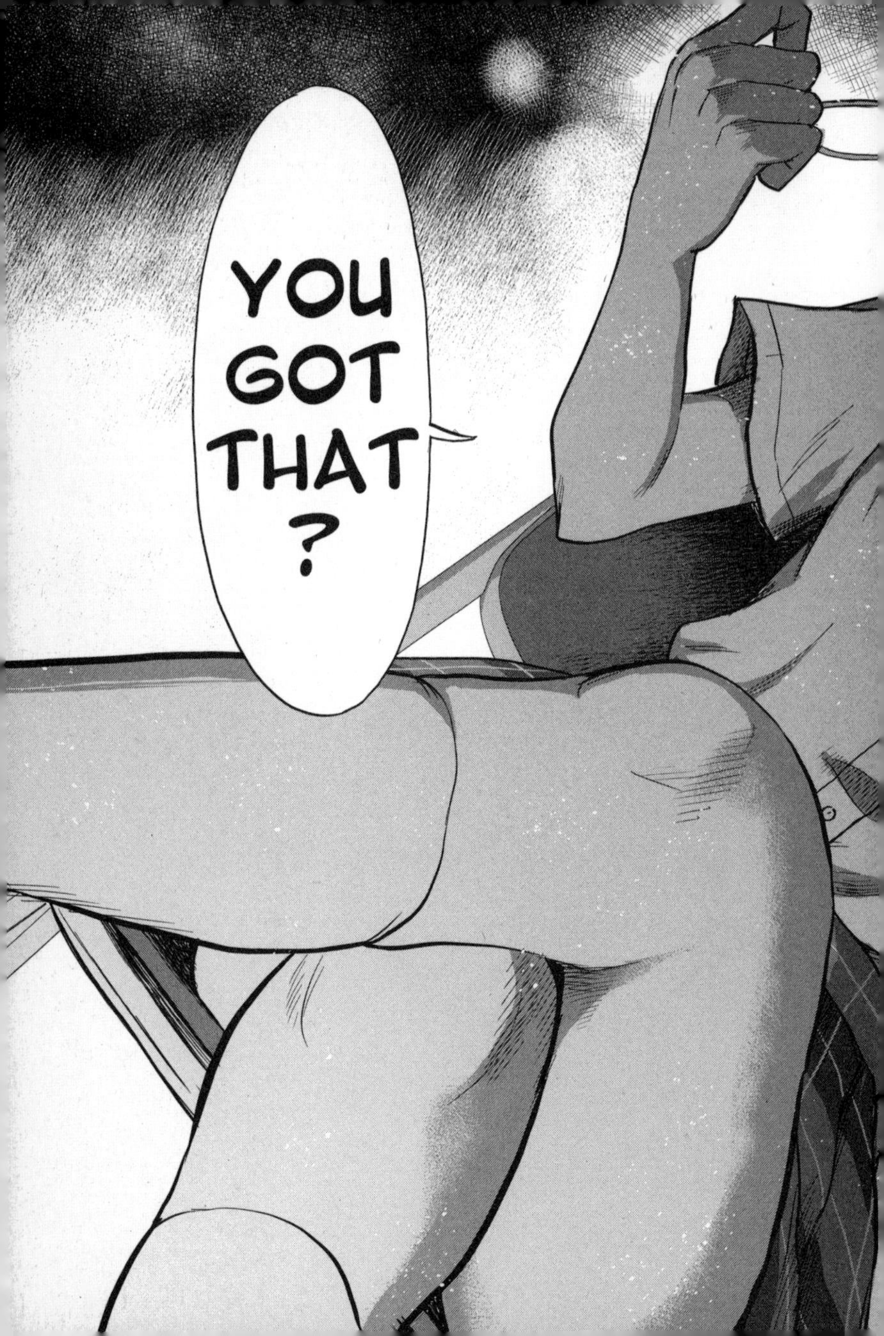
YOU GOT THAT ?

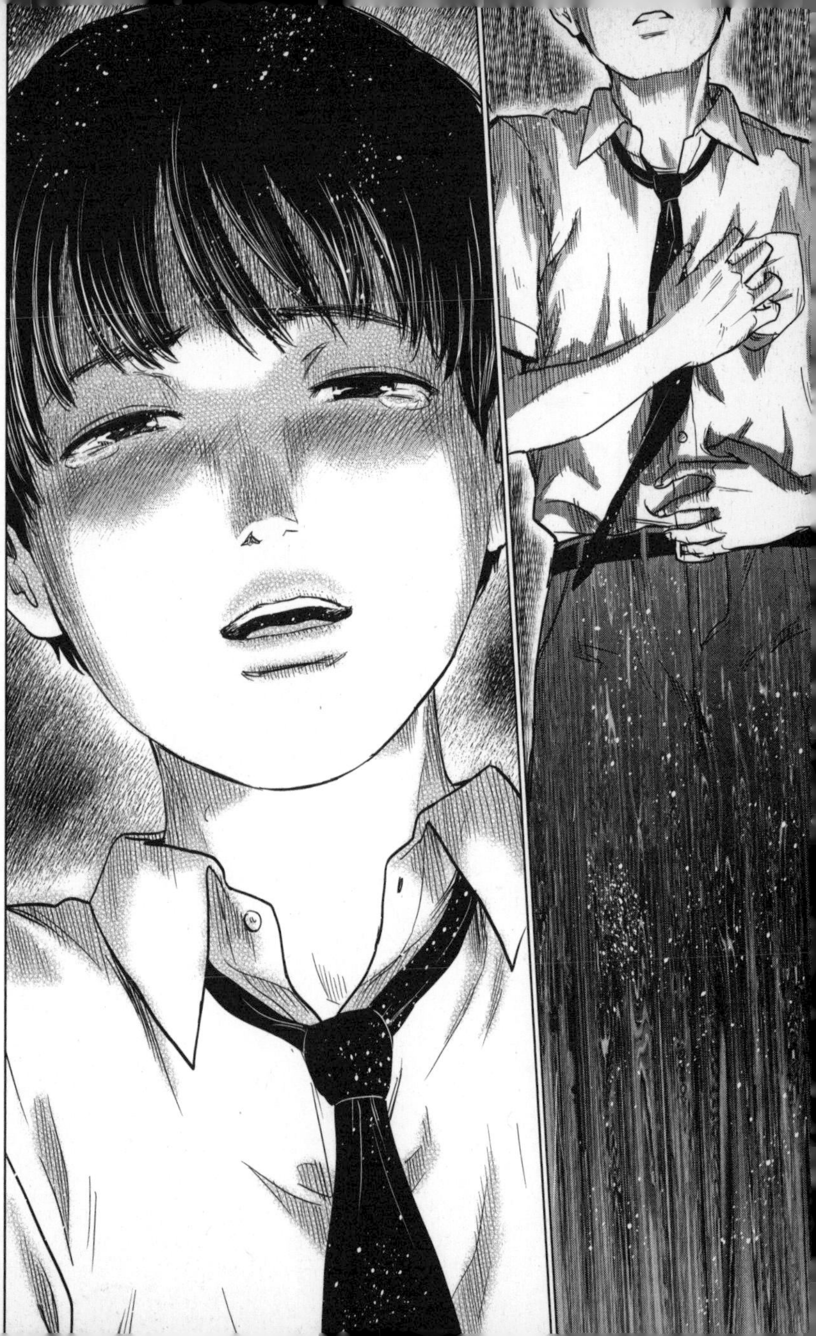

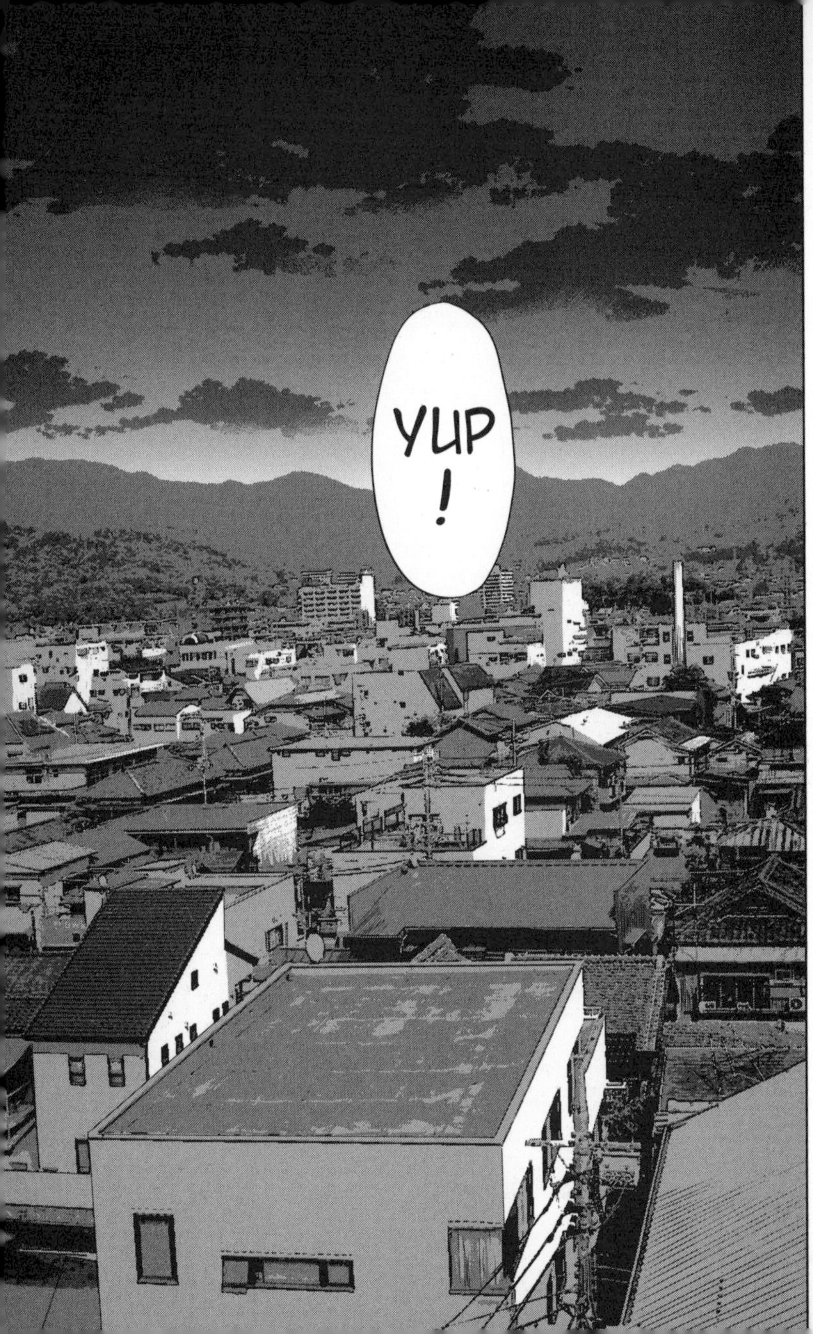
YUP!

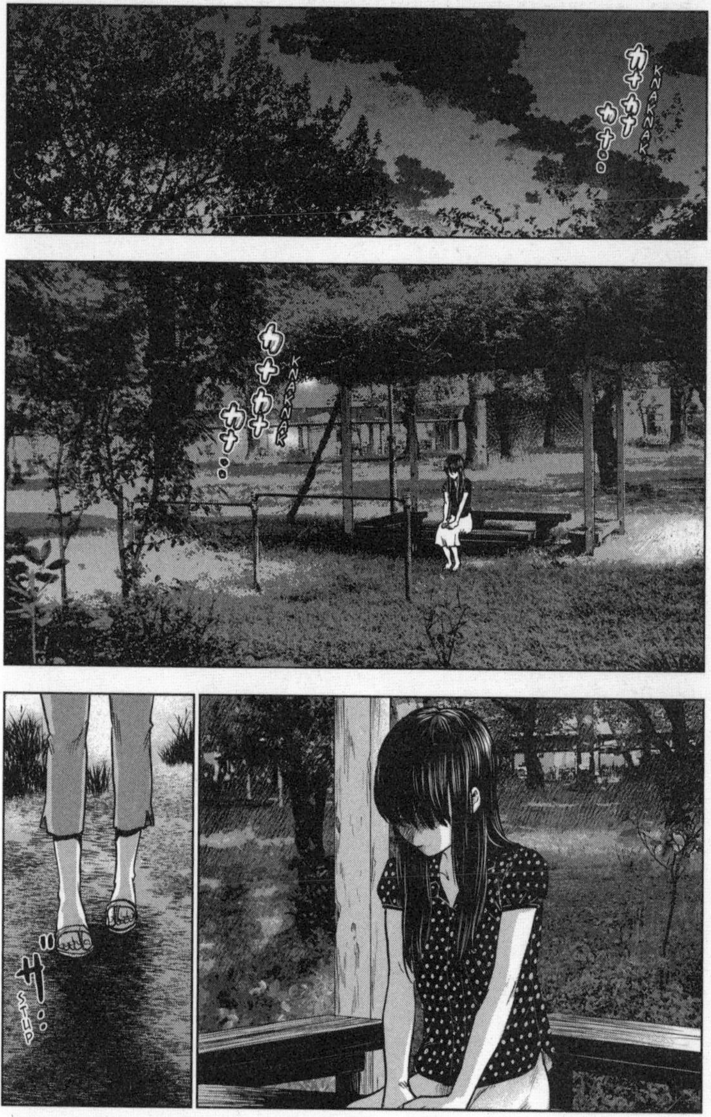
カナカナカナ‥
KNAKNAK
カナカナカナ‥
KNAKNAK
ザ‥
STUP

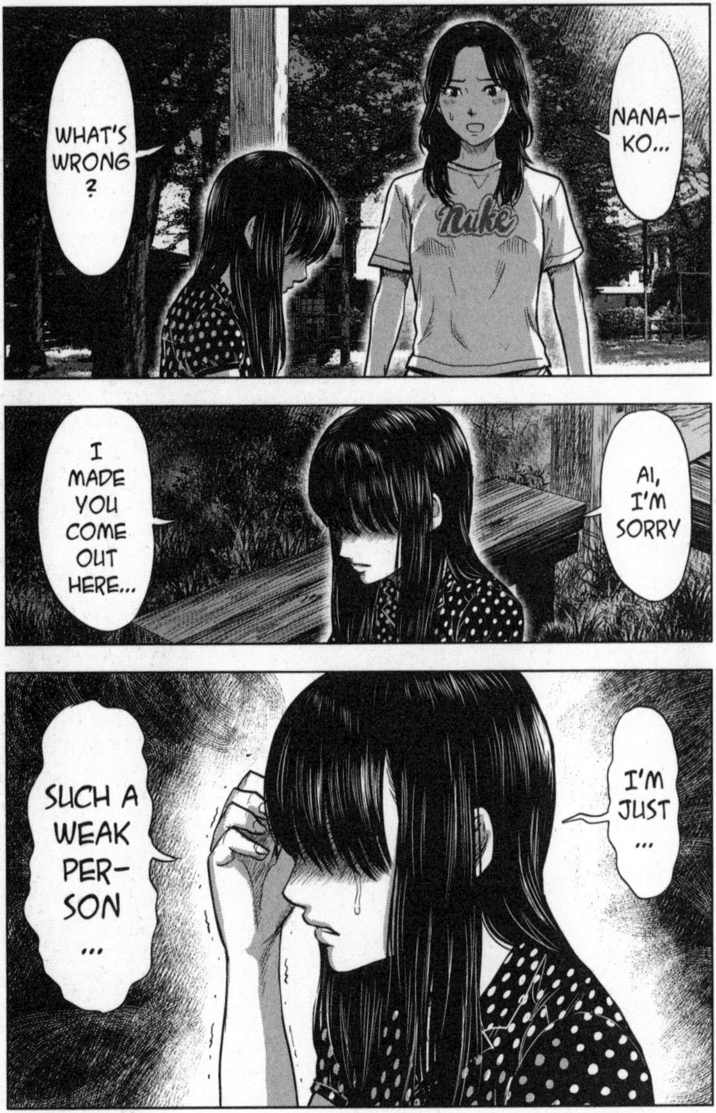
NANA-KO...
Nuke
WHAT'S WRONG?
AI, I'M SORRY
I MADE YOU COME OUT HERE...
I'M JUST...
SUCH A WEAK PER-SON...

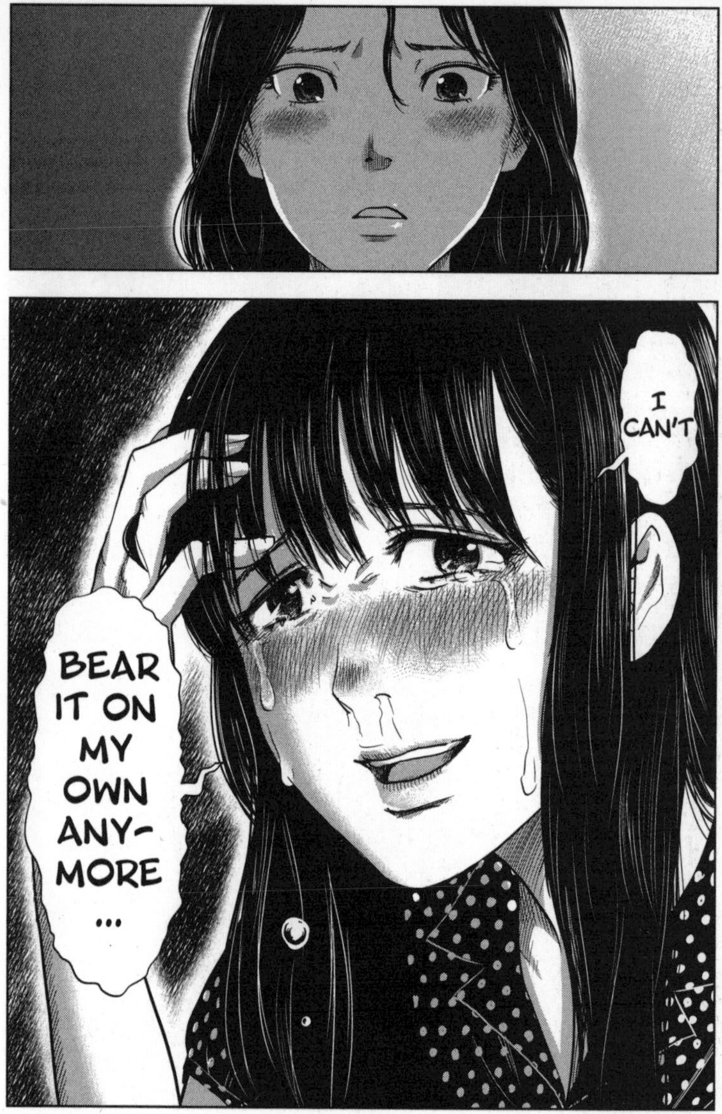
I CAN'T
BEAR IT ON MY OWN ANY-MORE...

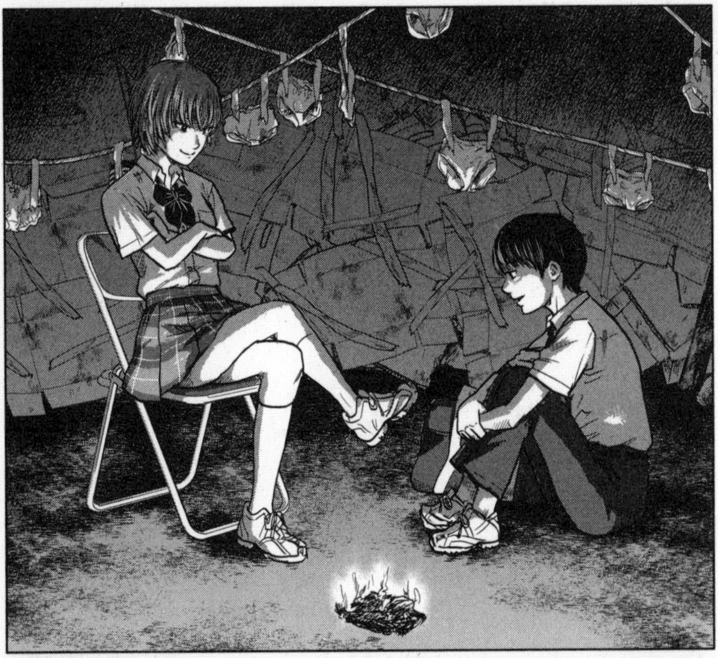

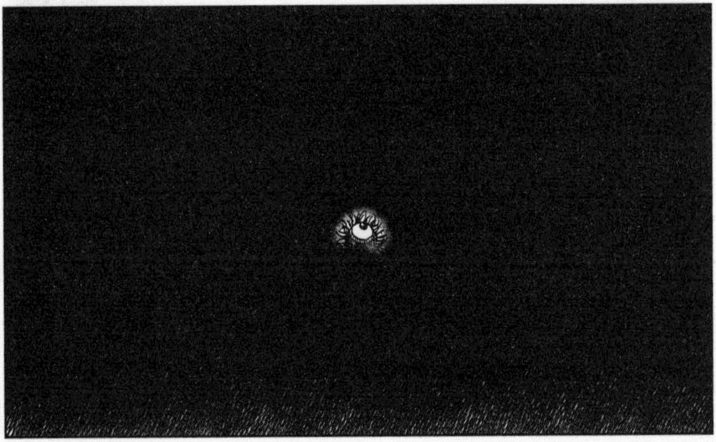

Continued in Volume 5

The
Flowers
of
Evil

Locations Tour

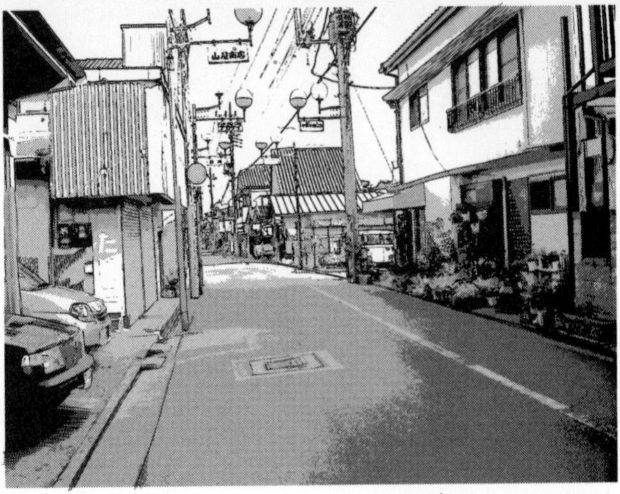

Kasuga's way to school.
It's close to my old house.

The view of the town from the roof of a department store.
You can see mountains no matter which way you face.

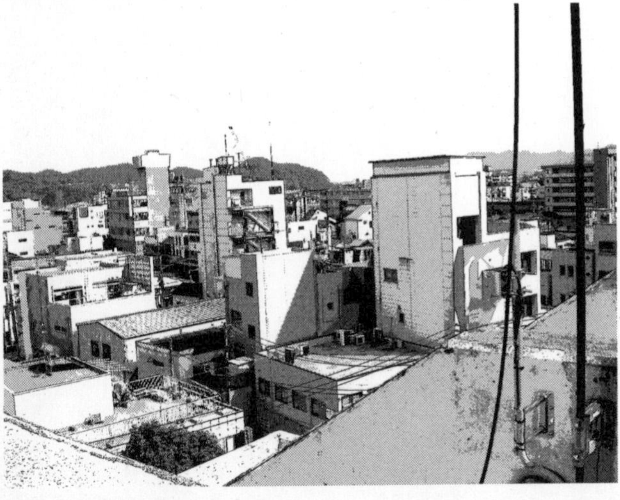

The park where
Kasuga confessed
to Saeki.

Old public housing
next to the park.

The middle school's field.

Below the elevated tracks that cut through the middle of town.
There was filthy graffiti in the public bathrooms here.

The main avenue in the heart of town.
Apparently it used to be quite lively.

There are lots of old buildings and storehouses.

The cycling path
along the river
embankment.

It's a maze of narrow streets.

This is the Watase River, which appears in a Chisato Moritaka song.

Thanks for
reading!